MW00957981

Speak Japanese in 90 Days:
A Self Study Guide to Becoming Fluent
Volume One
Copyright © Kevin Marx 2015

Also by Kevin Marx:

Speak Japanese in 90 Days: A Self Study Guide to Becoming Fluent (Volume 2)

Japanese Readings 1000: Master 1000 Words with 20 Short Stories

Japanese Readings 2000: Master 1000 More Words with 20 Short Stories

Japanese Study Guide: A Visual Reference for Beginning Japanese Grammar

Speak German in 90 Days: A Self Study Guide to Becoming Fluent

Speak German NOW: The Go-To Guide for Essential German Basics

Conner and the Telescope: Children's Multilingual Picture Book (Available in Spanish, Italian, French, Portuguese, German, Japanese, Mandarin Chinese, Korean, and Russian)

Table of Contents

Grammar Basics

Verb Basics

Intermediate Grammar

Adjectives

Numbers, Dates, Time

Special Words

Foreword

This is the first book in the series Speak Japanese in 90 Days. It covers all of the grammar tested in the JLPT5 (Japanese Language Proficiency Test) as well as most of the grammar in the JLPT4. Please read the following sections which will teach you how to study with this book. Thank you for your purchase, I hope you enjoy studying with this book!

How to Study

This book consists of 90 lessons that can be studied in one day each. Each lesson will present you with ten vocabulary words to memorize and most will also contain a grammar structure to memorize. To memorize vocabulary please use note cards, or some device to write down the vocabulary words. It is important that you have access to your vocabulary at all times during the day.

On both sides of the card write the numbers 1-10. On one side write the English word and on the other side write the Japanese equivalent. Read word number one **out loud**. Flip the card. Read the Japanese equivalent word **out loud.** Go on to the second word. Do this at least ten times for each word. You may notice, by the tenth time, that you can remember some of the words without making any effort. Please note that **out loud** is bold and underlined. It is extremely important that you say the words **out loud**.

Do this **at least** three times a day. The more often you do it, the easier it will be to recall the words. At the end of the day, try to make a sentence with the words you've memorized, or simply use the sample sentences provided in this book. Making sentences with your vocabulary words is just as important as saying everything **out loud.** If you do these two simple things, your progress will be much faster.

Practice each new card along with the old ones every day until you are able to freely use the vocabulary words on your own. Review all vocabulary at least once a week, even if you feel you have memorized it.

Your brain will play tricks on you, and you may begin to memorize the order of the words on the card, so it is important to mix them up, do the odd words, then do the even words. Do the words backwards. You can also switch the language you start with. Start on the English side to improve your speaking, start on the Japanese side to improve your reading and listening. Say everything **out loud**.

Motivation

The most difficult thing about learning a language is actually taking the time to study. Languages are different than most subjects, in that you cannot cram the information in one sitting. You must study as *often* as possible rather than as *long* as possible. It is imperative that you study and practice **every day**. You will gain more benefit from studying every day for fifteen minutes than you will from studying two hours once a week.

Your motivation for learning Japanese is very important. Ask yourself, why do I want to study Japanese? Remind yourself of the reason. Tell yourself *I want to study Japanese*. Say it, out loud, right now: *I want to study Japanese!* It is all a matter of will. You may find yourself one day feeling lazy, your thoughts telling you to relax, to procrastinate. Do not let this happen to you. Do not give in to negativity. If you feel this is happening, remind yourself of why you want to speak Japanese, remind yourself that you want to do this. You want to study. You want to improve.

It is my hope that you are able to finish this book in 90 days, however, everyone has different learning curves and busy lives, so if you find that it may take you 180, or even 360 days to finish this book, do not feel down. This book was designed to be done at your own pace. You can do it! Good luck!

Practicing

You perfect what you practice. If you play video games all day, you will get good at playing video games, if you read books all day, you will become a fast reader. The same goes for language, if you practice reading, you will increase your reading skill, if you practice listening, you will increase your listening skill, if you practice speaking, you will increase your speaking skill. The problem for most people learning a language is that they waste time doing written grammar exercises, which makes you good at passing tests, but doesn't improve your speaking.

In order to practice, you need someone to speak with. If you don't have a Japanese speaking friend to practice with, this can be difficult. The solution to this problem: talk to yourself. Look around you. What do you see? Do you see a window, a door, a person, a bird? If you know the name of it in Japanese, say it, **out loud**. Ask yourself, *What am I doing*? Think of as many things as possible: *I am sitting, I am breathing, I am reading, I am thinking*. Say it **out loud**. Ask yourself, *What did I do yesterday*? *What will I do tomorrow*? You must do this if you want to improve your speaking, **you must speak**.

Japanese is Different

Japanese is linguistically distant from English. This means there are almost no similarities and it is difficult for native speakers of each language to learn the other one. For example, it is easier for English speakers to learn Spanish or German because they are similar to English. Japanese people will have an easier time learning Korean, because the grammar is similar to Japanese. It is said that learning a European language can take about 500-600 hours of study, while Japanese takes about 1100-1200 hours of study. A lot of this is because of the writing system, but also the lack of similarity in the vocabulary.

That being said, you're going to have to drastically change the way you think about language and how you express things in Japanese. Often times, simply knowing all the vocabulary and grammar of a sentence will not let you understand its meaning.

One thing that is unique about Japanese, is that **they drop every word from the sentence that can be understood from context**. For example, the sentence: *I am giving this to you*, will just be one word, the verb *ageru* あげる[上げる] (to give). This is because in this situation, it is understood who is doing the giving and receiving, and obviously someone is holding something in their hand and extending it outward, so we don't really need to say that, do we?

Another thing you must get used to is thinking *backwards*. Word order, verb placement, and clause position in Japanese is, for the most part, opposite that of English. This will take some getting used to, even if you are able to speak and read Japanese, it's going to take you an even longer time to start *thinking* in Japanese.

Japanese is a very hierarchical language. In this book polite and casual forms of verbs will be covered, but there are also a few other forms used when talking to someone of higher status than you, and even forms for talking to things below you, like your pets. It is also very gender specific, men and women talk differently in Japanese. These nuances will take time and practice, so just keep that in mind.

Though there are a lot of things that can make Japanese difficult, one easy thing to know is that Japanese has no plural form of nouns, so you don't need to memorize any grammar for that. Isn't it great?!

The Japanese Writing System and Pronunciation

Pronunciation is quite easy in Japanese. There are five basic vowel sounds: a-i-u-e-o.

A sounds like the *o* in *hot* or the *a* in *awesome*.
I sounds like saying the letter E.
U sounds like the *oo* in *zoo*.
E can sound like saying the letter A, or softer like the first E in *enter,* depending on the word. The true pronunciation is somewhere between the two.
O sounds like saying the letter O.

Japanese letters are called kana. Every kana in Japanese is a syllable. The vowel sounds are combined with the consonants k-s-t-n-h-m-y-r-w. There is also a lone sound *N*. You already know words like *karate* and *sushi*, so remember to pronounce every vowel in Japanese, like you do with these words: *ka-ra-te, su-shi.* In Japanese, the letter R and L are the same kana, that's why Japanese people have so much trouble pronouncing these. The sound in Japanese is really a combination of the two, and in linguistics, is called a palatal D. You make the sound by tapping your palate with your tongue. Speakers of Spanish and German make this sound when they roll their Rs, but that version has multiple hits on the palate, the Japanese version is just one hit. So try it right now, try to make the R and L sound at the same time by rolling your tongue. Start with the R sound and roll it into an L, tapping your palate. Another trick is to start by saying *la la la* out loud. Do you see how the tip of your tongue taps your teeth? Now trying saying *la la la* again, but this time move the tip of your tongue back a bit, and tap your palate instead. It's pretty easy, right?

Japanese has three forms of writing. They are: *hiragana* ひらがな *katakana* カタカナ and *kanji* 漢字. Hiragana is used for Japanese words. Katakana is used for foreign words. Kanji are the scary messy things that take some serious amount of time to study and learn. Writing words using the alphabet is called *romaji* ローマ字, and there are many different romaji systems! This book will use the Hepburn romaji style with a few Wapuro romaji modifications to make it as easy as possible for new students to read. Surprisingly, hiragana and katakana are pretty easy to learn. If you haven't learned them already, make that your first priority. I highly recommend that you write using the Japanese system on your note cards. The faster you stop using the English alphabet, the better. The basic way to learn hiragana and katakana is to just write them over and over. I recommend doing five kana a day. There are about 50 of each, so you can do this in less than three weeks.

Kanji are quite difficult. Basically, each kanji is comprised of about 200 different possible parts. You can try to memorize these parts and then construct a meaning out of the kanji from its components, but that will not be covered at all in this book. The kanji themselves each have a few core meanings. Sometimes it can be helpful to look up the core meaning of a kanji when you are having trouble using a vocabulary word, to help you get a better understanding of the root meaning. There are many other resources you can use for studying kanji, and in my opinion the best one available is the Kanji Learner's Course by Andrew Scott Conning (Kodansha USA, 2013), which can be used with an excellent series of graded reading sets and a sequential wall chart. These resources can be found at his website keystojapanese.com. Good luck!

Every vocabulary word and example sentence in this book will be written using the Japanese writing system as well as the equivalent pronunciation using the English system. So don't worry, even if you are a complete beginner and can't read Japanese, you will be able to speak it soon! Here is the Japanese writing system:

Hiragana ひらがな

a あ	i い	u う	e え	o お
ka か	ki き	ku く	ke け	ko こ
sa さ	shi し	su す	se せ	so そ
ta た	chi ち	tsu つ	te て	to と
na な	ni に	nu ぬ	ne ね	no の
ha は	hi ひ	fu ふ	he へ	ho ほ
ma ま	mi み	mu む	me め	mo も
ya や		yu ゆ		yo よ
ra ら	ri り	ru る	re れ	ro ろ
wa わ				wo を
n ん				

Katakana カタカナ

a ア	i イ	u ウ	e エ	o オ
ka カ	ki キ	ku ク	ke ケ	ko コ
sa サ	shi シ	su ス	se セ	so ソ
ta タ	chi チ	tsu ツ	te テ	to ト
na ナ	ni ニ	nu ヌ	ne ネ	no ノ
ha ハ	hi ヒ	fu フ	he へ	ho ホ
ma マ	mi ミ	mu ム	me メ	mo モ
ya ヤ		yu ユ		yo ヨ
ra ラ	ri リ	ru ル	re レ	ro ロ
wa ワ				wo ヲ
n ン				

There are a few things to take note of when looking at these kana. The first is that some of the kana are limited, there is no *yi, ye, wi, we,* or *wu.* The second is that the pronunciation changes with a few of the kana. *Si* becomes *shi, ti* becomes *chi, tu* becomes *tsu, hu* becomes *fu.* The last thing to take note of is the pronunciation of *wo* をヲ. When written in hiragana, don't pronounce the *w,* it has the same pronunciation as *o* お.

Some of the kana are unvoiced. Each kana can be changed to its voiced equivalent by adding two dots that look like quotation marks to the top right of the kana. Here are the changes:

K becomes G	ka → ga	か → が
S becomes Z	sa → za	さ → ざ
T becomes D	ta → da	た → だ
H becomes B	ha → ba	は → ば

There are also a few irregular uses of this.

SH becomes J	shi → ji	し → じ
CH becomes J	chi → ji	ち → ぢ (written *di* on computers)
TS becomes Z	tsu → zu	つ → づ (written *du* on computers)

The P sound can be made by adding a small circle to *ha-hi-fu-he-ho*.

H becomes P	ha → pa	は → ぱ

There are a few contractions you can make with Japanese kana. Add a small version of ya-yu-yo to kana ending with *i* to change the vowel sound:

ki + yu = kyu	き ＋ ゆ ＝ きゅ
shi + ya = sha	し ＋ や ＝ しゃ
chi + yo = cho	ち ＋ よ ＝ ちょ

When done with *ji* じ, the romaji looks slightly different. Instead of *jya, jyu, jyo*, it will be *ja, ju, jo*. However, there are different styles of romaji, so you may see it written *jya, jyu, jyo*.

A small *tsu* つツ can be placed before a kana to double the consonant. For example *yokatta* よかった or *chotto* ちょっと.

Small versions of the vowels are sometimes written next to other kana. This is used in to write sounds that don't normally exist. For example *vi* ヴぃ. However, most people will just say *bi* びビ instead of *vi* ヴぃ because it is easier for them, so these sounds are quite rare. To write the small version of a vowel on an electronic device, precede the vowelwith an X. For example, to write *ti* テ ィ instead of *te* テ, type *t-e-x-i*.

The *o* おオ vowel sound can be extended by adding *u* うウ. For example, the word *chou* ちょう has the same pronunciation as *cho* ちょ, but the vowel is pronounced a bit longer. Any vowel sound can be extended, usually when using katakana カタカナ, by adding a dash that looks like this: ー
For example: *koohii* コーヒー (coffee).

When a kana ends in *a* あア and is combined with *i* いイ, the *ai* sound is pronounced like *eye*. For example, *zai* ざい is pronounced *z-eye*, not *za-ee*.

Another thing to note is that when *su* すス or *shi* しシ are at the end of a word, the vowel is often not pronounced. *su* すス at the end of a word will most always sound like *ss*. *Shi* しシ will sound like *sh* about fifty percent of the time, depending on the word, the region of Japan, and the gender of the speaker. This also happens to a lesser degree with *to* とト. Some people will pronounce the city Kyoto 京都 as *Kyot*.

Pronunciation is quite easy. However, spelling can sometimes be tough because you can't hear an extra consonant or vowel. If you are having troubling finding certain words in a dictionary, try adding an extra consonant somewhere, or add a *u* う to the *o* お vowel, and you might find it. Good luck!

Katakana Words

One good thing about Japanese, is the amazing amount of loan words from other languages. These are called *gairaigo* がいらいご[外来語] (foreign origin words) in Japanese. Many students of Japanese call these Katakana Words because they are written with katakana. When Japanese students first learn English, they learn to pronounce English words using their own writing system. Because of this, if you pronounce English words using Japanese pronunciation, someone will be able to more easily understand you. The following is a list of Katakana Words derived from English. If you can read katakana, please practice these words now. If not, practice pronouncing these words using Japanese pronunciation. A lot of these words also have a native Japanese equivalent, for example, the word **bag** *baggu* バッグ is used in addition to *fukuro* ふくろ[袋] (bag).

English Word	Romaji Spelling	Katakana Spelling
accessory	*akusesarii*	アクセサリー
Africa	*afurika*	アフリカ
album	*arubamu*	アルバム
alcohol	*arukooru*	アルコール
America	*amerika*	アメリカ
announcer	*anaunsaa*	アナウンサー
apartment	*apaato*	アパート
Asia	*ajia*	アジア
bag	*baggu*	バッグ
ball	*booru*	ボール
bed	*beddo*	ベッド
beer	*biiru*	ビール
bell	*beru*	ベル
belt	*beruto*	ベルト
bus	*basu*	バス
butter	*bataa*	バター
button	*botan*	ボタン
cake	*keeki*	ケーキ
calendar	*karendaa*	カレンダー
camera	*kamera*	カメラ
camp	*kyanpu*	キャンプ
card	*kaado*	カード

chance	chansu	チャンス
cheese	chiizu	チーズ
closet	kuroozetto	クローゼット
coach	koochi	コーチ
coffee	koohii	コーヒー
computer	konpyuutaa	コンピューター
concert	konsaato	コンサート
copy	kopii	コピー
cream	kuriimu	クリーム
cup	kappu	カップ
curtain	kaaten	カーテン
dance	dansu	ダンス
date	deeto	デート
department store	depaato	デパート
door	doa	ドア
drama	dorama	ドラマ
dress	doresu	ドレス
elevator	erebeetaa	エレベーター
energy	enerugii	エネルギー
engine	enjin	エンジン
escalator	esukareetaa	エスカレーター
Europe	yooroppa	ヨーロッパ
fax	fakkusu	ファックス
fork	fooku	フォーク
game	geemu	ゲーム
gas	gasu	ガス
glass	garasu	ガラス
goal	gooru	ゴール
gram	guramu	グラム
group	guruupu	グループ
guitar	gitaa	ギター
hiking	haikingu	ハイキング

hotel	*hoteru*	ホテル
ice cream	*aisu*	アイス
India	*indo*	インド
ink	*inku*	インク
iron	*airon*	アイロン
juice	*juusu*	ジュース
kilometer / kilogram	*kiro*	キロ
knife	*naifu*	ナイフ
knock	*nokku*	ノック
lettuce	*retasu*	レタス
lighter	*raitaa*	ライター
London	*rondon*	ロンドン
market	*maaketto*	マーケット
member	*menbaa*	メンバー
milk	*miruku*	ミルク
necktie	*nekutai*	ネクタイ
news	*nyuusu*	ニュース
notebook	*nooto*	ノート
orange	*orenji*	オレンジ
out	*auto*	アウト
page	*peeji*	ページ
party	*paatii*	パーティー
passport	*pasupooto*	パスポート
PC	*pasokon*	パソコン
pen	*pen*	ペン
percent	*paasento*	パーセント
pet	*petto*	ペット
piano	*piano*	ピアノ
picnic	*pikunikku*	ピクニック
plan	*puran*	プラン
plum	*puramu*	プラム
plus	*purasu*	プラス

pocket	poketto	ポケット
pool	puuru	プール
present	purezento	プレゼント
racket	raketto	ラケット
radio	rajio	ラジオ
record	rekoodo	レコード
register	reji	レジ
report	repooto	レポート
restaurant	resutoran	レストラン
robot	robotto	ロボット
rocket	roketto	ロケット
salad	sarada	サラダ
sandal	sandaru	サンダル
sandwich	sandoicchi	サンドイッチ
service	saabisu	サービス
shirt	shatsu	シャツ
shower	shawaa	シャワー
skate	sukeeto	スケート
skirt	sukaato	スカート
sofa	sofaa	ソファー
soup	suupu	スープ
Spain	supein	スペイン
speech	supiichi	スピーチ
spoon	supuun	スプーン
sports	supootsu	スポーツ
star	sutaa	スター
steak	suteeki	ステーキ
sterco	sutereo	ステレオ
stove	sutoobu	ストーブ
suit	suutsu	スーツ
sweater	seetaa	セーター
tobacco	tabako	タバコ

table	*teeburu*	テーブル
tape	*teepu*	テープ
taxi	*takushii*	タクシー
team	*chiimu*	チーム
television	*terebi*	テレビ
tennis	*tenisu*	テニス
test	*tesuto*	テスト
Thailand	*tai*	タイ
toilet	*toire*	トイレ
top	*toppu*	トップ
towel	*taoru*	タオル
truck	*torakku*	トラック
tunnel	*tonneru*	トンネル
video	*bideo*	ビデオ
violin	*baiorin*	バイオリン
vitamin	*bitamin*	ビタミン
whiskey	*uisukii*	ウイスキー
wine	*wain*	ワイン

Today we will learn some basic question words. Try saying these to your friends and watch at how amazed they are at your speaking ability! The format of the vocabulary section will be: **the English word in bold,** followed by the Japanese pronunciation using *the Alphabet in italics*, followed by the word using the Japanese writing system, followed by the kanji if one is available. Some words have a kanji but are usually written with only kana. If this is the case, (UK) will be placed next to the word. This means *usually kana.* Though I've chosen the word *usually*, some words are *never* written with kanji, and some words are only sometimes written with kanji. There really are no rules for when to use kanji and when not to, but in general, grammatical words, and words that are used very often, will be written with kana only.

Day 1 Vocabulary:

1. who	*dare*	だれ	誰
who (polite)	*donata*	どなた	何方 (UK)
2. what	*nani*	なに	何
3. where	*doko*	どこ	何処 (UK)
4. when	*itsu*	いつ	何時 (UK)
5. why	*naze*	なぜ	何故 (UK)
why	*nande*	なんで	何で
why (polite)	*doushite*	どうして	如何して (UK)

There are three different words for why, and you may be asking yourself which one is best to use. *Naze* なぜ is somewhat formal, used more often in writing. *Nande* なんで[何で] is casual, like the Japanese version of *what for*, or, *how come? Doushite* どうして[如何して] is polite.

6. how	*dou*	どう	如何 (UK)
how (polite)	*ikaga*	いかが	如何 (UK)
7. which (two choices)	*dochira*	どちら	何方 (UK)

In casual conversation this is shortened to *docchi* どっち.

8. which (three or more choices)	*dore*	どれ	
9. how many / how old	*ikutsu*	いくつ	幾つ(UK)
10. how much	*ikura*	いくら	幾ら (UK)

If you skipped the Foreword and came straight to this lesson, you missed some valuable information. Namely, Japanese sentences drop all unnecessary information. Many of the following example sentences were translated using *you*. However, *you* is not written in Japanese. Depending on the context, the first example sentence could be translated as *Who am I, Who are you, Who is he, Who is she, Who is it, Who are we, Who are they*?

Day 1 Example Sentences:

1. Who are you?

2. What are you doing?

3. Where are you?

4. When are you going?

5. Why did you do that?

6. How was it?

7. Which do you like, chocolate or vanilla?

8. Which do you like, chocolate, vanilla, or strawberry?

9. How old are you?

(Lit. How many are you?)

10. How much is this?

1. だれですか。

2. なにをしていますか。

3. どこですか。

4. いついきますか。

5. なぜそれをしましたか？

6. どうでしたか？

7. チョコかバニラ、どっちがすきですか。

8. チョコかバニラかストロベリー、どれがすきですか。

9. いくつですか。

10. これはいくらですか。

1. *Dare desu ka?*

2. *Nani o shite imasu ka?*

3. *Doko desu ka?*

4. *Itsu ikimasu ka?*

5. *Naze sore o shimashita ka?*

6. *Dou deshita ka?*

7. *Choko ka banira, docchi ga suki desu ka?*

8. *Choko ka banira ka sutoroberii, dore ga suki desu ka?*

9. *Ikutsu desu ka?*

10. *Kore wa ikura desu ka?*

1. 誰ですか。

2.何をしていますか。

3. どこですか。

4. いつ行きますか。

5. なぜそれをしましたか？

6. どうでしたか？

7. チョコかバニラ、どっちが好きですか。

8. チョコかバニラかストロベリー、どれが好きですか。

9. いくつですか。

10. これはいくらですか。

You may have noticed in sentence ten that *ha* は is pronounced as *wa* わ. We will cover why in another lesson.

Day 2: Greetings, Farewells, Yes and No

I hope you are enjoying saying some Japanese phrases. Today we will learn a few greetings and farewells to accompany the question words you learned yesterday. I bet you already know *konnichiwa* こんにちは[今日は]. Look at you! You can already speak Japanese!

Speaking of which, I bet you already know how to say *yes* in Japanese. Of course, you already know it's *hai* はい. How about *no*? *No* is *iie* いいえ. There are also casual versions of these words, similar to *yeah* and *nah* in English. In Japanese you can say *un* うん(yeah) and *uun* ううん(nah). Be careful because the pronunciation is the same, but you say the vowel longer with *nah*. Another way to say *yeah* is *ee* ええ, this is used generally by males only.

Remember, when you study, say everything out loud! Since a lot of today's words are phrases and not simple vocabulary words, they will be separated line by line for ease of reading.

Day 2 Vocabulary:

1. yes	*hai*	はい	
yeah	*un*	うん	
yeah	ee	ええ	
no	*iie*	いいえ	
nah	*uun*	ううん	
2. Good morning.	*Ohayou gozaimasu.*	おはようございます。	お早うございます。
3. Good evening.	*Konban wa.*	こんばんは。	今晩は。
4. Good night.	*Oyasuminasai.*	おやすみなさい。	お休みなさい。
5. Goodbye.	*Sayounara.*	さようなら。	
6. Bye.	*Jaa ne.*	じゃあね。	
7. See you later.	*Mata ne.*	またね。	
8. See you tomorrow.	*Mata ashita.*	またあした。	また明日。
9. Take care.	*Ki o tsukete.*	きをつけて。	気を付けて。
10. Hello (on the phone).	*Moshi moshi.*	もしもし。	
Some people pronounce this *mushi mushi* むしむし.			

Day 3: Meeting, Thanks, Sorry

You've made it to Day 3! It is my hope that with these first few lessons, you will become accustomed to the studying method that was previously outlined, so that in later lessons when grammar is introduced, you will already have mastered the vocabulary studying method. Today we will learn how to say *thank you*, *sorry*, and what to say when you meet someone. A lot of these words don't literally translate to their English counterparts, and require explanation.

Day 3 Vocabulary:

1. How do you do?	*Hajimemashite.*	はじめまして。	初めまして。

In English, the phrase *How do you do*, is not often used anymore. In Japanese, when people meet for the first time, they will say *hajimemashite* はじめまして[初めまして].

2. Nice to meet you.	*Yoroshiku onegaishimasu.*	よろしくおねがいします。	宜しくお願いします。

The first word *yoroshiku* よろしく[宜しく] means *good* or *alright*. The second word *onegaishimasu* おねがいします[お願いします] means *to beg*. So we are literally saying *I'm begging you to be good*. Sounds rather serious!

Please. (polite)	*Onegaishimasu.*	おねがいします。	お願いします。
3. How are you?	*Ogenki desu ka.*	おげんきですか。	お元気ですか。

This is literally asking *Are you healthy?*

4. I'm fine.	*Genki desu.*	げんきです。	元気です。
I'm so so.	*Maamaa desu.*	まあまあです。	

To answer *I'm fine*, or *I'm well*, say *hai, genki desu* はい、げんきです[はい、元気です].
If you are just *so so*, say *maamaa desu* まあまあです without *hai* はい.

5. I'm called ____. (polite)	____ *to moushimasu.*	____ともうします。	____と申します。

Name in Japanese is *namae* なまえ[名前]. I bet after reading this just now, you've already memorized it. To say *my name is*, simply say your name and add *desu* です. The phrase above is the formal version. If you use this, a Japanese person will be very impressed!

6. Excuse me. / I'm sorry.	*Sumimasen.*	すみません。	

Like in English, this can also double as *sorry*. Japanese people like to be polite, and are always apologizing, so you will probably hear this word very often in contexts where you wouldn't think to say it.

7. Excuse me. (polite) / Goodbye.	*Shitsurei shimasu.*	しつれいします。	失礼します。

This is the formal version of *excuse me*. This word can be used to say *goodbye* when you are at work, and you are leaving before your other coworkers. In this sense, it translates to *excuse me for leaving*.

8. Sorry.	*Gomennasai.*	ごめんなさい。	御免なさい。 **(UK)**

This can be shortened to *gomen* ごめん[御免].

| 9. Thank you very much. | *Doumo arigatou gozaimasu.* | どうもありがとう
ございます。 | |

You probably already know that *thank you* in Japanese is *arigatou* ありがとう. This is actually a shortened version of *arigatou gozaimasu* ありがとうございます. The word *doumo* どうも can be added for a more polite version. *doumo* どうも said by itself is a quick and very casual version: *thanks*.

| 10. You're welcome. | *Dou itashimashite.* | どういたしまして。 | |
| No problem. | *Iie iie.* | いいえいいえ。 | |

This literally means *no no,* but translates to *no problem.*

Day 4: Common Phrases

Day 4 Vocabulary:

1. I'm leaving.	*Ittekimasu.*	いってきます。	行って来ます。
This is said when you are leaving somewhere to the people who are staying behind. It literally means *I will go and come back.* In English we usually just say *bye.*			
2. Have a good one.	*Itterasshai.*	いってらっしゃい。	行ってらっしゃい。
This is the response to *ittekimasu* いってきます[行って来ます]. If you are staying at a location, you will say this to the person leaving. It can be translated as something like *Have a good one.*			
3. I'm home.	*Tadaima.*	ただいま。	只今。 **(UK)**
This is used as a greeting when you come home. It means *I'm home,* or *I'm back.*			
4. Welcome back.	*Okaerinasai.*	おかえりなさい。	お帰りなさい。
This is the response to *tadaima* ただいま[只今]. It means *welcome back.*			
5. Let's eat.	*Itadakimasu.*	いただきます。	頂きます。
Say this before you start eating. It is the honorific form of the verb *to receive.* It is often said whenever something is received, even if it isn't food.			
6. Thank you for the meal.	*Gochisousama deshita.*	ごちそうさまでした。	ご馳走様でした **(UK)**
Say this when you've finished eating to say *thank you for the meal.*			
7. Please come in.	*Irasshaimase.*	いらっしゃいませ。	
You will hear this word more often than you would like. It is constantly being said by store clerks and it means *please come in,* or *welcome.*			
8. I'm bothering you.	*Ojamashimasu.*	おじゃまします。	お邪魔します。
This is said when entering someone's home, asking forgiveness for the intrusion.			
9. Good work today.	*Otsukaresama deshita.*	おつかれさまでした。	お疲れ様でした。
This is used to say *goodbye* in the workplace. It can be translated as *you worked hard today* and is often used in other contexts anytime someone does some hard work.			
10. Please. (Do as you like.)	*Douzo.*	どうぞ。	
This is not *please* when giving a command. This please means *go ahead* or *do as you like.*			

Day 5: Pronouns, Politeness, and Suffixes

Japanese is very different from English in that there are different ways to say things depending on your politeness level. There are five different levels of politeness: 1. Talking down to something of lower status, like a pet. 2. Casual speech, used with your friends. 3. Polite speech, used with coworkers or strangers. 4. Honorific speech, used to show you honor someone. 5. Humble speech, used to show that you feel humble in someone's presence.

In English, we use more polite speech during formal situations or with strangers. The same is true in Japanese, however, there is one more use. Though we call it *polite* and *casual,* in Japanese we should really call it *soft* and *rough.* When Japanese people use casual or polite phrases, often, it isn't because they want to be polite, but the words themselves sound *soft* or *rough,* the speaker may want to appear to be *gentle,* so they will use polite words. This is why women will most often use polite speech, and have entirely different words in some instances. They want to appear *soft* or *gentle,* whereas men may want to appear to be *rough* and *rugged.* Of course, it's up to the speaker, and men and women can use whatever they want to make themselves appear *soft* or *rough.*

In this book, we will only cover casual and polite speech, because they are the most common. There are a few phrases that are very common with honorific and humble speech, which will be covered later. That being said, there are many ways to say *I* depending on how polite you want to be. The following words are listed in order from casual to polite.

Women can choose:

atashi (slang)	あたし	
watashi	わたし	私
watakuski	わたくし	私

Men can choose:

ore	おれ	俺
boku	ぼく	僕
watashi	わたし	私
washi (old person slang)	わし	私
watakushi	わたくし	私

In casual conversations, most men will rarely say *watashi* わたし[私] or *watakushi* わたくし[私] because these words are mostly used by women, but if they did use these words, it would usually be in a formal situation. Most men will say *ore* おれ[俺] with their friends, *boku* ぼく[僕] is less common. It is also possible to simply say your own name in place of *I.* This might sound strange to an English speaker, but sometimes Japanese people will refer to themselves in the third-person, instead of saying *I.*

To say *you* is a bit more complicated. The fact is, calling someone *you* is sort of impolite, and most Japanese people will try to find a way around it. People are most always referred to their names or titles if known. It's a bit strange sounding in English. Let's say your friend's name was John, instead of saying *I like you*, Japanese people will say *I like John*, even if John is standing right in front of them! However, if you absolutely must say *you*, there are a few ways we can say it. The most common are *kimi* きみ[君] for casual speech and *anata* あなた for polite speech. You may also often hear people say *omae* おまえ[お前] which used to be an honorific form of *you*, but has since changed into casual, or even sometimes derogatory, similar to English when calling someone *your highness* or *master*. Some people use *omae* おまえ[お前] to be polite, as well as to be rude, so you really have to understand the context. Some less common forms of *you* are *temae* てまえ[手前] and *sochira* そちら. There is also *kisama* きさま[貴様] which used to be an honorific word but is now a bad word, that means *you bastard*, or *you son of a bitch*. As you can see there are many ways to say *I* and *you*, depending on how polite you want to be.

The pronoun *he* is *kare* かれ[彼]. *She* is *kanojo* かのじょ[彼女]. These also can be translated as *boyfriend* or *girlfriend*. A casual form of *he* or *she* is *aitsu* あいつ. This is used by people of higher status talking down to someone, for example a parent to a child.

To make plural forms, as in *we* or *you all*, add the suffix *tachi* たち to the pronouns for *I* or *you*. For example *we* is *watashitachi* わたしたち[私たち]. There is also a formal version of *we*: *wareware* われわれ[我々].

To make the words for *they*, add *ra* ら to *he* or *she*: *karera* かれら [彼ら] for a group of men, *kanojora* かのじょら[彼女ら] for women. If the group is mixed, use the male version.

Let's talk a bit more about suffixes. You've seen The Karate Kid, right? Mr. Miyage always calls Daniel, Daniel-san. This can be translated as *mister*, but usually it shouldn't be translated at all. Japanese people will most always add a suffix to a name to show their politeness level and relationship with that person.

Polite suffix.	*san*	さん
Humble suffix, used often with customer.	*sama*	さま
Casual suffix for boys.	*kun*	くん
Casual suffix for girls, though sometimes used with boys to sound cute.	*chan*	ちゃん
Suffix for teachers or doctors.	*sensei*	せんせい
Suffix meaning *my senior*. Used in schools to address someone in a higher grade level than you, or in business to address a coworker who has been at the company longer.	*senpai*	せんぱい
Opposite suffix of *senpai* せんぱい. Used to talk to your juniors.	*kouhai*	こうはい

Nouns can be made more polite by adding the prefixes *o* お or *go* ご. For example, the word sushi is often called *o-sushi*. This makes the word polite and shows respect to the word. Some nouns almost always have this polite prefix, for example, *okane* おかね[お金] (money). People respect money so much that they will almost never say the word without the polite prefix!

Day 5 Vocabulary:

1. I (male only)	*ore*	おれ	俺
I (male only)	*boku*	ぼく	僕
I	*watashi*	わたし	私
I (polite)	*watakushi*	わたくし	私
2. you	*kimi*	きみ	君
you (polite)	*anata*	あなた	貴方 (UK)
3. you (rude)	*omae*	おまえ	お前
you (rude)	*kisama*	きさま	貴様
4. he / boyfriend	*kare*	かれ	彼
5. she / girlfriend	*kanojo*	かのじょ	彼女
6. humble suffix	*sama*	さま	様
7. plural suffix	*tachi*	たち	達 (UK)
plural suffix	*ra*	ら	等 (UK)
8. boy suffix	*kun*	くん	君
girl suffix	*chan*	ちゃん	
9. teacher / doctor suffix	*sensei*	せんせい	先生
10. senior suffix	*senpai*	せんぱい	先輩
junior suffix	*kouhai*	こうはい	後輩

Since you haven't learned any verbs yet, having example sentences isn't the best way to practice today's vocabulary. A great way to practice is to think of the appropriate pronoun and suffix of every person you meet as you go about your day. Go meet some people!

You've made it to the first grammar lesson! Are you excited? In Japanese, the verb always comes at the end of the sentence. Verbs do not conjugate with the subject, the same verb form is used when the subject is *I, you, he, she, it, they, we*. However, there are various politeness levels.

(to be)

Casual	*da*	だ
Polite	*desu*	です
Honorific / Humble	*de gozaimasu*	でございます

(not to be)

Casual	*dewa nai*	ではない
Polite	*dewa arimasen*	ではありません
Honorific / Humble	*dewa gozaimasen*	ではございません

But wait, there's more! *dewa* では is often shortened to *ja* じゃ. This makes it even more casual. This means that the casual and polite versions have a slightly more casual flavor if you say *ja* じゃ instead of *dewa* では. This is a lot of information, so let's look at some examples:

It's Jim. (casual)
Jimu da.
ジムだ。

It's not Jim. (casual)
Jimu ja nai.
ジムじゃない。

It's Jim. (polite)
Jimu desu.
ジムです。

It's not Jim. (polite)
Jimu dewa arimasen.
ジムではありません。

It's Jim. (honorific / humble)
Jimu de gozaimasu.
ジムでございます。

It's not Jim. (honorific / humble)
Jimu dewa gozaimasen.
ジムではございません。

desu です can be added to the end of a sentence with other verbs to slightly raise the politeness level. As you continue your studies, you may see sentences that have an extra *desu* です after the verb. This is a way to raise the politeness level of the sentence. You may also see *nodesu* のです or *ndesu* んです. These give the sentence an explanatory tone, it is being said as an answer or explanation to something. Don't worry yourself if this sounds confusing. For now, it's not important.

I'm going to introduce grammar cards in this lesson. In addition to your vocabulary cards, I want you to make grammar cards. They will be used a lot more in future lessons, and this will really help you memorize grammar. On one side of the card, write the English grammar, and on the other side, the Japanese equivalent. Write at least one example sentence on each grammar card, in Japanese on one side, and English on the other. Don't forget, say everything out loud.

Day 6 Grammar Cards:

1. to be (casual)	da	だ
not to be (casual)	dewa (ja) nai	では(じゃ)ない
2. to be (polite)	desu	です
not to be	dewa arimasen	ではありません
3. to be (honorific / humble)	de gozaimasu	でございます
not to be	dewa gozaimasen	ではございません

Day 6 Vocabulary:

1. adult	otona	おとな	大人
2. child	kodomo	こども	子供
3. person	hito	ひと	人
people	hitobito	ひとびと	人々
person (humble)	kata	かた	方
4. everyone	minna / mina	みんな・みな	皆

This word has two spellings, but is most always paired with *san* さん, and when it is, will take the shorter spelling: *minasan* みなさん[皆さん]

5. doctor	isha	いしゃ	医者
physician	ishi	いし	医師
6. dentist	shikai	しかい	歯科医
7. professor / teacher	kyouju	きょうじゅ	教授
8. school student	gakusei	がくせい	学生
9. police man	keikan	けいかん	警官
police man	omawarisan	おまわりさん	

omawarisan おまわりさん is a friendly word for *police,* often used by children.

10. business man	sarariiman	サラリーマン	
business woman	ooeru	オーエル	OL

As you can see, these words are taken from English. OL stands for *Office Lady.*

Day 6 Example Sentences:

1. **He is an adult.**

2. **She is not a child.**

3. **It is a person.**

4. **Everyone is not beautiful.**

5. **I am a doctor.**

6. **I am not a dentist.**

7. **We are professors.**

8. **They are not students.**

9. **I am a police man.**

10. **She is a business person.**

1. かれはおとなだ。

2. かのじょはこどもじゃない。

3. ひとです。

4. みなさんはきれいではありません。

5. わたしはいしゃです。

6. わたくしはしかいではございません。

7. わたしたちはきょうじゅです。

8. かれらはがくせいではありません。

9. おれはけいかんです。

10. かのじょはオーエルでございます。

1. *Kare wa otona da.*

2. *Kanojo wa kodomo ja nai.*

3. *Hito desu.*

4. *Minasan wa kirei dewa arimasen.*

5. *Watashi wa isha desu.*

6. *Watakushi wa shikai dewa gozaimasen.*

7. *Watashitachi wa kyouju desu.*

8. *Karera wa gakusei dewa arimasen.*

9. *Ore wa keikan desu.*

10. *Kanojo wa ooeru de gozaimasu.*

1. 彼は大人だ。

2. 彼女は子供じゃない。

3. 人です。

4. 皆さんはきれいではありません。

5. 私は医者です。

6. 私は歯科医ではございません。

7. 私たちは教授です。

8. 彼らは学生ではありません。

9. 俺は警官です。

10. 彼女はオーエルでございます。

In Japanese, most countries are written using *katakana* カタカナ. Some countries have both a *kanji* 漢字 and *katakana* カタカナ writing, for example, America can be said as *amerika* アメリカ or *beikoku* べいこく[米国], but most people will use the katakana version.

Let's take a second to talk about kanji. Kanji are difficult not only because of their various shapes, but they have various pronunciations. For example, in Japanese, the word for *country* is *kuni* くに [国]. However, in all of the words learned today, it will be pronounced *koku* こく[国]. Kanji have two main pronunciations called *kun* くん[訓] (Japanese reading) and *on* おん[音] (Chinese reading). In general, the Japanese reading will be used for the word itself, while the Chinese reading will be used for compound words. Because the words learned today are all compound words, the Chinese reading will be used. This is an advanced topic that you don't need to worry about until you begin trying to read kanji.

To say that you are a person from a country, add the suffix *jin* じん[人] to the country name.

America → American	*amerika → amerikajin*	アメリカ → アメリカじん	アメリカ → アメリカ人
Japan → Japanese	*nihon → nihonjin*	にほん → にほんじん	日本 → 日本人

To say the language of a country, add the suffix *go* ご[語] to the name of the country. English is an exception to this rule and has a different pronunciation. This is because the kanji version of England is *eikoku* えいこく[英国].

England → English	*igirisu → eigo*	イギリス → えいご	イギリス → 英語
Japan → Japanese	*nihon → nihongo*	にほん → にほんご	日本 → 日本語

You may have heard the word for Japan being pronounced as *nippon* instead of *nihon*. This is an example of Japanese speakers changing a kana to its voiced version. In this case *ho* changes to *ppo*. There is no difference in meaning, just as there is no difference between the USA, the US, America, the United States.

Day 7 Grammar Cards:

1. nationality suffix	*jin*	じん	人
2. language suffix	*go*	ご	語

Day 7 Vocabulary:

1. Japan	*nihon*	にほん	日本
2. China	*chuugoku*	ちゅうごく	中国
3. Korea	*kankoku*	かんこく	韓国
4. England	*igirisu*	イギリス	
5. Germany	*doitsu*	ドイツ	
6. USA	*amerika*	アメリカ	
7. country	*kuni*	くに	国
8. foreign country	*gaikoku*	がいこく	外国
9. foreign student	*ryuugakusei*	りゅうがくせい	留学生
10. abroad	*kaigai*	かいがい	海外

<u>Day 7 Example sentences</u>:

1. I am not Japanese.	1. ぼくはにほんじんじゃない。
2. She can speak Chinese.	2. かのじょはちゅうごくごをはなせます。
3. He is from Korea.	3. かれはかんこくからきました。
4. Do you speak English?	4. えいごをはなせますか。
5. Are you German?	5. あなたはドイツじんですか。
6. English is spoken in America.	6. アメリカではえいごがはなされる。
7. What kind of country is Japan?	7. にほんはどんなくにですか。
8. I am a foreigner.	8. わたしはがいこくじんです。
9. I am a foreign student.	9. ぼくはりゅうがくせいです。
10. Have you been abroad?	10. かいがいにいったことはありますか。

1. *Boku wa nihonjin ja nai.*	1. 僕は日本人じゃない。
2. *Kanojo wa chuugokugo o hanasemasu.*	2. 彼女は中国語を話せます。
3. *Kare wa kankoku kara kimashita.*	3. 彼は韓国から来ました。
4. *Eigo o hanasemasu ka?*	4. 英語を話せますか。
5. *Anata wa doitsujin desu ka?*	5. あなたはドイツ人ですか。
6. *Amerika de wa eigo ga hanasareru.*	6. アメリカでは英語が話される。
7. *Nihon wa donna kuni desu ka?*	7. 日本はどんな国ですか。
8. *Watashi wa gaikokujin desu.*	8. 私は外国人です。
9. *Boku wa ryuugakusei desu.*	9. 僕は留学生です。
10. *Kaigai ni itta koto wa arimasu ka?*	10. 海外に行ったことはありますか。

Day 8: Sentence Structure, Particles は, が, も

In English, there are special words called *prepositions*. Japanese has no prepositions, but has words called *particles*, which have many of the same functions as prepositions.

Basic word order for Japanese is: subject, indirect object, direct object, verb. Japanese uses particles after words to mark the grammar. Particles will follow the words they modify. There are many more particles and many more uses for the particles introduced today, but for now, let's just learn the basics:

Topic particle	*wa*	は
written as *ha* は, pronounced *wa* わ		
Subject particle	*ga*	が
Object particle	*o*	を
written as *wo* を, pronounced *o* お		
Indirect object particle	*ni*	に

The following is an example English sentence using Japanese sentence structure:

I は my mother に flowers を bought.

You may be asking yourself why *wa* は and not *ga* が was used. This is probably the hardest part about Japanese for non-native speakers. Japanese is what linguists call a Topic-Prominent Language, or a Topic-Comment language. This means that speakers will introduce a topic, and then comment on it. This sounds complicated, but there is really only one thing to keep in mind: The basic translation for *wa* は is **as for.** In fact, *wa* は can take the place of almost any other particle. It can be used more than once in a sentence. It can even combine with other particles. The following sentences use *wa* は in different places for slightly different translations:

As for me, I bought my mother flowers.
I は my mother に flowers を bought.

As for my mother, I bought her flowers.
My mother は I が flowers を bought.

As for the flowers, I bought them for my mother.
Flowers は I が my mother に bought.

In this way, *wa* は can be used to place emphasis on different parts of a sentence. As far as translating, *as for* will almost never be included in the English version. This is because it sounds unnatural in English. However, in Japanese, this is exactly what using *wa* は implies.

The particle *mo* も attaches to the subject of sentences in place of *wa* は or *ga* が, and when we use it, it will translate as *too* or *also*.

You are <u>also</u> cute.
You're cute <u>too</u>.
Anata <u>mo</u> kawaii desu.
あなたもかわいいです。

The next topic is omission. In Japanese, if the context can be understood, all unnecessary information will be dropped from a sentence. Often, people won't even say the topic or subject of a sentence. You may have noticed this in some of the example sentences in the previous lessons. In spoken Japanese, particles are often dropped and replaced with a pause. Study the following examples:

1. You are cute.
Anata wa kawaii desu.
あなたはかわいいです。

4. You are cute.
Anata, kawaii.
あなた、かわいい。

2. You are cute.
Anata ga kawaii desu.
あなたがかわいいです。

5. You are cute.
Kawaii.
かわいい。

3. You are cute.
Anata, kawaii desu.
あなた、かわいいです。

Sentence one translates to "As for you, you are cute." We would use this if we were discussing something else, and we wanted to change the topic to you, and then add that you are indeed cute. In sentence two, the topic is something else and already known, and you being cute somehow relates to that known topic. Sentence three shows how, in spoken Japanese, particles are often dropped. Sentence four shows that even the verb *to be* can be dropped if understood from context. Sentence five shows how the subject, particle, and verb can be dropped if understood from context. Sentence five also illustrates the most common form of spoken Japanese, that is, everything that can be understood from context will be dropped from the sentence.

Day 8 Grammar Cards:

1. Topic particle	wa	は
2. Subject particle	ga	が
3. Object particle	o	を
4. Indirect object particle	ni	に
5. also / too particle	mo	も

Day 8 Vocabulary:

1. head	atama	あたま	頭
2. body	karada	からだ	体
3. arm	ude	うで	腕
4. hand	te	て	手
5. leg / foot	ashi	あし	足
6. finger	yubi	ゆび	指
toe	ashiyubi	あしゆび	足指

For toes, literally *foot finger*.

7. eye	me	め	目
8. ear	mimi	みみ	耳
9. nose	hana	はな	鼻
10. mouth	kuchi	くち	口

Mouth in Japanese can refer to many types of openings. For example: *deguchi* でぐち[出口] (exit).

As stated previously, in Japanese, unnecessary information is dropped, because of this, today's sentences will all have an understood subject. Though the written translation may say *My head hurts*, it could also be translated as *your / his / her.* Additionally, *my* is also dropped, because it can be understood from context.

<u>Day 8 Example sentences:</u>

1. My head hurts.	**1.** あたまがいたいです。
2. My body also hurts.	**2.** からだもいたいです。
3. My right arm hurts.	**3.** みぎのうでがいたいです。
4. My hand also hurts.	**4.** てもいたい。
5. As for my leg, it's alright.	**5.** あしはだいじょうぶです。
6. My toes are okay too.	**6.** あしゆびもだいじょうぶです。
7. My eye hurts.	**7.** めがいたいです。
8. As for my ears, they are okay.	**8.** みみはだいじょうぶです。
9. My nose hurts.	**9.** はながいたいです。
10. As for my mouth, it's okay.	**10.** くちはだいじょうぶです。

1. *Atama ga itai desu.*	**1.** 頭が痛いです。
2. *Karada mo itai desu.*	**2.** 体も痛いです。
3. *Migi no ude ga itai desu.*	**3.** 右の腕が痛いです。
4. *Te mo itai.*	**4.** 手も痛い。
5. *Ashi wa daijoubu desu.*	**5.** 足は大丈夫です。
6. *Ashiyubi mo daijoubu desu.*	**6.** 足指も大丈夫です。
7. *Me ga itai desu.*	**7.** 目が痛いです。
8. *Mimi wa daijoubu desu.*	**8.** 耳は大丈夫です。
9. *Hana ga itai desu.*	**9.** 鼻が痛いです。
10. *Kuchi wa daijoubu desu.*	**10.** 口は大丈夫です。

Day 9: Particles を and で

As we learned yesterday, *wo* を is the particle that marks direct objects. Don't forget, it is pronounced as *o* お.

I bought a video.	I ate pizza.
Bideo o katta.	*Piza o tabeta.*
ビデオをかった。	ぴざをたべた。
ビデオを買った。	ピザを食べた。

It can be used with motion verbs and a location. This translates as *around / across / through / over*, basically all the prepositions besides *to*.

I walked <u>around / through</u> the park.
Kouen o sanpo shita.
こうえんをさんぽした。
公園を散歩した。

Though *wo* を is always used to mark the object of the verb, Japanese has a few verbs that function differently than in English. What we might consider to be the object of a verb in English isn't always the object of a verb in Japanese. Some verbs will take *ga* が or *ni* に instead of *wo* を even though they would be considered direct objects of the verb in English. But don't worry, this topic is for more advanced speakers. Even if you use the wrong particle, a Japanese person will most likely be able to understand what you said. Remember, in Japanese, you can often drop particles, so if you aren't sure about which one to use, don't worry, you can just say nothing at all!

The particle *de* で is used to indicate where, how, or with what.

Used to indicate by what means you did something:

I came <u>by</u> car.
Kuruma de kimashita.
くるまできました。
車で来ました。

Used to indicate what something is done with:

I eat sushi <u>with</u> chopsticks.
Hashi de sushi o tabemasu.
はしですしをたべます。
箸で寿司を食べます。

Used with time to show how long something took to complete:

It was finished <u>in</u> five minutes.
Gofun <u>de</u> owarimashita.
ごふん<u>で</u>おわりました。
五分<u>で</u>終わりました。

Used to indicate where something took place:

I drank coffee <u>at</u> the cafe.
Kafe <u>de</u> koohii o nonda.
カフェ<u>で</u>コーヒーをのんだ。
カフェ<u>で</u>コーヒーを飲んだ。

To change the meaning to *without*, add *nashi* なし[無し] to *de* で. This can only be used with nouns. It cannot be used with verbs.

I ate <u>without</u> chopsticks.
Ohashi <u>nashi de</u> tabemashita.
おはし<u>なし</u>でたべました。
お箸<u>無し</u>で食べました。

Of course, every great language has exceptions to the rules to confuse you! An exception for *de* で is in the context of people. To say you are *with* a person, use the particle *to* と.

I walked <u>with</u> Jim.
Jimu <u>to</u> arukimashita.
ジム<u>と</u>あるきました。
ジム<u>と</u>歩きました。

Though *de* で is used to show a location, like *wo* を it will sometimes be replaced with *ni* に, even though we think it shouldn't be. A useful example of this is the verb *to live / reside* すむ[住む]. This verb will always use *ni* に instead of *de* で.

I live <u>in</u> Japan.
Watashi wa nihon <u>ni</u> sunde imasu.
わたしはにほん<u>に</u>すんでいます。
私は日本<u>に</u>住んでいます。

Day 9 Grammar Cards:

1. where / how / with particle	*de*	で	
2. with (person) particle	*to*	と	
3. without (noun)	(noun) + *nashide*	(noun) + なしで	(noun) + 無しで

Day 9 Vocabulary:

1. food	*tabemono*	たべもの	食べ物
2. drinks	*nomimono*	のみもの	飲み物
3. meat	*niku*	にく	肉
4. vegetables	*yasai*	やさい	野菜
5. fruit	*kudamono*	くだもの	果物
6. rice	*kome*	こめ	米
rice	*gohan*	ごはん	ご飯

kome こめ[米] refers to the rice itself. *gohan* ごはん[ご飯] refers to a bowl of rice.

7. breakfast	*asagohan*	あさごはん	朝ご飯
breakfast	*choushoku*	ちょうしょく	朝食

Japanese people traditionally eat rice with every meal, therefore *morning rice bowl* became the word for *breakfast*. The second word, *choushoku* ちょうしょく[朝食] means *early meal*, and is used more often to refer to anything that is eaten in the morning. The same rule applies to the next two words.

8. lunch	*hirugohan*	ひるごはん	昼ご飯
lunch	*chuushoku*	ちゅうしょく	昼食
9. dinner	*bangohan*	ばんごはん	晩ご飯
dinner	*yuushoku*	ゆうしょく	夕食
10. chopsticks	*hashi*	はし	箸

<u>Day 9 Example sentences</u>:

1. **I buy food at the supermarket.**

2. **As for drinks, I buy them from a vending machine.**

3. **I eat meat with my hands.**

4. **I eat vegetables with a fork.**

5. **I buy fruits at the vegetable store.**

6. **I cook rice without a pot.**

7. **I eat breakfast at a cafe.**

8. **I eat lunch at home.**

9. **I eat dinner at a restaurant.**

10. **I eat rice without chopsticks.**

1. スーパーでたべものをかいます。

2. のみものはじどうはんばいきでかいます。

3. てでにくをたべます。

4. フォークでやさいをたべます。

5. やおやでくだものをかいます。

6. なべなしでこめをたきます。

7. カフェでちょうしょくをたべます。

8. うちでちゅうしょくをたべます。

9. レストランでゆうしょくをたべます。

10. はしなしでごはんをたべます。

1. *Suupaa de tabemono o kaimasu.*

2. *Nomimono wa jidouhanbaiki de kaimasu.*

3. *Te de niku o tabemasu.*

4. *Fooku de yasai o tabemasu.*

5. *Yaoya de kudamono o kaimasu.*

6. *Nabe nashi de kome o takimasu.*

7. *Kafe de choushoku o tabemasu.*

8. *Uchi de chuushoku o tabemasu.*

9. *Resutoran de yuushoku o tabemasu.*

10. *Hashi nashi de gohan o tabemasu.*

1. スーパーで食べ物を買います。

2. 飲み物は自動販売機で買います。

3. 手で肉を食べます。

4. フォークで野菜を食べます。

5. 八百屋で果物を買います。

6. 鍋無しで米を炊きます。

7. カフェで朝食を食べます。

8. 家で昼食を食べます。

9. レストランで夕食を食べます。

10. 箸無しでご飯を食べます。

We've already learned in the previous lesson that *ni* に is used to indicate the indirect object of a sentence. Let's find out why. In reality, *ni* に is like an arrow, it is always pointing towards something. In fact, many people will call *ni* に the *target particle*. If you think about it this way, it will be easier to know when to use it. Study the following examples:

Used as an indirect object marker:

I bought you a cake.
Watashi wa anata ni keeki o katta.
わたしはあなたにケーキをかった。
私はあなたにケーキを買った。

Used after time expressions to mean *at*:

Let's meet at seven.
Shichiji ni aimashou.
しちじにあいましょう。
七時に会いましょう。

Used with directions or movements to mean *to*:

I will go to Japan.
Nihon ni ikimasu.
にほんにいきます。
日本に行きます。

When *ni* に is used with directions, *e* へ can be substituted. Though written as *he* へ, it is pronounced *e* え. The difference between *ni* に and *e* へ in this usage, is that *e* へ is more vague. Perhaps you will be going somewhere, but then going somewhere else after that. The final destination is unknown. The preference is really up to the speaker.

I will go to Japan (and maybe somewhere else after that).
Nihon e ikimasu.
にほんへいきます。
日本へ行きます。

Day 10 Grammar Cards:

1. target particle	ni	に
2. direction particle	e	へ

Day 10 Vocabulary:

1. hospital	byouin	びょういん	病院
2. post office	yuubinkyoku	ゆうびんきょく	郵便局
3. police box	kouban	こうばん	交番

Japan is crowded, so instead of having central police stations, they have small scattered police stations called *boxes* throughout the cities.

4. park	kouen	こうえん	公園
5. movie theater	eigakan	えいがかん	映画館
6. station	eki	えき	駅
7. house	uchi	うち	家
house	ie	いえ	家

uchi うち[家] refers to your home. *ie* いえ[家] refers to someone else's home, and also the physical building itself. Don't confuse this word with *iie* いいえ(no).

8. shop	mise	みせ	店
9. town	machi	まち	町
city	shi	し	市

machi まち[町] can mean *town* or *city*. *shi* し[市] is the suffix used for cities. For example, *Yokohama City* is pronounced *yokohama-shi*.

10. village	mura	むら	村

Day 10 Example Sentences:

1. Let's go to the hospital.

2. I'm going to the post office.

3. I'm headed toward the police box.

4. We're going to the park.

5. He went toward the movie theater.

6. This train goes to Tokyo Station.

7. I'm going back home.

8. She is walking to that shop over there.

9. I live in this town.

10. I will move to this village.

1. びょういんにいきましょう。

2. ゆうびんきょくへいきます。

3. こうばんへむかっています。

4. わたしたちはこうえんにいきます。

5. かれはえいがかんへいった。

6. このでんしゃはとうきょうえきへいきます。

7. うちにかえります。

8. かのじょはあのみせにあるいてむかっています。

9. このまちにすんでいます。

10. このむらにひっこします。

1. *Byouin ni ikimashou.*

2. *Yuubinkyoku e ikimasu.*

3. *Kouban e mukatte imasu.*

4. *Watashitachi wa kouen ni ikimasu.*

5. *Kare wa eigakan e itta.*

6. *Kono densha wa Toukyou eki e ikimasu.*

7. *Uchi ni kaerimasu.*

8. *Kanojo wa ano mise ni aruite mukatte imasu.*

9. *Kono machi ni sunde imasu.*

10. *Kono mura ni hikkoshimasu.*

1. 病院に行きましょう。

2. 郵便局へ行きます。

3. 交番へ向かっています。

4. 私たちは公園に行きます。

5. 彼は映画館へ行った。

6. この電車は東京駅へ行きます。

7. 家に帰ります。

8. 彼女はあの店に歩いて向かっています。

9. この町に住んでいます。

10. この村に引っ越します。

Day 11: End of Sentence Particles か, の, よ

Today's particles will always appear at the end of a sentence. To form a question in Japanese, add the particle *ka* か after *desu* です, or the verb. In casual speech, *no* の can also be used to form a question. Doing so changes *da* だ to *na* な. *ka* か and *no* の act as question marks. There is no question mark in Japanese punctuation, however, because of the influence of English, many people write question marks in casual settings, such as a cell phone text message. In formal writing, question marks won't appear. Study the following examples:

Where is it? (casual)	Where is it? (polite)
Doko na no? どこなの?	*Doko desu ka?* どこですか。

Like *ka* か functioning as a question mark, *yo* よ functions as an exclamation point. However, it doesn't always need to be used in a sentence that you are yelling. It can be used just to draw attention. Again, English punctuation won't be used in formal Japanese writing.

It's Jim! (casual)	It's Jim! (polite)
Jimu da yo! ジムだよ。	*Jimu desu yo!* ジムですよ。

Day 11 Grammar Cards:

1. question particles	*ka / no*	か・の
2. Change *da* to *na* with question particle *no*	*da + no → na no*	だ＋の　→　なの
3. attention particle	*yo*	よ

Day 11 Vocabulary:

1. water	*mizu*	みず	水
2. milk	*gyuunyuu*	ぎゅうにゅう	牛乳
3. green tea	*ocha*	おちゃ	お茶
4. black tea	*koucha*	こうちゃ	紅茶
5. bread	*pan*	パン	
6. egg	*tamago*	たまご	卵
7. fish	*sakana*	さかな	魚
8. plate / bowl /dish	*osara*	おさら	お皿
9. small bowl	*chawan*	ちゃわん	茶碗
This is a small bowl used for rice or tea. The word itself actually means *tea bowl*.			
10. boxed lunch	*obentou*	おべんとう	お弁当

Day 11 Example Sentences:

1. **Is this water?**
2. **Is this milk?**
3. **It's green tea!**
4. **It's black tea!**
5. **Is it bread?**
6. **Is it an egg?**
7. **Is this a fish?**
8. **That is not a plate!**
9. **Is it a small bowl?**
10. **That is a boxed lunch!**

1. これはみずですか。
2. これはぎゅうにゅうなの？
3. おちゃだよ。
4. こうちゃですよ。
5. パンなの？
6. たまごですか。
7. これはさかなですか。
8. それはおさらじゃないよ。
9. ちゃわんですか。
10. それはおべんとうですよ。

1. *Kore wa mizu desu ka?*
2. *Kore wa gyuunyuu na no?*
3. *Ocha da yo!*
4. *Koucha desu yo!*
5. *Pan na no?*
6. *Tamago desu ka?*
7. *Kore wa sakana desu ka?*
8. *Sore wa osara ja nai yo!*
9. *Chawan desu ka?*
10. *Sore wa obentou desu yo!*

1. これは水ですか。
2. これは牛乳なの？
3. お茶だよ。
4. 紅茶ですよ。
5. パンなの？
6. 卵ですか。
7. これは魚ですか。
8. それはお皿じゃないよ。
9. 茶碗ですか。
10. それはお弁当ですよ。

Day 12: Ownership, Particle の

The particle *no* の can be used like the English preposition *of* to show ownership. To say things like *my, your, his, her,* simply add the particle *no* の to the pronoun. Study the following examples:

I → my	*watashi → watashi no*	わたし → わたしの	私 → 私の
you → your	*anata → anata no*	あなた → あなたの	
who → whose	*dare → dare no*	だれ → だれの	誰→誰の

This is used in the words for *boy, girl, man,* and *woman,* which, if translated literally would be *male of child, female of child, male of person,* and *female of person*:

boy	*otoko no ko*	おとこのこ	男の子
girl	*onna no ko*	おんなのこ	女の子
man	*otoko no hito*	おとこのひと	男の人
woman	*onna no hito*	おんなのひと	女の人

There are many words that will use the *no hito* のひと[の人] construction to express the type of person. It has a bit of a special pronunciation, the *hi* ひ sound will actually be pronounced like an *sh*. The words *man* and *woman* actually sound like *otoko no shto* and *onna no shto*.

The particle *no* の is also used in many location words. Study the following example:

desk	*tsukue*	つくえ	机
above	*ue*	うえ	上
on the desk	*tsukue no ue*	つくえのうえ	机の上

The last phrase literally says *desk of above*. This means something is *on the desk* or *above the desk*. With locations in Japanese, the particle *no* の is used like this. *Below the desk,* is literally, *desk of under. To the right of the desk,* is literally, *desk of right,* and so on.

In the Day 6 lesson, we learned that sentences can sometimes end with *nodesu* のです to add an explanatory tone. This is actually using the *no* の ownership particle along with *desu* です. Literally, this translation would sound something like: (sentence) *of is*. A better translation is: *It is so, that* (sentence). A sentence like *I went to the store*, when ended with *nodesu* のです, changes to: *It is so that I went to the store,* which sounds very strange in English. In Japanese, people often do this to politely offer an explanation. The *nodesu* のです is often shortened to *ndesu* んです, or just *no* の. This can sometimes be confusing because *no* の also can act like a question mark. Actually, when using *no* の as a question mark, it is a contraction of *nodesuka* のですか. Sentences can end with *no* の to add an explanatory tone, or to act as a question mark, so pay attention to the context!

Day 12 Vocabulary:

1. male	*otoko*	おとこ	男
2. female	*onna*	おんな	女
3. above	*ue*	うえ	上
4. below	*shita*	した	下
5. in / middle	*naka*	なか	中
6. right	*migi*	みぎ	右
7. left	*hidari*	ひだり	左
8. behind	*ushiro*	うしろ	後ろ
9. in front of / before	*mae*	まえ	前
This word is also used with time.			
10. room	*heya*	へや	部屋

Day 12 Example Sentences:

1. That man is Jim.	1. あのおとこのひとはジムです。
2. That woman is Mary.	2. あのおんなのひとはメアリーです。
3. My hat is on the desk.	3. わたしのぼうしはつくえのうえです。
4. His cell phone is under the chair.	4. かれのケイタイはいすのしたです。
5. Her cell phone is in the desk.	5. かのじょのケイタイはつくえのなかです。
6. Your lunch is to the right of the TV.	6. あなたのおべんとうはてれびのみぎです。
7. My lunch is to the left of the TV.	7. おれのおべんとうはテレビのひだりです。
8. His lunch is behind the TV.	8. かれのおべんとうはてれびのうしろです。
9. Her lunch is in front of the TV.	9. かのじょのおべんとうはてれびのまえです。
10. This is your room.	10. ここはあなたのへやです。

1. *Ano otoko no hito wa jimu desu.*	1. あの男の人はジムです。
2. *Ano onna no hito wa mearii desu.*	2. あの女の人はメアリーです。
3. *Watashi no boushi wa tsukue no ue desu.*	3. 私の帽子は机の上です。
4. *Kare no keitai wa isu no shita desu.*	4. 彼のケイタイは椅子の下です。
5. *Kanojo no keitai wa tsukue no naka desu.*	5. 彼女のケイタイは机の中です。
6. *Anata no obentou wa terebi no migi desu.*	6. あなたのお弁当はテレビの右です。
7. *Ore no obentou wa terebi no hidari desu.*	7. 俺のお弁当はテレビの左です。
8. *Kare no obentou wa terebi no ushiro desu.*	8. 彼のお弁当はテレビの後ろです。
9. *Kanojo no obentou wa terebi no mae desu.*	9. 彼女のお弁当はテレビの前です。
10. *Koko wa anata no heya desu.*	10. ここはあなたの部屋です。

Day 13: Family

In Japanese, there are three different ways to refer to family members. One to reference your own family members, another when talking to that family member, and a third when talking about someone else's family member. Study the following cxample:

older brother	*ani*	あに	兄
older brother	*niisan*	にいさん	兄さん
older brother	*oniisan*	おにいさん	お兄さん

The first word *ani* あに[兄] is used to refer to your own older brother when conversing with someone else. Think of it as *my older brother*. The second word *niisan* にいさん[兄さん] is the title. In English, usually only our mother and father are called by their titles: Mom and Dad, but in Japanese, not only parents are called by their titles, but every other family member as well. The third word simply adds *o* お, to make the word polite, when referring to other people's family members: *oniisan* おにいさん[お兄さん]. As you probably noticed, this word was *older brother*. In Japanese, there are different words for *older* and *younger* siblings.

Day 13 Vocabulary:

1. my father	*chichi*	ちち	父
father	*tousan*	とうさん	父さん
2. my mother	*haha*	はは	母
mother	*kaasan*	かあさん	母さん
3. my older brother	*ani*	あに	兄
older brother	*niisan*	にいさん	兄さん
4. my older sister	*ane*	あね	姉
older sister	*neesan*	ねえさん	姉さん
5. parents	*ryoushin*	りょうしん	両親
6. my younger brother	*otouto*	おとうと	弟
younger brother	*otoutosan*	おとうとさん	弟さん
7. my younger sister	*imouto*	いもうと	妹
younger sister	*imoutosan*	いもうとさん	妹さん
8. my grandfather	*sofu*	そふ	祖父
grandfather / old man	*jiisan*	じいさん	祖父さん・爺さん **(UK)**
The second kanji is used as a title for a male senior citizen, "old man".			
9. my grandmother	*sobo*	そぼ	祖母
grandmother / old woman	*baasan*	ばあさん	祖母さん・婆さん **(UK)**

The second kanji is used as a title for a female senior citizen, "old woman".			
10. family	*kazoku*	かぞく	家族

Day 13 Example Sentences:

1. My father is tall.

2. Your mother is short.

3. My older brother is cruel.

4. His older sister is beautiful.

5. My parents are always busy.

6. My younger brother is annoying.

7. My younger sister is very annoying.

8. My grandfather likes to sleep.

9. My grandmother likes reading books.

10. My family lives in Kyoto.

1. ちちはせがたかいです。

2. あなたのおかあさんはせがひくいです。

3. あにはざんこくです。

4. かれのおねえさんはきれいです。

5. ぼくのりょうしんはいつもいそがしいです。

6. おとうとはわずらわしいです。

7. いもうとはとてもわずらわしいです。

8. そふはねることがすきです。

9. そぼはほんをよむのがすきです。

10. かぞくはきょうとにすんでいます。

1. *Chichi wa se ga takai desu.*

2. *Anata no okaasan wa se ga hikui desu.*

3. *Ani wa zankoku desu.*

4. *Kare no oneesan wa kirei desu.*

5. *Boku no ryoushin wa itsumo isogashii desu.*

6. *Otouto wa wazurawashii desu.*

7. *Imouto wa totemo wazurawashii desu.*

8. *Sofu wa neru koto ga suki desu.*

9. *Sobo wa hon o yomu no ga suki desu.*

10. *Kazoku wa kyouto ni sunde imasu.*

1. 父は背が高いです。

2. あなたのお母さんは背が低いです。

3. 兄は残酷です。

4. 彼のお姉さんはきれいです。

5. 僕の両親はいつも忙しいです。

6. 弟は煩わしいです。

7. 妹はとても煩わしいです。

8. 祖父は寝ることが好きです。

9. 祖母は本を読むのが好きです。

10. 家族は京都に住んでいます。

Day 14: Family Part 2

The words learned today are a bit different. For some of the words, instead of adding *o* お to the beginning when talk about someone else's family, there will be entirely different words.

Day 14 Vocabulary:

1. my husband	*otto*	おっと	夫
your husband	*goshujin*	ごしゅじん	ご主人
2. my wife	*tsuma*	つま	妻
your wife	*okusan*	おくさん	奥さん
3. my son	*musuko*	むすこ	息子
your son	*musukosan*	むすこさん	息子さん
4. my daughter	*musume*	むすめ	娘
your daughter	*ojousan*	おじょうさん	お嬢さん
5. grandchild	*mago*	まご	孫
your grandchild	*omagosan*	おまごさん	お孫さん
6. uncle	*oji*	おじ	伯父・叔父
your uncle	*ojisan*	おじさん	伯父さん・叔父さん

Don't confuse this word with grandfather. The first kanji is for an uncle older than your parent, the second for an uncle younger than your parent. The same applies to aunt.

7. aunt	*oba*	おば	伯母・叔母
your aunt	*obasan*	おばさん	伯母さん・叔母さん

Don't confuse this word with grandmother.

8. cousin	*itoko*	いとこ	従兄弟・従兄・従弟・従姉妹・従姉・従妹

The kanji for this word depends on the gender of the cousin. It can be written six different ways, but is always pronounced the same. The word is usually just written without kanji, however. The order above is as follows: male cousins, older male cousin, younger male cousin, female cousins, older female cousin, younger female cousin.

9. siblings	*kyoudai*	きょうだい・しまい	兄弟・兄妹・姉妹・姉弟

Similar to cousin, the kanji for this word can be written four different ways, however, the kanji for two brothers is most often used, even when referring to women. If the two female kanji is used, it has the alternate pronunciation *shimai* しまい[姉妹]. The order above is male siblings, mixed siblings with younger sister, female siblings, mixed siblings with younger brother.

10. in law	*girino*	ぎりの	義理の

Here, the *no* の is the ownership particle.

Day 14 Example sentences:

1. My husband is lazy.

2. Your wife is kind.

3. My son is a hard worker.

4. My daughter is smart.

5. I have no grandchildren.

6. Is your uncle a dentist?

7. Is your aunt a doctor?

8. I have many cousins.

9. Siblings sometimes fight.

10. My brother in law is rich.

1. おっとはなまけものだ。

2. おくさんはしんせつです。

3. むすこははたらきものです。

4. むすめはあたまがいいです。

5. まごはいません。

6. おじさんはしかいですか。

7. おばさんはいしゃですか。

8. たくさんいとこがいます。

9. きょうだいはときどきけんかします。

10. ぎりのあにはおかねもちです。

1. *Otto wa namakemono da.*

2. *Okusan wa shinsetsu desu.*

3. *Musuko wa hatarakimono desu.*

4. *Musume wa atama ga ii desu.*

5. *Mago wa imasen.*

6. *Ojisan wa shikai desu ka?*

7. *Obasan wa isha desu ka?*

8. *Takusan itoko ga imasu.*

9. *Kyoudai wa tokidoki kenka shimasu.*

10. *Giri no ani wa okane mochi desu.*

1. 夫は怠け者だ。

2. 奥さんは親切です。

3. 息子は働き者です。

4. 娘は頭が良いです。

5. 孫はいません。

6. 叔父さんは歯科医ですか。

7. 叔母さんは医者ですか。

8. たくさんいとこがいます。

9. 兄弟は時々喧嘩します。

10. 義理の兄はお金持です。

Day 15: There is, There are, to Exist

To say that something exists, Japanese has two words: *iru* いる and *aru* ある. *Iru* いる is used for animate objects, living things. *Aru* ある is used for inanimate objects, non-living things. The polite forms of these verbs are *imasu* います and *arimasu* あります. The negative casual forms are *inai* いない and *nai* ない, and *imasen* いません and *arimasen* ありません for polite speech. Study the following examples:

Animate Casual | Animate Polite

There is a cat.
Neko ga iru.
ねこがいる。
猫がいる。

There is a cat.
Neko ga imasu.
ねこがいます。
猫がいます。

There is no cat.
Neko ga inai.
ねこがいない。
猫がいない。

There is no cat.
Neko ga imasen.
ねこがいません。
猫がいません。

Inanimate Casual | Inanimate Polite

There is a chair.
Isu ga aru.
いすがある。
椅子がある。

There is a chair.
Isu ga arimasu.
いすがあります。
椅子があります。

There is no chair.
Isu ga nai.
いすがない。
椅子がない。

There is no chair.
Isu ga arimasen.
いすがありません。
椅子がありません。

These two verbs also have secondary meanings. *Iru* いる and *aru* ある can be used in place of the verb *to be* when talking about locations. These sentences will be used with the particle *ni* に. Study the following example:

A: Is he here? (Lit. Is he existing here?)
B: No, he is in his room.

A: *Kare wa koko ni imasu ka?*
B: *Iie, heya ni imasu.*

A: かれはここにいますか。
B: いいえ、へやにいます。

A: 彼はここにいますか。
B: いいえ、部屋にいます。

Iru いる and *Aru* ある can also used in place of *to have*, for animate and inanimate objects respectively.

A: **Do you have scissors? (Lit. Do scissors exist?)** B: **No, I don't.**
A: *Hasami wa arimasu ka?* B: *Arimasen.*
A: ハサミはありますか。 B: ありません。

A: **Do you have a dog? (Lit. Does a dog exist?)** B: **No, I don't.**
A: *Inu ga imasu ka?* B: *Imasen.*
A: いぬがいますか。 B: いません。
A: 犬がいますか。 B: いません。

Now that you have learned *aru* ある, we can dive a bit deeper into the true meaning of *da* だ and *desu* です. *Da* だ and *desu* です don't actually mean *to be*, they are the *copula*. In linguistics, a copula is a word that links a subject and a verb. In English, we use *be* as the copula, but really, *be* means *exist*, right? *Da* だ is actually just shortened version of *de aru* である, and *desu* です a shortened version of *de arimasu* であります. In writing especially, you may see *da* だ or *desu* です written as *de aru* である. This will be important when learning verb conjugation in future lessons.

Day 15 Grammar Cards:

1. There is / are (animate casual)	*iru*	いる	居る (UK)
There is / are (animate polite)	*imasu*	います	居ます (UK)
2. There is / are not (animate casual)	*inai*	いない	居ない (UK)
There is / are not (animate polite)	*imasen*	いません	居ません (UK)
3. There is / are (inanimate casual)	*aru*	ある	有る (UK)
There is / are (inanimate polite)	*arimasu*	あります	有ります (UK)
4. There is / are not (inanimate casual)	*nai*	ない	無い
There is / are not (inanimate polite)	*arimasen*	ありません	有りません (UK)

Day 15 Vocabulary:

1. chair	*isu*	いす	椅子
2. desk	*tsukue*	つくえ	机
3. pencil	*enpitsu*	えんぴつ	鉛筆
4. paper	*kami*	かみ	紙
5. book	*hon*	ほん	本
6. phone	*denwa*	でんわ	電話
cell phone	*keetai*	ケータイ	携帯

Cell phone is a rare word that uses sometimes uses katakana. It doesn't refer to a cell phone specifically, but rather, anything carried in your hand.

7. wallet	*saifu*	さいふ	財布
8. dog	*inu*	いぬ	犬
9. cat	*neko*	ねこ	猫
10. bird	*tori*	とり	鳥

Day 15 Example Sentences:

1. There are no chairs.
2. There is a desk in the room.
3. Do you have a pencil?
4. I don't have any paper.
5. I have many books.
6. Do you have a cell phone?
7. I don't have a wallet.
8. There is a dog in the park.
9. I have a cat.
10. There are no birds on the moon.

1. いすはありません。
2. へやのなかにつくえがある。
3. えんぴつはありますか。
4. かみがない。
5. たくさんほんがあります。
6. ケータイはありますか。
7. さいふがない。
8. こうえんにはいぬがいます。
9. ねこがいる。
10. つきにはとりがいません。

1. *Isu wa arimasen.*
2. *Heya no naka ni tsukue ga aru.*
3. *Enpitsu wa arimasu ka?*
4. *Kami ga nai.*
5. *Takusan hon ga arimasu.*
6. *Keetai ga arimasu ka?*
7. *Saifu ga nai.*
8. *Kouen ni wa inu ga imasu.*
9. *Neko ga iru.*
10. *Tsuki ni wa tori ga imasen.*

1. 椅子はありません。
2. 部屋の中に机がある。
3. 鉛筆はありますか。
4. 紙がない。
5. たくさん本があります。
6. 携帯はありますか。
7. 財布がない。
8. 公園には犬がいます。
9. 猫がいる。
10. 月には鳥がいません。

Day 16: こそあど Words

In Japanese, the proximity of things to the speaker or listener is very important. Depending on the proximity, different prefixes will be used. For example, in the word *doko* どこ (where), *do* ど is actually a prefix used with *ko* こ. Study the following prefixes:

Indicates something is near the speaker	*ko*	こ
Indicates something in near the listener	*so*	そ
Indicates something is away from both the listener and the speaker	*a*	あ
Used to make a question word	*do*	ど

Study the following words using *ko* こ to show location:

here (near the speaker)	*koko*	ここ
there (near the listener)	*soko*	そこ
over there (away from the speaker and listener)	*asoko*	あそこ
Over there is irregular.		
where	*doko*	どこ

For demonstratives, *re* れ is used. Like the pronouns *he* and *she*, *ra* ら can be added to make them plural:

this (near the speaker)	*kore*	これ
that (near the listener)	*sore*	それ
these (near the speaker)	*korera*	これら
those (near the listener)	*sorera*	それら
that over there (away from the speaker and listener)	*are*	あれ
are あれ is also used if something unexpected happens, meaning, *Huh?* or *Wait, what?*		
which (among three or more)	*dore*	どれ
dore どれ and *docchi* どっち both mean *which*, but *dore* どれ is used with three or more objects, whereas *docchi* どっち is used to choose between two objects		

Kore これ *sore* それ and *are* あれ refer to an object without a noun attached. As in: *What is this? What is that? How about this? How about that?* When connected to a noun, *re* れ becomes *no* の:

What about <u>this</u> banana?
<u>Kono</u> banana wa?
<u>この</u>バナナは?

Additionally, *ano* あの can be used to state that you are thinking. In English, *umm* or *uhh* are common. Just like in English, the vowel sound will trail off. Another word to use for thinking is *etto* えっと.

The remaining こそあど words are as follows:

Referring to direction:

this way	kochira	こちら
that way	sochira	そちら
that way over there	achira	あちら
which way	dochira	どちら

The final *ra* ら at the end of these words can be dropped for the casual form: *kocchi* こっち *socchi* そっち *acchi* あっち *docchi* どっち. These directional words are also used when referring to people standing next to you. For example, the sentence, *This is my friend Dave,* will use *kochira* こちら, not *kore* これ. As mentioned in the Day 5 lesson, *sochira* そちら can mean *you*. Perhaps now you can see why.

Referring to a way of doing something:

like this	kou	こう
like that	sou	そう
like that over there (irregular)	aa	ああ
how	dou	どう

To be an active listener, people will often say, *sou desu ka* そうですか while listening, which translates to: *Oh, I see,* but literally means, *Is it like that?* This is will be covered in detail in Volume Two.

Referring to a type or kind:

this kind of	konna	こんな
that kind of	sonna	そんな
that kind of (over there)	anna	あんな
what kind of	donna	どんな

Referring to a degree or level:

this (much) / such	konnani	こんなに
that (much) / such	sonnani	そんなに
that (much) / such	annani	あんなに
how(much) / such	donnani	どんなに

Day 16 Vocabulary:

1. here	*koko*	ここ
there	*soko*	そこ
over there	*asoko*	あそこ
where	*doko*	どこ
2. this	*kore / kono*	これ・この
that	*sore / sono*	それ・その
that over there	*are / ano*	あれ・あの
which (of 2)	*docchi*	どっち
which (3+)	*dore*	どれ
3. this way	*kochira*	こちら
that way	*sochira*	そちら
that way over there	*achira*	あちら
which way	*dochira*	どちら
here and there	*achikochi*	あちこち
4. like this	*kou*	こう
like that	*sou*	そう
like that over there	*aa*	ああ
how	*dou*	どう
5. this kind of	*konna*	こんな
that kind of	*sonna*	そんな
that kind of (over there)	*anna*	あんな
what kind of	*donna*	どんな
6. this (much) / such	*konnani*	こんなに
that (much) / such	*sonnani*	そんなに
that (much) / such	*annani*	あんなに
how(much) / such	*donnani*	どんなに
7. Huh? / Wait, what?	*Are?*	あれ。
8. Umm / uhh	*ano / etto*	あの・えっと
9. Well, uhh...	*saa / jaa*	さあ・じゃあ
10. With that...	*dewa*	では
Similarly to *saa* さあ and *jaa* じゃあ, this will be used at the beginning of a sentence to move on to some new topic.		

Day 16 Example Sentences:

1. **This is Japan.**

(Lit. This location is Japan.)

2. **What's that over there?**

3. **The hospital is this way.**

4. **Do I do it like this?**

5. **That kind of thing is not alright!**

6. **Such a delicious food doesn't exist.**

7. **Huh? What's that?**

8. **Uhh, I forgot.**

9. **Well, shall we go?**

10. **Okay, with that finished, shall we go?**

1. ここはにほん。

2. あれはなんですか。

3. びょういんはこちらです。

4. こうしますか。

5. そんなことはだめだよ。

6. あんなにおいしいたべものはない。

7. あれ、なにそれ？

8. えっとね、わすれました。

9. じゃあ、いきましょうか。

10. では、いきましょうか。

1. *Koko wa nihon.*

2. *Are wa nan desu ka?*

3. *Byouin wa kochira desu.*

4. *Kou shimasu ka?*

5. *Sonna koto wa dame da yo!*

6. *Annani oishii tabemono wa nai.*

7. *Are? Nani sore?*

8. *Etto ne, wasuremashita.*

9. *Jaa, ikimashou ka?*

10. *Dewa, ikimashou ka?*

1. ここは日本。

2. あれは何ですか。

3. 病院はこちらです。

4. こうしますか。

5. そんなことはだめだよ。

6. あんなに美味しい食べ物はない。

7. あれ、何それ？

8. えっとね、忘れました。

9. じゃあ、行きましょうか。

10. では、行きましょうか。

Day 17: こそあど Words Part 2

There are additional, more abstract, usages of *this* and *that*. This is a bit of an advanced lesson at this stage, but it is important to learn everything about こそあど words at once.

The timing of an event is important when using こそあど words to express concepts and ideas. こそあど words can be used to reference when something took place, with *ko* こ being now, or very recently, and *a* あ being a long time ago. *So* そ is somewhere in the middle, but is more often used with something that didn't happen very long ago in the past, that is, it's closer to *ko* こ than *a* あ. *Sore* それ is also often used to reference previous statements that the speaker just made. So in this sense, it is not referring to the listener, but the speaker's previously mentioned statement. Think of it like a time line, with you in the center, and events happening next to you, or distant from you. Study the following example:

I was living alone in Tokyo. <u>This</u> was a hard time for me. *Hitori de Toukyou ni sunde ita. <u>Kono</u> toki wa taihen datta.* ひとりでとうきょうにすんでいた。<u>この</u>ときはたいへんだった。 一人で東京に住んでいた。<u>この</u>時は大変だった。

In this sentence, when the speaker says *this*, he is referring to his state of mind at the time of living in Tokyo, that is, he is reliving the memory, and expressing how he felt about it at the time it took place.

I was living alone in Tokyo. <u>That</u> was a hard time for me. *Hitori de Toukyou ni sunde ita. <u>Sono</u> toki wa taihen datta.* ひとりでとうきょうにすんでいた。<u>その</u>ときはたいへんだった。 一人で東京に住んでいた。<u>その</u>時は大変だった。

In this sentence, when the speaker says *that*, he is referring to his current feelings about the situation, which happened in the past.

I was living alone in Tokyo a long time ago. <u>That</u> was a hard time for me. *Mukashi wa hitori de Toukyou ni sunde ita. <u>Ano</u> toki wa taihen datta.* むかしはひとりでとうきょうにすんでいた。<u>あの</u>ときはたいへんだった。 昔は一人で東京に住んでいた。<u>あの</u>時は大変だった。

In this sentence, the speaker is expressing his current feelings about the situation, which happened a long time ago in the past.

Day 17 Vocabulary:

1. refrigerator	*reizouko*	れいぞうこ	冷蔵庫
2. glasses	*megane*	めがね	眼鏡
3. fountain pen	*mannenhitsu*	まんねんひつ	万年筆
4. ashtray	*haizara*	はいざら	灰皿
5. things / luggage	*nimotsu*	にもつ	荷物

This often refers to luggage but also just things you are carrying or taking with you somewhere.

6. watch / clock	*tokei*	とけい	時計
7. train	*densha*	でんしゃ	電車

This refers to an electric train, opposed to a steam engine. Most all public trains in Japan are electric.

8. subway	*chikatetsu*	ちかてつ	地下鉄
9. letter	*tegami*	てがみ	手紙
10. newspaper	*shinbun*	しんぶん	新聞

Day 17 Example Sentences:

1. We didn't have refrigerators back then.

2. My glasses broke yesterday. That was bad luck.

3. I got a fountain pen after graduation. That was a happy time.

4. There is no ashtray. This is bad!

5. You lost my luggage? That is terrible!

6. I bought a gold watch today. It was a great experience.

7. The train crashed. It was terrible.

8. They built a subway. It was a great thing.

9. The letter burned in the fire. That was bad luck.

10. Newspapers didn't exist back then.

1. あのときはれいぞうこがなかった。

2. きのうめがねがこわれた。それはざんねん。

3. そつぎょうのあと、まんねんひつをもらいました。あのときはしあわせでした。

4. はいざらがない。これはたいへん。

5. わたしのにもつをなくしたの。それはひどいよ。

6. きょうはきんのとけいをかいました。これはすばらしいけいけんだった。

7. でんしゃがしょうとつした。それはおそろしかった。

8. ちかてつをたてた。あれはすばらしかった。

9. かさいでてがみがもえました。それはざんねんだった。

10. あのときはしんぶんがなかった。

1. *Ano toki wa reizouko ga nakatta.*

2. *Kinou megane ga kowareta. Sore wa zannen.*

3. *Sotsugyou no ato, mannenhitsu o moraimashita. Ano toki wa shiawase deshita.*

4. *Haizara ga nai. Kore wa taihen.*

5. *Watashi no nimotsu o nakushita no? Sore wa hidoi yo!*

6. *Kyou wa kin no tokei o kaimashita. Kore wa subarashii keiken datta.*

7. *Densha ga shoutotsu shita. Sore wa osoroshikatta.*

8. *Chikatetsu o tateta. Are wa subarashikatta.*

9. *Kasai de tegami ga moemashita. Sore wa zannen datta.*

10. *Ano toki wa shinbun ga nakatta.*

1. あの時は冷蔵庫がなかった。

2. 昨日眼鏡が壊れた。それは残念。

3. 卒業の後、万年筆をもらいました。あの時は幸せでした。

4. 灰皿がない。これは大変。

5. 私の荷物を無くしたの。それは酷いよ。

6. 今日は金の時計を買いました。これは素晴らしい経験だった。

7. 電車が衝突した。それは恐ろしかった。

8. 地下鉄を建てた。あれは素晴らしかった。

9. 火災で手紙が燃えました。それは残念だった。

10. あの時は新聞がなかった。

Day 18: Some, Any, No

Today's lesson will cover how to say things like, *someone, anyone, no one, something, anything, nothing,* etc. It's actually quite easy. Simply attach a suffix to the correlating question word. Study the following suffixes:

Some	ka	か
Any	demo	でも
No	mo	も

When using the words with *no*, like *no one, nothing, no where*, a negative verb must be used. For example, instead of saying: *No one knows,* Japanese people say: *No one doesn't know.* In English, we call these double negative sentences, which are grammatically incorrect.

Study these suffixes attached to *dare* だれ[誰] (who):

who	dare	だれ	誰
someone	dareka	だれか	誰か
anyone	daredemo	だれでも	誰でも
no one	daremo	だれも	誰も

Now, think of the other question words in your head. Attach the suffixes and try to think of the translations yourself, without looking at the following list. Once completed, look at the following list to confirm your answers. It is likely that you got at least one wrong, because there are a few exceptions:

what	nani	なに	何
something	nanka*	なんか*	何か*
anything	nandemo*	なんでも*	何でも*
nothing	nanimo	なにも	何も

Additionally, *nantoka* なんとか[何とか], means *something* or *somehow*.

where	doko	どこ
somewhere	dokoka	どこか
anywhere	dokodemo	どこでも
nowhere	dokomo	どこも

when	*itsu*	いつ
sometime	*itsuka*	いつか
anytime	*itsudemo*	いつでも
never	*kesshite**	けっして＊

Never is completely different word, because *itsumo* いつも actually has the opposite meaning: *always*.

which	*dore*	どれ
one of them	*doreka*	どれか
any of them	*doredemo*	どれでも
none of them	*doremo*	どれも

which direction	*dochira*	どちら
some direction	*dochiraka*	どちらか
any direction	*dochirademo*	どちらでも
no direction	*dochiramo*	どちらも

how much	*ikura*	いくら
some amount of	*ikuraka*	いくらか
any amount of	*ikurademo*	いくらでも
almost no amount of / not much / a lot of	*ikuramo*	いくらも

Instead of *no amount of*, this means *almost no amount of*, there is still a small amount. With a positive verb, *ikuramo* いくらも means *a lot of*.

how many	*ikutsu*	いくつ
some number of	*ikutsuka*	いくつか
any number of	*ikutsudemo*	いくつでも
almost none / few / many / several	*ikutsumo*	いくつも

Instead of *none*, this means *almost none* or *few*. With a positive verb, *ikutsumo* いくつも means *many / several*.

These suffixes can be used with every question word except *why*, but sometimes translate differently in English. Study the following words:

how	*dou*	どう
somehow*	*douka*	どうか

douka どうか usually translates to *please,* and is used when making requests. To say *somehow* like the English version, use *dounikashite* どうにかして.

anyhow*	*doudemo*	どうでも

Anyhow in English is usually used colloquially to trail off from a sentence, or connect to separate ideas. For example: *I talked to him yesterday. Anyhow, I have to get going.* In Japanese it is not used like this. It really means *anyhow,* as in: *any way* you do something, *how ever* something is accomplished, or *no matter how*. For example: (*Any way / how ever / no matter how) you fix it is fine, just do it quickly!*

nohow*	*dounimo**	どうにも

Similarly, *nohow* isn't used in English like the Japanese word. Think of it as: *no possible way.*

Day 18 Vocabulary:

1. some (prefix)	*ka*	か (suffix)	
2. any (prefix)	*demo*	でも (suffix)	
3. no (prefix)	*mo*	も (suffix)	
4. never	*kesshite*	けっして	決して
5. always	*itsumo*	いつも	
6. almost no amount of / not much / a lot of	*ikuramo*	いくらも	
7. almost none / few / many / several	*ikutsumo*	いくつも	
8. no matter how / any how	*doudemo*	どうでも	

The phrase *doudemoii* どうでもいい translates to *However is fine,* or *Anyway is okay,* but in Japanese has a very negative connotation, similar to the English: *I don't give a f---.*

9. no possible way	*dounimo*	どうにも	
10. not many / not often	*amari*	あまり	

This word will be used with a negative verb. It can also be pronounced as *anmari* あんまり.

Day 18 Example Sentences:

1. **Sometime, somewhere, I'll find someone!**

2. **Anytime, anywhere, it's alright.**

3. **There's no one there.**

4. **I never eat meat.**

5. **I'm always eating vegetables.**

6. **I have almost no money at all!**

7. **I have several hobbies.**

8. **Do it quickly! However you do it is fine!**

9. **No matter what I do, my Japanese won't improve.**

10. **There aren't many snacks left.**

1. いつか、どこかで、どうにかして、だれかをみつける。

2. いつでも、どこでも、だいじょうぶだ。

3. だれもいない。

4. おにくはけっしてたべません。

5. やさいはいつもたべています。

6. おかねはいくらもないですよ。

7. しゅみがいくつもあります。

8. はやくして。どうでもいいから。

9. にほんごがどうにもうまくならない。

10. おかしがあまりない。

1. *Itsuka, dokoka de, dounikashite, dareka o mitsukeru!*

2. *Itsudemo, dokodemo, daijoubu da.*

3. *Daremo inai.*

4. *Oniku wa kesshite tabemasen.*

5. *Yasai wa itsumo tabete imasu.*

6. *Okane wa ikuramo nai desu yo!*

7. *Shumi ga ikutsumo arimasu.*

8. *Hayaku shite! Doudemo ii kara!*

9. *Nihongo ga dounimo umaku naranai.*

10. *Okashi ga amari nai.*

1. いつか、どこかで、どうにかして、誰かを見つける。

2. いつでも、どこでも、大丈夫だ。

3. 誰もいない。

4. お肉は決して食べません。

5. 野菜はいつも食べています。

6. お金はいくらもないですよ。

7. 趣味がいくつもあります。

8. 早くして。どうでも良いから。

9. 日本語がどうにも上手くならない。

10. お菓子があまりない。

Day 19: Vocabulary Practice

Now that you've learned the basics, spend the next few lessons focusing on vocabulary. Use these lessons to practice and review everything you have studied thus far.

The final few words in today's lesson will be the names of different regions. In America, from small to big, it goes: *city, county, state*. In Japan, they don't have states, they have prefectures. Some cities are so big that they are divided into wards, while smaller cities are divided into districts. Tokyo itself is so big that it isn't a prefecture, it is a *metropolis*. Osaka and Kyoto also have special names because of their size and history. As far as governmental organization, the largest organizational structure is a prefecture, of which there are forty-seven. However, even bigger than that, are the *regions* of Japan, of which there are nine. Finally, there are the four islands. When someone tells you where they are from, they may give any combination of these words. In order from small to big, it goes: town, ward / district, city, prefecture, region, island.

Day 19 Vocabulary:

1. temple	*tera*	てら	寺
This refers to temples for the Buddhist religion.			
2. Shinto shrine	*jinja*	じんじゃ	神社
Shinto is a religion that is native to Japan, which was popular before Buddhism. Though most Japanese people are non-religious, it is still customary to go to shrines and temples on certain occasions.			
3. harbor / port	*minato*	みなと	港
4. parking lot	*chuushajou*	ちゅうしゃじょう	駐車場
5. Japanese hotel	*ryokan*	りょかん	旅館
Compared to something in western culture, this is similar to a bed and breakfast.			
6. countryside	*inaka*	いなか	田舎
7. airport	*kuukou*	くうこう	空港
8. ward	*ku*	く	区
district	*gun*	ぐん	郡
Wards are used for large cities, while districts are used for smaller cities.			
9. prefecture	*ken*	けん	県
10. metropolis	*to*	と	都

Day 19 Example Sentences:

1. Japan has many temples.

2. Kyoto has many temples and shrines.

3. Yokohama has a big port.

4. In Japan, parking lots are very important.

5. If you go to Japan, you should stay at a Japanese style hotel.

6. The countryside is so peaceful.

7. I'm meeting my friend at the airport.

8. I live in Shibuya.

9. They live in Saitama prefecture.

10. I want to live in the Tokyo metropolis.

1. にほんはおてらがおおいです。

2. きょうとはおてらとじんじゃがおおいです。

3. よこはまはおおきいみなとがあります。

4. にほんではちゅうしゃじょうがたいせつなものだ。

5. にほんにいったら、りょかんにとまるべきだ。

6. いなかはとてものどかです。

7. わたしはくうこうでともだちとあいます。

8. しぶやくにすんでいます。

9. かれらはさいたまけんにすんでいる。

10. とうきょうとにすみたいです。

1. *Nihon wa otera ga ooi desu.*

2. *Kyouto wa otera to jinja ga ooi desu.*

3. *Yokohama wa ookii minato ga arimasu.*

4. *Nihon de wa chuushajou ga taisetsu na mono da.*

5. *Nihon ni ittara, ryokan ni tomaru beki da.*

6. *Inaka wa totemo nodoka desu.*

7. *Watashi wa kuukou de tomodachi to aimasu.*

8. *Shibuya-ku ni sunde imasu.*

9. *Karera wa Saitama-ken ni sunde iru.*

10. *Toukyou-to ni sumitai desu.*

1. 日本はお寺が多いです。

2. 京都はお寺と神社が多いです。

3. 横浜は大きい港があります。

4. 日本では駐車場が大切なものだ。

5. 日本に行ったら、旅館に泊まるべきだ。

6. 田舎はとても長閑です。

7. 私は空港で友達と会います。

8. 渋谷区に住んでいます。

9. 彼らは埼玉県に住んでいる。

10. 東京都に住みたいです。

Day 20: Vocabulary Practice

Day 20 Vocabulary:

1. grass	kusa	くさ	草
2. cloud	kumo	くも	雲
3. woods	hayashi	はやし	林
This kanji is two trees.			
4. forest	mori	もり	森
This kanji is three trees, an even bigger amount!			
5. star	hoshi	ほし	星
6. lake	mizuumi	みずうみ	湖
7. coast	kaigan	かいがん	海岸
8. air / atmosphere	kuuki	くうき	空気
9. factory	koujou	こうじょう	工場
10. island	shima	しま	島

Day 20 Example Sentences:

1. They are allergic to grass.

2. That cloud is huge!

3. She ran into the woods.

4. Many animals live in the forest.

5. You can see the stars from here.

6. They are swimming in the lake.

7. We walked along the coast.

8. I like the smell of the air in the mountains.

9. These factories create a lot of pollution.

10. Japan is an island nation.

1. かれらはくさのアレルギーがあります。

2. あのくもはでかいよ。

3. かのじょははやしにはしった。

4. もりにはたくさんどうぶつがすんでいます。

5. ここからほしがみえます。

6. かれらはみずうみをおよいでいる。

7. わたしたちはかいがんをさんぽしました。

8. やまのくうきのにおいがすきです。

9. このこうじょうはたくさんおせんをつくります。

10. にほんはしまのくにです。

1. *Karera wa kusa no arerugi ga arimasu.*

2. *Ano kumo wa dekai yo!*

3. *Kanojo wa hayashi ni hashitta.*

4. *Mori ni wa takusan doubutsu ga sunde imasu.*

5. *Koko kara hoshi ga miemasu.*

6. *Karera wa mizuumi o oyoide iru.*

7. *Watashitachi wa kaigan o sanpo shimashita.*

8. *Yama no kuuki no nioi ga suki desu.*

9. *Kono koujou wa takusan osen o tsukurimasu.*

10. *Nihon wa shima no kuni desu.*

1. 彼らは草のアレルギーがあります。

2. あの雲はでかいよ。

3. 彼女は林に走った。

4. 森にはたくさん動物が住んでいます。

5. ここから星が見えます。

6. 彼らは湖を泳いでいる。

7. 私たちは海岸を散歩しました。

8. 山の空気の匂いが好きです。

9. この工場はたくさん汚染を作ります。

10. 日本は島の国です。

Day 21: Vocabulary Practice

Day 21 Vocabulary:

1. question	*shitsumon*	しつもん	質問
2. dictionary	*jisho*	じしょ	辞書
3. homework	*shukudai*	しゅくだい	宿題
4. lesson / class	*jugyou*	じゅぎょう	授業
5. student / pupil	*seito*	せいと	生徒
This refers to any type of student, whereas *gakusei* がくせい[学生] refers to a school student.			
6. word	*tango*	たんご	単語
word	*kotoba*	ことば	言葉
tango たんご[単語] refers to vocabulary and individual words. *kotoba* ことば[言葉] refers to a language or a dialect.			
7. sentence	*bun*	ぶん	文
8. composition / essay	*sakubun*	さくぶん	作文
9. writing / article	*bunshou*	ぶんしょう	文章
This can refer to someone's writing style, as well as any small composition, as in, a collection of sentences. The difference between this and *sakubun* さくぶん[作文] is the length.			
10. grammar	*bunpou*	ぶんぽう	文法

Day 21 Example Sentences:

1. **Do you have a question?**

2. **Dictionaries are very handy.**

3. **Did you do your homework?**

4. **Class is starting soon.**

5. **Students must study every day.**

6. **Do you know this word?**

7. **I don't understand this sentence very well.**

8. **I've written three essays this year.**

9. **I respect his writing style.**

10. **Japanese grammar and English grammar are different.**

1. しつもんがありますか。

2. じしょはとてもべんりです。

3. しゅくだいをしましたか?

4. じゅぎょうがすぐにはじまるよ。

5. せいとはまいにちべんきょうしなくちゃ。

6. このたんごをしっていますか。

7. このぶんはよくわかりません。

8. ことしはみっつのさくぶんをかきました。

9. かれのぶんしょうをそんけいします。

10. にほんのぶんぽうとえいごのぶんぽうはちがいます。

1. *Shitsumon ga arimasu ka?*

2. *Jisho wa totemo benri desu.*

3. *Shukudai o shimashita ka?*

4. *Jugyou ga suguni hajimaru yo.*

5. *Seito wa mainichi benkyou shinakucha.*

6. *Kono tango o shitte imasu ka?*

7. *Kono bun wa yoku wakarimasen.*

8. *Kotoshi wa mittsu no sakubun o kakimashita.*

9. *Kare no bunshou o sonkei shimasu.*

10. *Nihon no bunpou to Eigo no bunpou wa chigaimasu.*

1. 質問がありますか。

2. 辞書はとても便利です。

3. 宿題をしましたか?

4. 授業がすぐに始まるよ。

5. 生徒は毎日勉強しなくちゃ。

6. この単語を知っていますか。

7. この文は良く分かりません。

8. 今年は三つの作文を書きました。

9. 彼の文章を尊敬します。

10. 日本の文法と英語の文法は違います。

Day 22: Vocabulary Practice

Day 22 Vocabulary:

1. photograph	*shashin*	しゃしん	写真
2. gate	*mon*	もん	門
3. picture / drawing / painting	*e*	え	絵
4. movie / film	*eiga*	えいが	映画
5. music	*ongaku*	おんがく	音楽
6. ticket	*kippu*	きっぷ	切符
7. flower	*hana*	はな	花
8. postcard	*hagaki*	はがき	葉書
A postcard with a picture is a combination of this word and *picture*: *ehagaki* えはがき[絵葉書].			
9. stamp	*kitte*	きって	切手
10. envelope	*fuutou*	ふうとう	封筒

Day 22 Example Sentences:

1. **Will you take a picture for me please?**

2. **This gate is red.**

3. **I like drawing pictures.**

4. **Let's watch a movie.**

5. **What kind of music do you like?**

6. **Buy me a ticket please.**

7. **There are flowers in my garden.**

8. **These postcards are expensive.**

9. **This needs two stamps.**

10. **I have no envelopes.**

1. しゃしんをとってくれませんか。

2. このもんはあかいです。

3. えをかくのがすきです。

4. えいがをみましょう。

5. どんなおんがくがすきですか。

6. わたしにきっぷをかってください。

7. わたしのにわにははながあります。

8. これらのはがきはたかいです。

9. これはにまいのきってがひつようです。

10. ふうとうがない。

1. *Shashin o totte kuremasen ka?*

2. *Kono mon wa akai desu.*

3. *E o kaku no ga suki desu.*

4. *Eiga o mimashou.*

5. *Donna ongaku ga suki desu ka?*

6. *Watashi ni kippu o katte kudasai.*

7. *Watashi no niwa ni wa hana ga arimasu.*

8. *Korera no hagaki wa takai desu.*

9. *Kore wa nimai no kitte ga hitsuyou desu.*

10. *Fuutou ga nai.*

1. 写真を撮ってくれませんか。

2. この門は赤いです。

3. 絵を描くのが好きです。

4. 映画を観ましょう。

5. どんな音楽が好きですか。

6. 私に切符を買って下さい。

7. 私の庭には花があります。

8. これらの葉書は高いです。

9. これは二枚の切手が必要です。

10. 封筒がない。

Day 23: Vocabulary Practice

Day 23 Vocabulary:

1. **north**	*kita*	きた	北
2. **south**	*minami*	みなみ	南
3. **east**	*higashi*	ひがし	東
4. **west**	*nishi*	にし	西
5. **map**	*chizu*	ちず	地図
6. **river**	*kawa*	かわ	川
stream	*kawa*	かわ	河
7. **mountain**	*yama*	やま	山
8. **bank**	*ginkou*	ぎんこう	銀行
9. **library**	*toshokan*	としょかん	図書館
10. **embassy**	*taishikan*	たいしかん	大使館

Day 23 Example Sentences:

1. **Hokkaido is in northern Japan.**

2. **Okinawa is the southern most location in Japan.**

3. **The meaning of Tokyo's kanji is "East Capital."**

4. **Fukuoka is in western Japan.**

5. **Let's look at the map.**

6. **Japan has many rivers.**

7. **Mt. Fuji is not a mountain, but a volcano!**

8. **I have to go to the bank.**

9. **Libraries have disappeared.**

10. **This is the American embassy.**

1. ほっかいどうはきたにほんにあります。

2. おきなわはにほんのいちばんみなみのばしょです。

3. とうきょうのかんじのいみはひがしのみやこです。

4. ふくおかはにしにほんにあります。

5. ちずをみましょう。

6. にほんはたくさんかわがある。

7. ふじさんはやまじゃなくて、かざんです。

8. ぎんこうにいかなければなりません。

9. としょかんはなくなりました。

10. ここはアメリカのたいしかんです。

1. *Hokkaidou wa kita Nihon ni arimasu.*

2. *Okinawa wa Nihon no ichiban minami no basho desu.*

3. *Toukyou no kanji no imi wa higashi no miyako desu.*

4. *Fukuoka wa nishi Nihon ni arimasu.*

5. *Chizu o mimashou.*

6. *Nihon wa takusan kawa ga aru.*

7. *Fujisan wa yama ja nakute, kazan desu!*

8. *Ginkou ni ikanakereba narimasen.*

9. *Toshokan wa nakunarimashita.*

10. *Koko wa Amerika no taishikan desu.*

1. 北海道は北日本にあります。

2. 沖縄は日本の一番南の場所です。

3. 東京の漢字の意味は東の京です。

4. 福岡は西日本にあります。

5. 地図を見ましょう。

6. 日本はたくさん川がある。

7. 富士山は山じゃなくて、火山です。

8. 銀行に行かなければなりません。

9. 図書館は無くなりました。

10. ここはアメリカの大使館です。

Day 24: Vocabulary Practice

Day 24 Vocabulary:

1. bathroom	*otearai*	おてあらい	お手洗い

The kanji for this word literally mean, *hand washing*. The word borrowed from English, *toire* トイレ, can also be used. Most Japanese homes separate the toilet from the room with the bath, which is called *furoba* ふろば[風呂場].

2. kitchen	*daidokoro*	だいどころ	台所
3. window	*mado*	まど	窓
4. entrance / entry hall	*genkan*	げんかん	玄関

This refers to the entrance itself as well as the area around the entrance.

5. door	*to*	と	戸

This refers to a Japanese style sliding door.

6. classroom	*kyoushitsu*	きょうしつ	教室
7. school	*gakkou*	がっこう	学校
8. textbook	*kyoukasho*	きょうかしょ	教科書
9. pillow	*makura*	まくら	枕
10. car	*kuruma*	くるま	車

<u>Day 24 Example Sentences</u>:

1. **Where is the bathroom?**

2. **My kitchen is big.**

3. **His window is small.**

4. **There is no entrance over there.**

5. **Please open the door.**

6. **The students are in the classroom.**

7. **I'm going to school!**

8. **Do you have a textbook?**

9. **I have no pillows.**

10. **I bought a car.**

1. おてあらいはどこですか。

2. わたしのだいどころはおおきいです。

3. かれのまどはちいさいです。

4. あちらにはげんかんがありません。

5. とをあけてください。

6. せいとはきょうしつにいます。

7. がっこうにいきますよ。

8. きょうかしょをもっていますか。

9. おれはまくらがない。

10. ぼくはくるまをかった。

1. *Otearai wa doko desu ka?*

2. *Watashi no daidokoro wa ookii desu.*

3. *Kare no mado wa chiisai desu.*

4. *Achira ni wa genkan ga arimasen.*

5. *To o akete kudasai.*

6. *Seito wa kyoushitsu ni imasu.*

7. *Gakkou ni ikimasu yo!*

8. *Kyoukasho o motte imasu ka?*

9. *Ore wa makura ga nai.*

10. *Boku wa kuruma o katta.*

1. お手洗いはどこですか。

2. 私の台所は大きいです。

3. 彼の窓は小さいです。

4. あちらには玄関がありません。

5. 戸を開けて下さい。

6. 生徒は教室にいます。

7. 学校に行きますよ。

8. 教科書を持っていますか。

9. 俺は枕がない。

10. 僕は車を買った。

Day 25: Verbs and U-Form

The next few lessons will teach you how to conjugate verbs into their various forms. Honestly, it is quite a bit of information and you shouldn't expect to completely memorize the grammar in one day. Simply familiarize yourself with each verb form, and practice each verb form every day. Eventually it will become second nature. How to use all of these different forms will be explained in greater detail in later lessons. For now, concentrate on how to conjugate the verbs. Short explanations of their uses will be included in each lesson.

There are two types of verbs in Japanese. Verbs that end with *iru* いる or *eru* える are called either *ichidan* いちだん verbs, *vowel-stem* verbs, or *ru* る verbs. Verbs that end with *u* う *tsu* つ *ru* る *mu* む *bu* ぶ *ku* く *gu* ぐ or *su* す (basically all other verbs) are called either *godan* ごだん verbs, *consonant-stem* verbs, or *u* う verbs. That is a lot of names! Unfortunately, there is no consensus in the Japanese teaching community as to what to call the verbs. This is why I prefer to just use the Japanese names. The names *ichidan* いちだん and *godan* ごだん literally mean *level one* and *level five* verbs.

All *ichidan* いちだん verbs follow the same rules, and all *godan* ごだん verbs follow slightly different rules. The differences aren't that big. But be careful, a few verbs can appear to be *ichidan* いちだん when in fact they are *godan* ごだん. An example of this is *kaeru* かえる[帰る] (to return), which appears to be *ichidan* いちだん, because it ends with *eru* える, but in fact is *godan* ごだん. Don't worry about it too much for now, these verbs will be covered later.

There are two special verbs in Japanese that follow their own rules, *suru* する(to do), and *kuru* くる [来る] (to come). These verbs always have an irregular conjugation. There are a few other verbs that have some irregular conjugations in different forms, which will be covered later.

Every verb has five basic grammatical forms. Some people call them Form 1, Form 2, etc. Some people attribute their forms to their function, Negative-Form, Polite-Form, Dictionary-Form. I prefer the easiest method, calling them: U-I-A-E-O-Form. When a *godan* ごだん verb is in the U-Form, the stem will end with a U, when it is in I-Form, it will end with an I, and so on.

Today's lesson covers the U-Form. This is the most basic form a verb can take. It requires no conjugation. This is also called the Dictionary-Form, because it is the form of verbs that you will see in the dictionary. Every verb in Japanese ends with U. The U-Form is used in casual speech for present and future tense sentences.

This is quite a lot of information, so review it once more:

1. Every verb ends with the sound *u* う.
2. Verbs that end with *iru* いる or *eru* える are called *ichidan* いちだん verbs.
3. Most all other verbs are called *godan* ごだん verbs.
4. Verbs have five basic conjugations, which can be called the U-I-A-E-O forms.
5. The U-Form of a verb is also called the Dictionary-Form. No conjugation is necessary.
6. The U-Form is used in casual speech, for present and future tense sentences.

You've actually already learned two verbs, *iru* いる and *aru* ある. Though they both mean *there is / there are*, *iru* いる is an *ichidan* いちだん verb, and *aru* ある is a *godan* ごだん verb. Starting with this lesson *ichidan* いちだん verbs will be marked with **(I)**. If a verb appears to be an *ichidan* いちだん verb, but is actually a *godan* ごだん verb, it will be marked with **(G)**.

Day 25 Vocabulary:

1. to eat	*taberu*	たべる	食べる **(I)**
to eat (male only)	*kuu*	くう	食う
2. to see / to look / to watch	*miru*	みる	見る・観る **(I)**

The second kanji is used when watching something and focusing your attention. For example, both can be used for watching TV, but the second kanji implies you are watching intently. Because of this, it will be usually be used when you are watching things in theaters or sports arenas.

3. to buy	*kau*	かう	買う
4. to wait	*matsu*	まつ	待つ
5. to return	*kaeru*	かえる	帰る **(G)**

This verb almost always refers to returning home.

6. to read	*yomu*	よむ	読む
7. to play	*asobu*	あそぶ	遊ぶ
8. to work	*hataraku*	はたらく	働く

This verb implies working hard, or doing physical labor. It can be used with the particle *de* で to say that you work at a company.

9. to hurry	*isogu*	いそぐ	急ぐ
10. to speak	*hanasu*	はなす	話す

<u>Day 25 Example Sentences</u>:

1. **Do you eat fish?**	1. さかなをたべるの？
2. **I watch TV every day.**	2. まいにちテレビをみる。
3. **I buy eggs every morning.**	3. まいあさたまごをかう。
4. **I'll wait here.**	4. ここでまつ。
5. **I'll go home now.**	5. いまからかえる。
6. **I read a book every day.**	6. まいにちほんをよむ。
7. **Do you play games?**	7. ゲームであそぶの。
8. **I always work hard!**	8. いつもはたらく。
9. **He hurries.**	9. かれはいそぐ。
10. **Do you speak Japanese?**	10. にほんごをはなすの。

1. *Sakana o taberu no?*	1. 魚を食べるの？
2. *Mainichi terebi o miru.*	2. 毎日テレビを見る。
3. *Maiasa tamago o kau.*	3. 毎朝卵を買う。
4. *Koko de matsu.*	4. ここで待つ。
5. *Ima kara kaeru.*	5. 今から帰る。
6. *Mainichi hon o yomu.*	6. 毎日本を読む。
7. *Geemu de asobu no?*	7. ゲームで遊ぶの。
8. *Itsumo hataraku!*	8. いつも働く。
9. *Kare wa isogu.*	9. 彼は急ぐ。
10. *Nihongo o hanasu no?*	10. 日本語を話すの。

Day 26: I-Form

The I-Form could also be called the Polite-Form, because it is used to make the polite form of verbs. This will be used when talking to strangers, or to sound more polite with friends. The I-form can be used to talk about the present or the future.

To make the I-Form for *ichidan* いちだん verbs, drop *ru* る.

Ichidan いちだん verbs

taberu → tabe	たべる → たべ	食べる → 食べ
miru → mi	みる → み	見る → 見

To make the I-Form for *godan* ごだん verbs, replace the final *u* う sound with *i* い.

Godan ごだん verbs

kau → kai	かう → かい	買う → 買い
matsu → machi	まつ → まち	待つ → 待ち
kaeru → kaeri	かえる → かえり	帰る → 帰り
yomu → yomi	よむ → よみ	読む → 読み
asobu → asobi	あそぶ → あそび	遊ぶ → 遊び
hataraku → hataraki	はたらく → はたらき	働く → 働き
isogu → isogi	いそぐ → いそぎ	急ぐ → 急ぎ
hanasu → hanashi	はなす → はなし	話す → 話し

Special verbs

suru → shi	する → し	
kuru → ki	くる → き	来る → 来

Remember, the words *da* だ and *desu* です(to be), are actually *de aru* である and *de arimasu* でありま す, so the I-Form is *de ari* であり. Again, this is used in writing, but not often in conversation.

These I-Form stems by themselves will turn most verbs into a noun. For example *shinu* しぬ[死ぬ] (to die) can change into a noun with the I-Form: *shini* しに[死に] (death). Some of the noun translations are slightly different than the verb itself. For example, *hanasu* はなす[話す] means *to speak*, but *hanashi* はなし[話] can mean: *story, speech,* or *conversation*.

These I-Form stems are used primarily for the Polite-Form. To make the Polite-Form with these stems, add *masu* ます to the I-Form. In addition to the Polite-Form, this will be called the Masu-Form. To make any of these verbs negative, change *masu* ます to *masen* ません.

Study the following conjugation:

Ichidan いちだん verbs

| *tabe → tabemasu* | たべ → たべます | 食べ → 食べます |
| *mi → mimasu* | み → みます | 見 → 見ます |

Godan ごだん verbs

kai → kaimasu	かい → かいます	買い → 買います
machi → machimasu	まち → まちます	待ち → 待ちます
kaeri → kaerimasu	かえり → かえります	帰り → 帰ります
yomi → yomimasu	よみ → よみます	読み → 読みます
asobi → asobimasu	あそび → あそびます	遊び → 遊びます
hataraki → hatarakimasu	はたらき → はたらきます	働き → 働きます
isogi → isogimasu	いそぎ → いそぎます	急ぎ → 急ぎます
hanashi → hanashimasu	はなし → はなします	話し → 話します

Special verbs

| *shi → shimasu* | し → します | |
| *ki → kimasu* | き → きます | 来 → 来ます |

Day 26 Grammar Cards:

1. U-Form → I-Form (ichidan)	drop *ru*	drop る	
2. U-Form → I-Form (godan)	replace *u* sound with *i*	replace う sound with い	
3. I-Form of *suru*	*shi*	し	
I-Form of *kuru*	*ki*	き	来
I-Form of *desu*	*deari*	であり	
4. I-Form → Masu-Form	add *masu*	add ます	

Day 26 Vocabulary:

1. to come	*kuru*	くる	来る
2. to die	*shinu*	しぬ	死ぬ

This is the only verb that ends in *nu* ぬ. It conjugates just like *mu* む verbs.

3. to say / to tell / to be called	*iu*	いう	言う

In Japanese, *say* and *tell* are the same word. To say *tell*, use a noun + *ni* に to show who or what you are telling it to. Your name + *toiu* という[と言う] means *I'm called...* Remember from Day 3, *to moushimasu* ともうします[と申します] also means *I'm called... Mousu* もうす[申す] is the humble form of *iu* いう[言う].

4. to ask / to listen	*kiku*	きく	聞く

Ask and *listen* are the same word. In context, it is easy to understand which meaning is being used. In general, but not always, *ask* will use the particle *ni* に and *listen* will use the particle *o* を.

5. to drink	*nomu*	のむ	飲む
6. to talk	*shaberu*	しゃべる	喋る **(G)**
7. to request	*tanomu*	たのむ	頼む
8. to use	*tsukau*	つかう	使う
9. to answer	*kotaeru*	こたえる	答える **(I)**
10. to write	*kaku*	かく	書く

The kanji for this word will often be used for types of books, or written things, or as a suffix to indicate a written version. In these cases, it is pronounced *sho* しょ[書].

1. **Are you coming to the party?**

2. **Everyone will die someday.**

3. **I will tell your mother.**

4. **I will listen to your story.**

5. **Do you drink coffee?**

6. **I will talk to him later.**

7. **The customers request food.**

8. **Do you use a computer for work?**

9. **Will you answer this question?**

10. **I will write a book.**

1. パーティにきますか。

2. みんなはいつかしにます。

3. おかあさんにいいます。

4. あなたのはなしをききます。

5. コーヒーをのみますか。

6. あとでかれとしゃべります。

7. おきゃくはたべものをたのみます。

8. しごとはぱそこんをつかいますか。

9. このしつもんにこたえますか。

10. ほんをかきます。

1. *Paati ni kimasu ka?*

2. *Minna wa itsuka shinimasu.*

3. *Okaasan ni iimasu.*

4. *Anata no hanashi o kikimasu.*

5. *Koohii o nomimasu ka?*

6. *Ato de kare to shaberimasu.*

7. *Okyaku wa tabemono o tanomimasu.*

8. *Shigoto wa pasokon o tsukaimasu ka?*

9. *Kono shitsumon ni kotaemasu ka?*

10. *Hon o kakimasu.*

1. パーティに来ますか。

2. 皆はいつか死にます。

3. お母さんに言います。

4. あなたの話を聞きます。

5. コーヒーを飲みますか。

6. 後で彼と喋ります。

7. お客は食べ物を頼みます。

8. 仕事はパソコンを使いますか。

9. この質問に答えますか。

10. 本を書きます。

Day 27: A-Form

This form is sometimes called the Negative-Form or Nai-Form, because it is used to negate verbs in casual speech: to say you didn't do something.

To make the A-Form for *ichidan* いちだん verbs, drop *ru* る.

Ichidan いちだん verbs

taberu → tabe	たべる → たべ	食べる → 食べ
miru → mi	みる → み	見る → 見

To make the A-Form of *godan* ごだん verbs, replace the final *u* う sound with *a* あ. Verbs that end with *u* う change to *wa* わ.

Godan ごだん verbs

kau → kawa	かう → かわ	買う → 買わ
matsu → mata	まつ → また	待つ → 待た
kaeru → kaera	かえる → かえら	帰る → 帰ら
yomu → yoma	よむ → よま	読む → 読ま
asobu → asoba	あそぶ → あそば	遊ぶ → 遊ば
hataraku → hataraka	はたらく → はたらか	働く → 働か
isogu → isoga	いそぐ → いそが	急ぐ → 急が
hanasu → hanasa	はなす → はなさ	話す → 話さ

Special verbs

suru → shi	する → し	
kuru → ko	くる → こ	来る → 来

These A-Form stems have no meaning by themselves. *nai* ない must be added to put the verb in its Negative-Form, or Nai-Form. Study the following conjugations:

Ichidan いちだん verbs

tabe → tabenai	たべ → たべない	食べ → 食べない
mi → minai	み → みない	見 → 見ない

Godan ごだん verbs

kau → kawanai	かう → かわない	買う → 買わない
matsu → matanai	まつ → またない	待つ → 待たない
kaeru → kaeranai	かえる → かえらない	帰る → 帰らない
yomu → yomanai	よむ → よまない	読む → 読まない
asobu → asobanai	あそぶ → あそばない	遊ぶ → 遊ばない
hataraku → hatarakanai	はたらく → はたらかない	働く → 働かない
isogu → isoganai	いそぐ → いそがない	急ぐ → 急がない
hanasu → hanasanai	はなす → はなさない	話す → 話さない

Special verbs

suru → shinai	する → しない	
kuru → konai	くる → こない	来る → 来ない

Aru ある has a special A-Form conjugation. It becomes *nai* ない. So remember, the negative forms of *da* だ and *desu* です are *dewa nai* ではない (usually pronounced *ja nai* じゃない), and *dewa arimasen* ではありません.

Day 27 Grammar Cards:

1. U-Form → A-Form (ichidan)	drop *ru*	drop る	
2. U-Form → A-Form (godan)	replace *u* sound with *a* (exception: *u→wa*)	replace う sound with あ (exception: う→わ)	
3. A-Form of *suru*	*shi*	し	
A-Form of *kuru*	*ko*	こ	来
4. A-Form → Nai-Form	*add nai*	add ない	

Day 27 Vocabulary:

1. to wash	*arau*	あらう	洗う
2. to sing	*utau*	うたう	歌う
3. to lie down / to sleep / to go to bed	*neru*	ねる	寝る **(I)**

The verb *to sleep* is actually *nemuru* ねむる[眠る], but *neru* ねる[寝る] is used far more often.

4. to get up / to rouse	*okiru*	おきる	起きる **(I)**
5. to wake up / to open your eyes	*samasu*	さます	覚ます

This literally means to open your eyes, not get out of bed, and is usually paired with *me* め[目] (eye). It is also used to say *sober up*, as in, the opposite of *drunk*.

6. to understand / to know	*wakaru*	わかる	分かる

Similar to saying *I dunno* in English, many speakers will drop the *ra* ら and say this negatively as *wakanai* わかない, instead of *wakaranai* わからない.

7. to rest	*yasumu*	やすむ	休む
8. to learn	*narau*	ならう	習う
9. to lose / to misplace	*nakusu*	なくす	無くす
10. to fly	*tobu*	とぶ	飛ぶ

1. I don't wash my hands.

2. She doesn't sing.

3. He never sleeps.

4. I won't get up early tomorrow.

5. He won't wake up at 7:00.

6. I don't understand this kanji.

7. She doesn't rest at all!

8. I don't learn math at school.

9. I won't lose this.

10. Pigs don't fly.

1. てはあらわないです。

2. かのじょはうたわない。

3. かれはけっしてねない。

4. あしたははやくおきない。

5. かれはしちじにめをさまさない。

6. このかんじはわからない。

7. かのじょはぜんぜんやすまないよ。

8. がっこうではすうがくをならわないです。

9. これをなくさない。

10. ぶたはとばないです。

1. *Te wa arawanai desu.*

2. *Kanojo wa utawanai.*

3. *Kare wa kesshite nenai.*

4. *Ashita wa hayaku okinai.*

5. *Kare wa shichiji ni me o samasanai.*

6. *Kono kanji wa wakaranai.*

7. *Kanojo wa zenzen yasumanai yo!*

8. *Gakkou de wa suugaku o narawanai desu.*

9. *Kore o nakusanai.*

10. *Buta wa tobanai desu.*

1. 手は洗わないです。

2. 彼女は歌わない。

3. 彼は決して寝ない。

4. 明日は早く起きない。

5. 彼は七時に目を覚まさない。

6. この漢字は分からない。

7. 彼女は全然休まないよ。

8. 学校では数学を習わないです。

9. これを無くさない。

10. 豚は飛ばないです。

Day 28: E-Form

The E-Form is also called the Imperative-Form, and in a later lesson will be used to make the Potential-Form, and in Volume Two, the Conditional-Form. It has many uses! Just a reminder, the Imperative-Form is used to give commands, to tell someone to do something. The Potential-Form shows what we *can do*. The Conditional-Form is used with *if*.

To make the E-Form for *ichidan* いちだん verbs, drop *ru* る.

Ichidan いちだん verbs

taberu → tabe	たべる → たべ	食べる → 食べ
miru → mi	みる → み	見る → 見

To make the E-Form for *godan* ごだん verbs, replace the final *u* う sound with *e* え.

Godan ごだん verbs

kau → kae	かう → かえ	買う → 買え
matsu → mate	まつ → まて	待つ → 待て
kaeru → kaere	かえる → かえれ	帰る → 帰れ
yomu → yome	よむ → よめ	読む → 読め
asobu → asobe	あそぶ → あそべ	遊ぶ → 遊べ
hataraku → hatarake	はたらく → はたらけ	働く → 働け
isogu → isoge	いそぐ → いそげ	急ぐ → 急げ
hanasu → hanase	はなす → はなせ	話す → 話せ

Special verbs

suru → sure	する → すれ	
kuru → kure	くる → くれ	来る → 来れ

Aru ある has an E-Form: *are* あれ, but this is not used like other verbs. *Are* あれ can not be used to give commands with *to be*.

The Imperative-Form for *godan* ごだん verbs is the same as the stem, no changes re necessary, however, the Imperative-Form for *ichidan* いちだん verbs requires adding *ro* ろ to the stem. This way to give a command is quite forceful, and should only be used when you are angry or have lost your patience.

Ichidan いちだん verbs

taberu → tabero	たべる → たべろ	食べる → 食べろ
miru → miro	みる → みろ	見る → 見ろ

Special verbs

suru → shiro	する → しろ	
kuru → koi	くる → こい	来る → 来い

Day 28 Grammar Cards:

1. U-Form → E-Form (ichidan)	drop *ru*	drop る	
2. U-Form → E-Form (godan)	replace *u* sound with *e*	replace う sound with え	
3. E-Form of *suru*	sure	すれ	
E-Form of *kuru*	kure	くれ	来れ
4. Imperative-Form (ichidan)	add *ro*	add ろ	
5. Imperative-Form of *suru*	shiro	しろ	
Imperative-Form of *kuru*	koi	こい	来い

Day 28 Vocabulary:

1. to turn on	*tsukeru*	つける	点ける **(I)**
2. to turn off / to extinguish / to erase	*kesu*	けす	消す

The intransitive version of this verb is *kieru* きえる[消える].

3. to make / to create	*tsukuru*	つくる	作る
4. to shower	*abiru*	あびる	浴びる **(I)**
5. to go	*iku*	いく	行く

An older pronunciation is *yuku* ゆく, often used at train stations.

6. to sell	*uru*	うる	売る
7. to put	*oku*	おく	置く
8. to push	*osu*	おす	押す
9. to swim	*oyogu*	およぐ	泳ぐ
10. to ride / to get on	*noru*	のる	乗る

Day 28 Example Sentences:

1. **Turn on the lights!**

2. **Turn off the lights!**

3. **Make a sandwich!**

4. **You're dirty! Take a shower!**

5. **Go fast!**

6. **Sell your clothes!**

7. **Put that on the desk!**

8. **Push this button!**

9. **Swim 100 meters!**

10. **Get on the train!**

1. でんきをつけろ。

2. でんきをけせ。

3. サンドイッチをつくれ。

4. きたないですよ。シャワーをあびろ。

5. はやくいけ。

6. ふくをうれ。

7. つくえにおけ。

8. このぼたんをおせ。

9. ひゃくメートルおよげ。

10. でんしゃにのれ。

1. *Denki o tsukero!*

2. *Denki o kese!*

3. *Sandoicchi o tsukure!*

4. *Kitanai desu yo. Shawaa o abiro!*

5. *Hayaku ike!*

6. *Fuku o ure!*

7. *Tsukue ni oke!*

8. *Kono botan o ose!*

9. *Hyaku meetoru oyoge!*

10. *Densha ni nore!*

1. 電気を点けろ。

2. 電気を消せ。

3. サンドイッチを作れ。

4. 汚いですよ。シャワーを浴びろ。

5. 速く行け。

6. 服を売れ。

7. 机に置け。

8. このボタンを押せ。

9. 百メートル泳げ。

10. 電車に乗れ。

Day 29: O-Form

The O-Form is also called the Volitional-Form or the Presumptive-Form. Volition means a conscious choice to do something. This form is used in casual speech when you want to say *Let's* or *Shall we*. Presumptive means you presume something to be true, you assume, you guess.

To make the O-Form for *ichidan* いちだん verbs, replace *ru* る with *you* よう.

Ichidan いちだん verbs

taberu → tabeyou	たべる → たべよう	食べる → 食べよう
miru → miyou	みる → みよう	見る → 見よう

To make the O-Form for *godan* ごだん verbs, replace the final *u* う sound with *ou* おう.

Godan ごだん verbs

kau → kaou	かう → かおう	買う → 買おう
matsu → matou	まつ → まとう	待つ → 待とう
kaeru → kaerou	かえる → かえろう	帰る → 帰ろう
yomu → yomou	よむ → よもう	読む → 読もう
asobu → asobou	あそぶ → あそぼう	遊ぶ → 遊ぼう
hataraku → hatarakou	はたらく → はたらこう	働く → 働こう
isogu → isogou	いそぐ → いそごう	急ぐ → 急ごう
hanasu → hanasou	はなす → はなそう	話す → 話そう

Special verbs

suru → shiyou	する → しよう	
kuru → koyou	くる → こよう	来る → 来よう

Technically, *desu* です has an O-Form: *da* だ changes to *darou* だろう, and *desu* です changes to *deshou* でしょう. These words have different uses, they aren't volitional, they don't mean: *Let's be,* or *shall we be?*

The O-Form is used in casual speech to say: *Let's,* or *Shall we?* The Volitional-Form can be used politely with the Masu-Form, by changing *masu* ます to *mashou* ましょう:

Let's go. (casual)	Let's go. (polite)
Ikou.	*Ikimashou.*
いこう。	いきましょう。
行こう。	行きましょう。
Let's eat.(casual)	**Let's eat. (polite)**
Tabeyou.	*Tabemashou.*
たべよう。	たべましょう。
食べよう。	食べましょう。

Day 29 Grammar Cards:

1. U-Form → O-Form (ichidan)	replace *ru* with *you*	replace る with よう	
2. U-Form → O-Form (godan)	replace *u* sound with *ou*	replace う sound with おう	
3. O-Form of *suru*	*shiyou*	しよう	
O-Form of *kuru*	*koyou*	こよう	来よう
O-Form of *masu*	*mashou*	ましょう	

Day 29 Vocabulary:

1. to brush teeth / to polish	*migaku*	みがく	磨く
2. to do	*yaru*	やる	

This is a more casual way to say *to do*. While *suru* する is used in many other grammar constructions, *yaru* やる is not.

3. to call over / to invite	*yobu*	よぶ	呼ぶ
4. to pray	*inoru*	いのる	祈る
5. to cut	*kiru*	きる	切る **(G)**
6. to smoke / to suck	*suu*	すう	吸う
7. to take	*toru*	とる	取る
8. to look for / to search	*sagasu*	さがす	探す
9. to climb	*noboru*	のぼる	登る
10. to investigate	*shiraberu*	しらべる	調べる **(I)**

Investigate is a bit formal in English. This word is more casual in Japanese, and can mean to *search for information* or *find out*. This word is also used to say *look up words*.

<u>Day 29 Example Sentences</u>:

1. Let's brush our teeth.	**1.** はをみがこう。
2. Let's do it from now on.	**2.** いまからやりましょう。
3. Let's invite our friends over.	**3.** ともだちをよぼう。
4. Let's pray with the monks.	**4.** おぼうさんといのりましょう。
5. Let's cut this paper.	**5.** このかみをきりましょう。
6. Let's smoke some cigarettes.	**6.** タバコをすおう。
7. Let's take these snacks.	**7.** このおかしをとりましょう。
8. Let's look for my keys.	**8.** わたしのかぎをさがしましょう。
9. Let's climb that mountain over there.	**9.** あのやまをのぼりましょう。
10. Let's look up this word in the dictionary.	**10.** じしょでこのたんごをしらべましょう。

1. *Ha o migakou.*	**1.** 歯を磨こう。
2. *Ima kara yarimashou.*	**2.** 今からやりましょう。
3. *Tomodachi o yobou.*	**3.** 友達を呼ぼう。
4. *Obousan to inorimashou.*	**4.** お坊さんと祈りましょう。
5. *Kono kami o kirimashou.*	**5.** この紙を切りましょう。
6. *Tabako o suou.*	**6.** タバコを吸おう。
7. *Kono okashi o torimashou.*	**7.** このお菓子を取りましょう。
8. *Watashi no kagi o sagashimashou.*	**8.** 私の鍵を探しましょう。
9. *Ano yama o noborimashou.*	**9.** あの山を登りましょう。
10. *Jisho de kono tango o shirabemashou.*	**10.** 辞書でこの単語を調べましょう。

Day 30: Te-Form

The Te-Form is a bit different than the other five forms of verbs. The Te-Form at its most basic level is the polite version of the Imperative-Form. The E-Form can be imperative, but it is rather rude. Te-Form imperative commands are more polite. It has many other uses. It is used to create sentences in the continuous tense, to link sentences with *and*, and a whole host of other things, which will be covered later. For now, study how to make the Te-Form.

To make the Te-Form for *ichidan* いちだん verbs, replace *ru* る with *te* て.

Ichidan いちだん verbs

taberu → tabete	たべる → たべて	食べる → 食べて
miru → mite	みる → みて	見る → 見て

The Te-Form for *godan* ごだん verbs is a bit different for each one. Unlike previous conjugations, making the Te-Form replaces <u>the entire last kana</u>.

Godan ごだん verbs
Verbs ending in *u* う, *tsu* つ, or *ru* る, replace the last kana with *tte* って.

kau → katte	かう → かって	買う → 買って
matsu → matte	まつ → まって	待つ → 待って
kaeru → kaette	かえる → かえって	帰る → 帰って

Verbs ending in *mu* む or *bu* ぶ, replace the last kana with *nde* んで.

yomu → yonde	よむ → よんで	読む → 読んで
asobu → asonde	あそぶ → あそんで	遊ぶ → 遊んで

Verbs ending in *ku* く or *gu* ぐ, replace the last kana with *ite* いて, or *ide* いで.

hataraku → hataraite	はたらく → はたらいて	働く → 働いて
isogu → isoide	いそぐ → いそいで	急ぐ → 急いで

Verbs ending in *su* す replace the last kana with *shite* して.

hanasu → hanashite	はなす → はなして	話す → 話して

Special verbs

suru → shite	する → して	
kuru → kite	くる → きて	来る → 来て
*iku → itte (to go)	いく → いって	行く → 行って

Technically, *desu* です has a Te-Form: *de* で. It is very limited in its uses. It is only used to connect sentence with *and*, which will be covered later.

The Te-Form is used to give commands. To make more polite requests, add *kudasai* ください. This translates as *please*.

Please study.
Benkyou shite kudasai.
べんきょうしてください。
勉強して下さい。

Day 30 Grammar Cards:

1. U-Form → Te-Form (ichidan)	replace *ru* with *te*	replace る with て	
2. U-Form → Te-Form (*u* う *tsu* つ *ru* る godan)	replace last kana with *tte*	replace last kana with って	
3. U-Form → Te-Form (*mu* む *bu* ぶ godan)	replace last kana with *nde*	replace last kana with んで	
4. U-Form → Te-Form (*ku* く *gu* ぐ godan)	replace last kana with *ite / ide*	replace last kana with いて・いで	
5. U-Form → Te-Form (*su* す godan)	replace last kana with *shite*	replace last kana with して	
6. Te-Form of *suru*	*shite*	して	
Te-Form of *kuru*	*kite*	きて	来て
Te-Form of *iku*	*itte*	いって	行って

Day 30 Vocabulary:

1. to throw away	*suteru*	すてる	捨てる (I)
2. to visit	*tazuneru*	たずねる	訪ねる (I)
3. to enjoy oneself / to have fun	*tanoshimu*	たのしむ	楽しむ

tanoshimi たのしみ[楽しみ] can be used to say: *to look forward to*. For example, *I'm looking forward to it*: *Tanoshimi desu.* たのしみです。[楽しみです。]

4. to stop (doing)	*yameru*	やめる	止める (I)
5. to continue	*tsuzukeru*	つづける	続ける (I)

The intransitive form of this word is used a lot at the end of television shows: *tsuzuku* つづく[続く] (to be continued)

6. to stay the night	*tomaru*	とまる	泊まる
7. to pay	*harau*	はらう	払う
8. to go back / to return	*modoru*	もどる	戻る

This is often interchangeable with *kaeru* かえる[帰る] (to return). The difference is that this word means simply to go back from where you came, as opposed to going back home.

9. to apologize	*ayamaru*	あやまる	謝る
10. to choose	*erabu*	えらぶ	選ぶ

Day 30 Example Sentences:

1. **Please throw away your trash.**

2. **Please visit your parents.**

3. **Have fun tomorrow.**

4. **Please stop doing that.**

5. **Please continue doing that.**

6. **Please stay here tonight.**

7. **Please pay 10,000 yen.**

8. **Please go back to your room.**

9. **Please apologize to your sister.**

10. **Please choose the one you like.**

1. ごみをすててください。

2. りょうしんをたずねてください。

3. あしたたのしんでください。

4. それをやめてください。

5. それをつづけてください。

6. こんやはここにとまってください。

7. いちまんえんはらってください。

8. へやにもどってください。

9. いもうとにあやまってください。

10. すきなものをえらんでください。

1. *Gomi o sutete kudasai.*

2. *Ryoushin o tazunete kudasai.*

3. *Ashita tanoshinde kudasai.*

4. *Sore o yamete kudasai.*

5. *Sore o tsuzukete kudasai.*

6. *Konya wa koko ni tomatte kudasai.*

7. *Ichi man en haratte kudasai.*

8. *Heya ni modotte kudasai.*

9. *Imouto ni ayamatte kudasai.*

10. *Suki na mono o erande kudasai.*

1. 塵を捨てて下さい。

2. 両親を訪ねて下さい。

3. 明日楽しんで下さい。

4. それを止めて下さい。

5. それを続けて下さい。

6. 今夜はここに泊まって下さい。

7. 一万円払って下さい。

8. 部屋に戻って下さい。

9. 妹に謝って下さい。

10. 好きなものを選んで下さい。

Day 31: Ta-Form

The Ta-Form is the casual past tense form of verbs. It is formed exactly like the Te-Form, but uses *ta* た and *da* だ instead of *te* て and *de* で.

To make the Ta-Form for *ichidan* いちだん verbs, replace *ru* る with *ta* た.

Ichidan いちだん verbs

taberu → tabeta	たべる → たべた	食べる → 食べた
miru → mita	みる → みた	見る → 見た

Godan ごだん verbs
Verbs ending in *u* う, *tsu* つ, or *ru* る, replace the last kana with *tta* った.

kau → katta	かう → かった	買う → 買った
matsu → matta	まつ → まった	待つ → 待った
kaeru → kaetta	かえる → かえった	帰る → 帰った

Verbs ending in *mu* む or *bu* ぶ, replace the last kana with *nda* んだ.

yomu → yonda	よむ → よんだ	読む → 読んだ
asobu → asonda	あそぶ → あそんだ	遊ぶ → 遊んだ

Verbs ending in *ku* く or *gu* ぐ, replace the last kana with *ita* いた or *ida* いだ.

hataraku → hataraita	はたらく → はたらいた	働く → 働いた
isogu → isoida	いそぐ → いそいだ	急ぐ → 急いだ

Verbs ending in *su* す, replace the last kana with *shita* した.

hanasu → hanashita	はなす → はなした	話す → 話した

Special verbs

suru → shita	する → した	
kuru → kita	くる → きた	来る → 来た
*iku → itta	いく → いった	行く → 行った

Now that you know the past tense of *suru* する, you should learn one idiomatic phrase: *dou shita* どうした. This literally means *How did it happen,* but actually translates to: *What's wrong?*

Desu です has a Ta-Form. The past tense forms are *datta* だった for casual, and *deshita* でした for polite speech.

Day 31 Grammar Cards:

1. U-Form → Ta-Form (ichidan)	replace *ru* with *ta*	replace る with た	
2. U-Form → Ta-Form (u う tsu つ ru る godan)	replace last kana with *tta*	replace last kana with った	
3. U-Form → Ta-Form (mu む bu ぶ godan)	replace last kana with *nda*	replace last kana with んだ	
4. U-Form → Ta-Form (ku く gu ぐ godan)	replace last kana with *ita / ida*	replace last kana with いた・いだ	
5. U-Form → Ta-Form (su す godan)	replace last kana with *shita*	replace last kana with した	
6. Ta-Form of suru	*shita*	した	
Ta-Form of kuru	*kita*	きた	来た
Ta-Form iku	*itta*	いった	行った
7. What's wrong?	*Dou shita?*	どうした。	

Day 31 Vocabulary:

1. to tie / to fasten	*shimeru*	しめる	締める **(I)**
This word is used for seat belts.			
2. to differ / to be wrong	*chigau*	ちがう	違う
Be careful with this word. It is used to say that two things are *different*, as in: *not the same*, and also used to say that something is *wrong*, as in: *not correct*.			
3. to become tired	*tsukareru*	つかれる	疲れる **(I)**
4. to arrive	*tsuku*	つく	着く
5. to photograph / to film	*toru*	とる	撮る
6. to chirp (animate)	*naku*	なく	鳴く
to chirp (inanimate)	*naru*	なる	鳴る
Chirp is chosen for this word because the kanji depicts the mouth of a bird, however, it is used for many different animals noises, as well as beeping electronics. When used for electronics, it will be the inanimate version, *naru* なる[鳴る].			
7. to become	*naru*	なる	成る **(UK)**
8. to stick / to glue / to attach	*haru*	はる	貼る
9. to pull	*hiku*	ひく	引く
10. to fall	*furu*	ふる	降る
This is used for the weather, referring to rain or snow falling.			

Day 31 Example Sentences:

1. I fastened my seat belt.

2. His answer was wrong.

3. I'm tired!

(Lit. I've become tired!)

4. I've arrived at Tokyo station.

5. I took many pictures.

6. The alarm clock buzzed.

7. She became a singer.

8. I stuck the paper to the wall.

9. I pulled the string.

10. It rained yesterday.

1. シートベルトをしめた。

2. かれのかいとうはちがった。

3. つかれたよ。

4. とうきょうえきについた。

5. たくさんしゃしんをとった。

6. めざましどけいがなった。

7. かのじょはかしゅになった。

8. かべにかみをはった。

9. いとをひいた。

10. きのうあめがふった。

1. *Shiitoberuto o shimeta.*

2. *Kare no kaitou wa chigatta.*

3. *Tsukareta yo.*

4. *Toukyou eki ni tsuita.*

5. *Takusan shashin o totta.*

6. *Mezamashidokei ga natta.*

7. *Kanojo wa kashu ni natta.*

8. *Kabe ni kami o hatta.*

9. *Ito o hiita.*

10. *Kinou ame ga futta.*

1. シートベルトを締めた。

2. 彼の解答は違った。

3. 疲れたよ。

4. 東京駅に着いた。

5. たくさん写真を撮った。

6. 目覚まし時計が鳴った。

7. 彼女は歌手になった。

8. 壁に紙を貼った。

9. 糸を引いた。

10. 昨日雨が降った。

Day 32: Suru Verbs

Many verbs in Japanese are so-called *suru* する verbs. *Suru* する means *to do*. You've already learned *yaru* やる (to do), but *yaru* やる is more casual, and not used in many other grammar constructions, while *suru* する has many uses. Many verbs in Japanese will use a noun plus *suru* する to express that action. For example, *benkyou suru* べんきょうする[勉強する] (to study). The word *benkyou* べんきょう[勉強] is the noun *studies* or *diligence,* but when combined with *suru* する, it becomes the verb *to study,* or more literally, *to do studying.*

Day 32 Vocabulary:

1. to do	*suru*	する	
2. to work (do work)	*shigoto suru*	しごとする	仕事する
3. to study (do studies)	*benkyou suru*	べんきょうする	勉強する
4. to clean (do cleaning)	*souji suru*	そうじする	掃除する
5. to exercise (do movement)	*undou suru*	うんどうする	運動する
6. to practice (do practice)	*renshuu suru*	れんしゅうする	練習する
7. to go for a walk (do walk)	*sanpo suru*	さんぽする	散歩する
8. to cook (do cuisine)	*ryouri suru*	りょうりする	料理する
9. to call (do phone)	*denwa suru*	でんわする	電話する
10. to drive (do motion)	*unten suru*	うんてんする	運転する

Day 32 Example Sentences:

1. I'll do it tomorrow.	1. あしたするよ。
2. I work on weekends.	2. しゅうまつはしごとする。
3. I study mornings.	3. あさべんきょうする。
4. I clean every day.	4. まいにちそうじする。
5. I exercise on Monday.	5. げつようびはうんどうする。
6. I practice baseball every day.	6. まいにちやきゅうをれんしゅうする。
7. I'll go for a walk tonight.	7. こんやさんぽする。
8. My wife cooks my food.	8. つまがりょうりする。
9. Will you call her?	9. かのじょにでんわするの。
10. I drive a car.	10. くるまをうんてんする。

1. *Ashita suru yo.*	1. 明日するよ。
2. *Shuumatsu wa shigoto suru.*	2. 週末は仕事する。
3. *Asa benkyou suru.*	3. 朝勉強する。
4. *Mainichi souji suru.*	4. 毎日掃除する。
5. *Getsuyoubi wa undou suru.*	5. 月曜日は運動する。
6. *Mainichi yakyuu o renshuu suru.*	6. 毎日野球を練習する。
7. *Konya sanpo suru.*	7. 今夜散歩する。
8. *Tsuma ga ryouri suru.*	8. 妻が料理する。
9. *Kanojo ni denwa suru no?*	9. 彼女に電話するの。
10. *Kuruma o unten suru.*	10. 車を運転する。

Day 33: Compound Verbs

Many verbs in Japanese are actually combinations of two verbs. You can't make compound verbs on your own, but you can use the following rules to easily identify them:

The first way to make compound verbs is by combining the I-Form of one verb with the U-Form of another. For example, *hanashiau* はなしあう[話し合う] (to discuss), which is a combination of *hanasu* はなす[話す] (to speak) and *au* あう[合う] (to fit / to unite). Another way is to use a noun or an I-Form verb with the particle *ni* に. For example, *maniau* まにあう[間に合う] (to be in time for), which combines *ma* ま[間] (time interval) with *au* あう[合う] (to fit / to unite). This verb literally means, *to fit into a time interval*. The I-Form combined with *ni* に is often paired with *iku* いく[行く] (to go) to say that you are going out to do that I-Form verb. For example, *tabeniiku* たべにいく[食べに行く] (to go out to eat). Finally, some compound verbs are made with the Te-Form. For example, *mottekuru* もってくる[持って来る] (to bring) which combines *motsu* もつ[持つ] (to hold) with *kuru* くる[来る] (to come).

Day 33 Vocabulary:

1. to fit / to unite	*au*	あう	合う

Be very careful with this word, not only is it a homonym with *au* あう[会う] (to meet), but the kanji look very similar as well.

2. to take out / to get out / to put out	*dasu*	だす	出す

This verb is the transitive form of *deru* でる[出る] (to exit). It is used in many contexts, whenever you are putting or taking something out. For example, it can mean *to submit, to reveal, to turn in, to publish, to send, to produce*.

3. to take out / to pull out	*hikidasu*	ひきだす	引き出す

This word is for taking things out of a container, and is not used in many other contexts like *dasu* だす[出す].

4. to discuss	*hanashiau*	はなしあう	話し合う
5. to be in time for	*maniau*	まにあう	間に合う
6. to make a mistake	*machigau*	まちがう	間違う
7. to bring	*mottekuru*	もってくる	持って来る
8. to take along	*motteiku*	もっていく	持って行く
9. to be packed (put into)	*komu*	こむ	込む
to be crowded	*komu*	こむ	混む

This first kanji is used for many compound verbs, and it has a sense of *inclusion*. The second kanji meaning is *crowded* or *mixture*.

10. to include / to insert	*kumikomu*	くみこむ	組み込む

The first kanji means *association* or *unite*, so this word has the sense of putting things together.

Day 33 Example Sentences:

1. These shoes don't fit.	1. このくつはあわない。
2. Please take out a pen.	2. ペンをだしてください。
3. I pulled out the papers from the desk.	3. つくえからかみをひきだした。
4. Let's discuss it after this.	4. あとではなしあいましょう。
5. We're not going to make it in time!	5. まにあわないよ。
6. Oops, I made a mistake.	6. おっと、まちがいました。
7. I brought apples.	7. リンゴをもってきました。
8. Take the report with you please.	8. レポートをもっていってください。
9. Tokyo is crowded, isn't it?	9. とうきょうはこんでいるね。
10. Please include this report.	10. このほうこくをくみこんでください。

1. *Kono kutsu wa awanai.*	1. この靴は合わない。
2. *Pen o dashite kudasai.*	2. ペンを出して下さい。
3. *Tsukue kara kami o hikidashita.*	3. 机から紙を引き出した。
4. *Ato de hanashiaimashou.*	4. 後で話し合いましょう。
5. *Maniawanai yo!*	5. 間に合わないよ。
6. *Otto, machigaimashita.*	6. おっと、間違いました。
7. *Ringo o mottekimashita.*	7. リンゴを持って来ました。
8. *Repooto o motteitte kudasai.*	8. レポートを持って行って下さい。
9. *Toukyou wa konde iru ne.*	9. 東京は混んでいるね。
10. *Kono houkoku o kumikonde kudasai.*	10. この報告を組み込んでください。

Day 34: Mono and Koto, Verbs as Nouns

Mono もの[物] can be attached to the I-Form of many, but not all verbs, to change them into nouns. *Mono* もの[物] is used for tangible objects. English expressions like *thing-a-ma-bob* or *what-do-call*-it can be used when you don't know the name of an object. In Japanese, words like this can be made using *mono* もの[物]. For example, *hanashimono* はなしもの[話物] (not actually a real word) would refer to a tangible thing that is used for speaking. It could be a written speech, or a microphone, it could be anything, so long as that thing is used for speaking. This fake word literally means: *tangible speaking thing*.

Koto こと[事] is used for intangible objects, or ideas. The kanji is only used for nouns, not nominative verbs. It can be attached to the U-Form of all verbs to make them nominative verbs, like in English using *-ing*. To say *Speaking is fun*, use *hanasukoto* はなすこと[話すこと], not *hanashi* はなし[話].

Many verbs can change into nouns in the I-Form, without adding *mono* もの[物] or *koto* こと[事]. Some examples of this are *hanashi* はなし[話] (conversation), from the verb *hanasu* はなす[話す] (to speak), and *yasumi* やすみ[休み] (day off / vacation), from the verb *yasumu* やすむ[休む] (to rest). Notice, however, that these noun versions are slightly different than their verb counterparts. Study the following examples:

to eat	*taberu*	たべる	食べる
food	*tabemono*	たべもの	食べ物
eating	*taberukoto*	たべること	食べること
to drink	*nomu*	のむ	飲む
drinks	*nomimono*	のみもの	飲み物
drinking	*nomukoto*	のむこと	飲むこと
to serve	*tsukaeru*	つかえる	仕える
work	*shigoto*	しごと	仕事
to work	*shigoto suru*	しごとする	仕事する
working	*shigoto surukoto*	しごとすること	仕事すること

Notice that in the case of *work*, the unvoiced *koto* こと[事] changed to the voiced *goto* ごと. This happens quite often in Japanese with suffixes and compound nouns.

While *mono* もの[物] is used primarily with objects, *koto* こと[事] has many more complex uses. It is used in many grammar constructions, which will be covered later.

Consider the phrase: *watashi no koto* わたしのこと[私の事], which literally means: *my intangible thing*. This can be roughly translated as: *my task*, *myself,* or *my very soul and existence*, or something along those lines. English doesn't really have a word like this, but keeping in mind that *mono* もの[物] and *koto* こと are basically the same word, used for tangible and intangible things, it may help you understand its meaning.

There is also a slang version of these words: *yatsu* やつ. It can be used in place of both *mono* もの[物] and *koto* こと[事], but it is a very casual form, so only use it with your friends.

Verbs can also become nouns by adding *no* の to the U-Form, instead of *koto* こと. There is no discernible difference when using *no* の, just as there is no major difference in meaning between the sentences, *I like speaking* and *I like to speak.* However, certain grammar constructions will always use *koto* こと, which we will learn about later.

I like <u>to</u> speak. I like speak<u>ing</u>. *Hanasu<u>koto</u> ga suki desu.* はなす<u>こと</u>がすきです 話す<u>こと</u>が好きです。	I like <u>to</u> speak. I like speak<u>ing</u>. *Hanasu <u>no</u> ga suki desu.* はなす<u>の</u>がすきです。 話す<u>の</u>が好きです。

Finally, written with a different kanji, *mono* もの[者] means *person*. This is usually used in set words, for example, *hatarakimono* はたらきもの[働き者] (a hard working person) and *namakemono* なまけもの[怠け者] (a lazy person). The kanji itself is more often pronounced as (*sha / ja*) (しゃ・じゃ) [者] and used as a suffix, in words such as *gakusha* がくしゃ[学者] (scholar) and *kanja* かんじゃ[患者] (patient).

You may also hear it in the phrase *nani mono da* なにものだ[何者だ] (Who is that? / What is that?). You may be asking yourself what is the difference between this phrase and *dare desu ka* だれですか [誰ですか] (Who is that?) This is usually used in contexts where the speaker is surprised or unsure about what they are looking at, or heard a sound and are unsure where it came from. The speaker has no information about the person or thing they are seeing or hearing.

Day 34 Grammar Cards:

1. **Verb → Tangible Noun**	I-Form + *mono*	I-Form + もの	I-Form + 物
2. **Verb → Intangible Noun (*ing*)**	U-Form + *koto / no*	U-Form + こと・の	
3. **Slang word for *mono* or *koto***	*yatsu*	やつ	
4. **person**	*mono / sha / ja*	もの・しゃ・じゃ	者

Day 34 Vocabulary:

1. **to build**	*tateru*	たてる	建てる **(I)**
2. **to forget**	*wasureru*	わすれる	忘れる **(I)**
3. **to meet**	*au*	あう	会う
4. **to walk**	*aruku*	あるく	歩く
5. **to run**	*hashiru*	はしる	走る **(G)**
6. **to enter**	*hairu*	はいる	入る **(G)**

A secondary meaning of this word is *to contain*. When people ask what ingredients were used to make a food, they will literally ask, *What has entered this dish?*

7. **to exit**	*deru*	でる	出る **(I)**
8. **to teach**	*oshieru*	おしえる	教える **(I)**

A secondary meaning of this word is *to tell*. As in, when *telling* someone some information, you are *teaching* them something they didn't know before.

9. **to stand**	*tatsu*	たつ	立つ
10. **to sit**	*suwaru*	すわる	座る

<u>Day 34 Example Sentences</u>:

1. This building is tall.

2. I forgot many things.

(Lit. There are many forgotten things.)

3. Meeting today will be difficult.

4. Walking is fun!

5. Running is not fun!

6. A key is required to enter.

(Lit. As for entering, a key is necessary.)

7. Exiting is impossible.

8. Teaching English is easy.

9. If you are tired, standing is tough.

10. We have chairs for sitting.

1. このたてものはたかいです。

2. わすれものがおおいです。

3. きょうあうのはむずかしいです。

4. あるくことはたのしいですよ。

5. はしるのはたのしくないですよ。

6. はいるのにかぎがひつようです。

7. でることはむりです。

8. えいごをおしえることはかんたんです。

9. つかれていたら、たつのはこんなんだ。

10. すわるためのいすがあります。

1. *Kono tatemono wa takai desu.*

2. *Wasuremono ga ooi desu.*

3. *Kyou au no wa muzukashii desu.*

4. *Aruku koto wa tanoshii desu yo!*

5. *Hashiru no wa tanoshikunai desu yo!*

6. *Hairu no ni kagi ga hitsuyou desu.*

7. *Deru koto wa muri desu.*

8. *Eigo o oshieru koto wa kantan desu.*

9. *Tsukarete itara, tatsu no wa konnan da.*

10. *Suwaru tame no isu ga arimasu.*

1. この建物は高いです。

2. 忘れ物が多いです。

3. 今日会うのは難しいです。

4. 歩くことは楽しいですよ。

5. 走るのは楽しくないですよ。

6. 入るのに鍵が必要です。

7. 出ることは無理です。

8. 英語を教えることは簡単です。

9. 疲れていたら、立つのは困難だ。

10. 座るための椅子があります。

Now that you've learned about all the forms verbs can take, it's time to explain Japanese grammar from an English perspective. To form a present tense, future tense, or habitual sentence, use the U-Form for casual speech, and the Masu-Form for polite speech. When talking about the future or habitual action, it can usually be understood from context. If not, a time word can be inserted to clarify. Study the following examples:

Casual

I _eat_ bread.
Watashi wa pan o taberu.
わたしはパンを<u>たべる</u>。
私はパンを<u>食べる</u>。

I will eat bread <u>tomorrow</u>.
Watashi wa ashita pan o taberu.
わたしは<u>あした</u>パンをたべる。
私は<u>明日</u>パンを食べる。

I eat bread <u>every day</u>.
Watashi wa mainichi pan o taberu.
わたしは<u>まいにち</u>パンをたべる。
私は<u>毎日</u>パンを食べる。

Polite

I _eat_ bread.
Watashi wa pan o tabemasu.
わたしはパンを<u>たべます</u>。
私はパンを<u>食べます</u>。

I will eat bread <u>tomorrow</u>.
Watashi wa ashita pan o tabemasu.
わたしは<u>あした</u>パンをたべます。
私は<u>明日</u>パンを食べます。

I eat bread <u>every day</u>.
Watashi wa mainichi pan o tabemasu.
わたしは<u>まいにち</u>パンをたべます。
私は<u>毎日</u>パンを食べます。

Negative sentences are made by using the Nai-Form, or the negative Masu-Form, which becomes _masen_ ません. Study the following examples:

Casual

I <u>don't eat</u> bread.
Watashi wa pan o tabenai.
わたしはパンを<u>たべない</u>。
私はパンを<u>食べない</u>。

I <u>won't eat</u> bread tomorrow.
Watashi wa ashita pan o tabenai.
わたしはあしたパンを<u>たべない</u>。
私は明日パンを<u>食べない</u>。

I <u>don't eat</u> bread every day.
Watashi wa mainichi pan o tabenai.
わたしはまいにちパンを<u>たべない</u>。
私は毎日パンを<u>食べない</u>。

Polite

I <u>don't eat</u> bread.
Watashi wa pan o tabemasen.
わたしはパンを<u>たべません</u>。
私はパンを<u>食べません</u>。

I <u>won't eat</u> bread tomorrow.
Watashi wa ashita pan o tabemasen.
わたしはあしたパンを<u>たべません</u>。
私は明日パンを<u>食べません</u>。

I <u>don't eat</u> bread every day.
Watashi wa mainichi pan o tabemasen.
わたしはまいにちパンを<u>たべません</u>。
私は毎日パンを<u>食べません</u>。

Day 35 Grammar Cards:

1. Present Tense, Future Tense, Habitual Action	U-Form (casual) Masu-Form (politc)
2. Negative Present Tense, Future Tense, Habitual Action	Nai-Form (casual) Negative Masu-Form (polite)

Day 35 Vocabulary:

1. to put in / to insert	*ireru*	いれる	入れる (I)
2. to play an instrument	*hiku*	ひく	弾く
This is limited to instruments that don't involve blowing air.			
3. to blow	*fuku*	ふく	吹く
This is used for playing wind instruments, as well as things are blowing, such as the wind.			
4. to finish / to end	*owaru*	おわる	終わる
The transitive form of this verb is *oeru* おえる[終える].			
5. to lend	*kasu*	かす	貸す
6. to borrow	*kariru*	かりる	借りる (I)
7. to be surprised	*odoroku*	おどろく	驚く
8. to be worried / to be in trouble	*komaru*	こまる	困る
9. to bloom	*saku*	さく	咲く
10. to shine	*sasu*	さす	差す
This word is a bit complicated. The core meaning of this word is *to put out*. The meaning *shine* is derived from the idea that the sun is *putting out* light. This word can mean *to wear* with swords (more important back in the day than now). It can mean *to serve / to offer,* as in a cup of tea. It can mean *to put your arms out*, and also used for *putting up* an umbrella.			

1. I put food in my mouth every day.

2. She plays the piano.

3. He plays the trumpet.

4. It ends at 7:00pm every day.

5. I sometimes lend him money.

6. I never borrow money.

7. I listened to the statement and was surprised.

8. I worry about not having money.

9. The flowers bloom every year.

10. The sun shines on bad days too.

1. まいにちくちにたべものをいれる。

2. かのじょはピアノをひきます。

3. かれはトランペットをふく。

4. まいにちじゅうくじにおわります。

5. わたしはときどきかれにおかねをかします。

6. わたしはけっしておかねをかりません。

7. せいめいをきいておどろいた。

8. おかねがなくてこまります。

9. まいとしはながさきます。

10. わるいひも、たいようがさします。

1. *Mainichi kuchi ni tabemono o ireru.*

2. *Kanojo wa piano o hikimasu.*

3. *Kare wa toranpetto o fuku.*

4. *Mainichi juuku ji ni owarimasu.*

5. *Watashi wa tokidoki kare ni okane o kashimasu.*

6. *Watashi wa kesshite okane o karimasen.*

7. *Seimei o kiite odoroita.*

8. *Okane ga nakute komarimasu.*

9. *Maitoshi hana ga sakimasu.*

10. *Warui hi mo, taiyou ga sashimasu.*

1. 毎日口に食べ物を入れる。

2. 彼女はピアノを弾きます。

3. 彼はトランペットを吹く。

4. 毎日十九時に終わります。

5. 私は時々彼にお金を貸します。

6. 私は決してお金を借りません。

7. 声明を聞いて驚いた。

8. お金が無くて困ります。

9. 毎年花が咲きます。

10. 悪い日も、太陽が差します。

Day 36: Continuous Tense

In English, continuous tense sentences are formed with (be) + *-ing.* In Japanese, the Te-Form + *iru* いる is used. To be polite, change *iru* いる to its Masu-Form: *imasu* います. In English, the Continuous-Form can be used to talk about the future, for example: *I am going somewhere tomorrow,* but in Japanese, it is not used this way. In Japanese, this form is <u>only</u> used for the present moment, or a current state resulting from a past action.

Casual	Polite
I <u>am eating</u> bread. *Watashi wa pan o <u>tabete iru</u>.* わたしはパンを<u>たべている</u>。 私はパンを<u>食べている</u>。	**I <u>am eating</u> bread.** *Watashi wa pan o <u>tabete imasu</u>.* わたしはパンを<u>たべています</u>。 私はパンを<u>食べています</u>。

Some verbs will <u>always</u> use the Continuous-Form. This is because they are resulting states from past actions. For example, *sumu* すむ [住む] (to live / reside), and *shiru* しる [知る] (to know). Study the following examples:

Casual	Polite
I <u>live</u> in Japan. *Nihon ni <u>sunde iru</u>.* にほんに<u>すんでいる</u>。 日本に<u>住んでいる</u>。	**I <u>know</u> that.** *Sore o <u>shitte imasu</u>.* それを<u>しっています</u>。 それを<u>知っています</u>。

To negate these sentences, use the Nai-Form of *iru* いる, which are *inai* いない, and *imasen* いません.

Casual	Polite
I <u>am not eating</u> bread. *Watashi wa pan o <u>tabete inai</u>.* わたしはパンを<u>たべていない</u>。 私はパンを<u>食べていない</u>。	**I <u>am not eating</u> bread.** *Watashi wa pan o <u>tabete imasen</u>.* わたしはパンを<u>たべていません</u>。 私はパンを<u>食べていません</u>。
I <u>don't live</u> in Japan. *Nihon ni <u>sunde inai</u>.* にほんに<u>すんでいない</u>。 日本に<u>住んでいない</u>。	**I <u>don't live</u> in Japan.** *Nihon ni <u>sunde imasen</u>.* にほんに<u>すんでいません</u>。 日本に<u>住んでいません</u>。

Shiru しる [知る] (to know) is a bit special, because the Continuous-Form is not used in the negative:

I <u>don't know</u> that. *Sore o <u>shiranai</u>.* それを<u>しらない</u>。 それを<u>知らない</u>。

Verbs that are almost always used in the continuous tense will be noted with **(Te-Iru).**

Day 36 Grammar Cards:

1. Continuous Action	Te-Form + *iru / imasu*	Te-Form + いる・います
2. Negative Continuous Action	Te-Form + *inai / imasen*	Te-Form + いない・いません

Day 36 Vocabulary:

1. to know	*shiru*	しる	知る (G) (Te-Iru)

There is a lot of confusion between this verb and *wakaru* わかる[分かる]. *Shiru* is used to say that some information is in your head at this moment. This is why it is always used in the continuous tense, you are literally saying that you are *in the state of holding the information*. In the negative, you are not talking about the state of your mind, but rather, you are saying *That information hasn't entered my brain*. This is why it is not in the continuous tense in the negative. *Wakaru* わかる[分かる] is used to show that you understand something about the information, you are familiar with it. The truth is, no amount of explanation is going to help you decide which one to use, you'll have to learn from trial and error, as well as listening to native Japanese speakers.

2. to live / to reside	*sumu*	すむ	住む (Te-Iru)
3. to hold / to possess	*motsu*	もつ	持つ (Te-Iru)

This can sometimes be interchanged with *aru* ある to say that you *have* something. The emphasis with this verb is that you are currently in possession of it, you are holding it.

4. to remember / to memorize	*oboeru*	おぼえる	覚える (I) (Te-Iru)

The emphasis on this word is information going into your head, as well as being in the state of being able to recall the information.

5. to remember / to recall / to recollect	*omoidasu*	おもいだす	思い出す

The emphasis on this word is the information coming out of your head. This compound verb literally means *exiting memory*. This is usually used with personal memories, not information.

6. to love	*ai suru*	あいする	愛する (Te-Iru)

In English there is the comical distinction between *loving* someone and being *in love* with someone. This word means *in love*.

7. to be married	*kekkon suru*	けっこんする	結婚する (Te-Iru)

To say that you are married, use the Te-Iru form of this verb. If you use the simple present tense, you are asking someone to marry you, so watch out!

8. to work for / at / as	*tsutomeru*	つとめる	勤める (I) (Te-Iru)

This verb literally means *to serve*, or *be employed by*. With companies use the particle *ni* に, with types of jobs, use the particle *o* を.

9. to get angry	*okoru*	おこる	怒る (Te-Iru)
10. to be similar / to look the same	*niru*	にる	似る (I) (Te-Iru)

1. I don't know the answer.	1. かいとうをしらない。
2. She lives in Tokyo.	2. かのじょはとうきょうにすんでいます。
3. I have many pens.	3. ペンをたくさんもっています。
4. I don't remember that.	4. それはおぼえていない。
5. Do you recall that day?	5. あのひをおもいだしているの。
6. I love you.	6. あいしているよ。
7. Are you married?	7. けっこんしていますか。
8. I work for Toyota.	8. とよたにつとめています。
9. He is really angry.	9. かれはすごくおこっているよ。
10. I look like my mother.	10. わたしはおかあさんににている。

1. *Kaitou o shiranai.*	1. 解答を知らない。
2. *Kanojo wa Toukyou ni sunde imasu.*	2. 彼女は東京に住んでいます。
3. *Pen o takusan motte imasu.*	3. ペンをたくさん持っています。
4. *Sore wa oboete inai.*	4. それは覚えていない。
5. *Ano hi o omoidashite iru no?*	5. あの日を思い出しているの。
6. *Ai shite iru yo.*	6. 愛しているよ。
7. *Kekkon shite imasu ka?*	7. 結婚していますか。
8. *Toyota ni tsutomete imasu.*	8. 豊田に勤めています。
9. *Kare wa sugoku okotte iru yo.*	9. 彼は凄く怒っているよ。
10. *Watashi wa okaasan ni nite iru.*	10. 私はお母さんに似ている。

Day 37: Past Tense

The Ta-Form for casual past tense. To be polite, use the Masu-Form, changing *masu* ます into its Ta-Form: *mashita* ました.

Casual	Polite
I <u>ate</u> bread. *Watashi wa pan o <u>tabeta</u>.* わたしはパンを<u>たべた</u>。 私はパンを<u>食べた</u>。	**I <u>ate</u> bread.** *Watashi wa pan o <u>tabemashita</u>.* わたしはパンを<u>たべました</u>。 私はパンを<u>食べました</u>。

For a continuous past action, do the same:

Casual	Polite
I <u>was eating</u> bread. *Watashi wa pan o <u>tabete ita</u>.* わたしはパンを<u>たべていた</u>。 私はパンを<u>食べていた</u>。	**I <u>was eating</u> bread.** *Watashi wa pan o <u>tabete imashita</u>.* わたしはパンを<u>たべていました</u>。 私はパンを<u>食べていました</u>。

To negate these sentences, use the past tense version of the Nai-Form and negative Masu-Form. *Nai* ない changes to *nakatta* なかった, and *mashita* ました changes to *masen deshita* ませんでした.

Casual	Polite
I <u>didn't eat</u> bread. *Watashi wa pan o <u>tabenakatta</u>.* わたしはパンを<u>たべなかった</u>。 私はパンを<u>食べなかった</u>。	**I <u>didn't eat</u> bread.** *Watashi wa pan o <u>tabemasen deshita</u>.* わたしはパンを<u>たべませんでした</u>。 私はパンを<u>食べませんでした</u>。
I <u>wasn't eating</u> bread. *Watashi wa pan o <u>tabete inakatta</u>.* わたしはパンを<u>たべていなかった</u>。 私はパンを<u>食べていなかった</u>。	**I <u>wasn't eating</u> bread.** *Watashi wa pan o <u>tabete imasen deshita</u>.* わたしはパンを<u>たべていませんでした</u>。 私はパンを<u>食べていませんでした</u>。

The past tense of *da* だ is *datta* だった. The past tense of *desu* です is *deshita* でした.

Casual	Polite
It <u>was</u> me. *Watashi <u>datta</u>.* わたし<u>だった</u>。 私<u>だった</u>。	**It <u>was</u> me.** *Watashi <u>deshita</u>.* わたし<u>でした</u>。 私<u>でした</u>。

The negative form of *datta* だった is *dewa nakatta* ではなかった. This is often abbreviated to *ja nakatta* じゃなかった. The negative form of *deshita* でした is *dewa arimasen deshita* ではありませんでした。

Casual

It <u>wasn't</u> me.
Watashi <u>ja nakatta</u>.
わたし<u>じゃなかった</u>。
私<u>じゃなかった</u>。

Polite

It <u>wasn't</u> me.
Watashi <u>dewa arimasen deshita</u>.
わたし<u>ではありませんでした</u>。
私<u>ではありませんでした</u>。

In English, time is very important for grammar. There are different grammar forms depending on when something took place, and whether it is still taking place. Compare the two sentences: *I was studying* and *I have been studying*. The first sentence talks about the past, and the second states that the action happened in the past, and has continued up until now. In Japanese, they don't make this distinction with grammar. The same past tense grammar is used for both sentences. Time words like *recently* or *since Monday* can be used to explicitly state when the action took place.

Day 37 Grammar Cards:

1. **Past Tense**	Ta-Form (casual) *masu → mashita* (polite)	ます → ました (polite)
2. **Negative Past Tense**	Nai-Form → *nakatta* (casual) *masen → masen deshita* (polite)	Nai-Form → なかった (casual) ません → ませんでした (polite)
3. **Continuous Past Tense**	Te-Form + *itta* (casual) Te-Form + *imashita* (polite)	Te-Form + いった (casual) Te-Form + いました (polite)
4. **Negative Continuous Past Tense**	Te-Form + *inakatta* (casual) Te-Form + *imasen deshita* (polite)	Te-Form + いなかった (casual) Te-Form + いませんでした (polite)
5. **was / were**	*datta*	だった
was / were	*deshita*	でした
was / were	*de gozaimashita*	でございました
6. **wasn't / weren't**	*dewa nakkata / ja nakkata*	ではなかった・じゃなかった
wasn't / weren't	*dewa arimasen deshita*	ではありませんでした
wasn't / weren't	*dewa gozaimasen deshita*	ではございませんでした

Day 37 Vocabulary:

1. **bath**	*ofuro*	おふろ	お風呂
Instead of *take*, Japanese say *enter* a bath.			
2. **stairs**	*kaidan*	かいだん	階段
3. **key / lock**	*kagi*	かぎ	鍵
This word is used for both the lock and your keys. To say that something is *locked* or *unlocked*, use the words *open* and *closed: aku* あく[開く] and *shimaru* しまる[閉まる].			
4. **umbrella**	*kasa*	かさ	傘
5. **bag / basket / purse**	*kaban*	かばん	鞄
6. **box**	*hako*	はこ	箱
7. **soap**	*sekken*	せっけん	石鹸
8. **bicycle**	*jitensha*	じてんしゃ	自転車
9. **automobile**	*jidousha*	じどうしゃ	自動車
10. **money**	*okane*	おかね	お金

1. **Were you taking a bath?**

2. **We ran up the stairs quickly.**

3. **He unlocked the door.**

4. **I lost my umbrella.**

5. **I found my bag.**

6. **I dropped the box.**

7. **I didn't use soap.**

8. **I didn't buy the bike.**

9. **He didn't drive the automobile.**

10. **I didn't have any money.**

1. おふろにはいっていましたか？

2. わたしたちはかいだんをはやくかけあがりました。

3. かれはかぎをあけました。

4. かさをなくした。

5. かばんがみつかりました。

6. はこをおとした。

7. せっけんをつかいませんでした。

8. じてんしゃをかわなかった。

9. かれはじどうしゃをうんてんしなかった。

10. おかねがありませんでした。

1. *Ofuro ni haitte imashita ka?*

2. *Watashitachi wa kaidan o hayaku kakeagarimashita.*

3. *Kare wa kagi o akemashita.*

4. *Kasa o nakushita.*

5. *Kaban ga mitsukarimashita.*

6. *Hako o otoshita.*

7. *Sekken o tsukaimasen deshita.*

8. *Jitensha o kawanakatta.*

9. *Kare wa jidousha o unten shinakatta.*

10. *Okane ga arimasen deshita.*

1. お風呂に入っていましたか？

2. 私たちは階段を早く駆け上がりました。

3. 彼は鍵を開けました。

4. 傘を無くした。

5. 鞄が見つかりました。

6. 箱を落とした。

7. 石鹸を使いませんでした。

8. 自転車を買わなかった。

9. 彼は自動車を運転しなかった。

10. お金がありませんでした。

Certainty can be expressed with specific words, or by using *darou* だろう and *deshou* でしょう, which are the Volitional-Form of *da* だ and *desu* です. Previously, you learned that the Volitional-Form can be translated as: *Shall we* or *Let's*, but *darou* だろう and *deshou* でしょう are not used like this. In Japanese, these words are used to express that you are uncertain about the sentence. Study the following examples:

Certain	Uncertain
Who is that?	**Who is that?**
Dare desu ka?	*Dare deshou ka?*
だれですか。	だれでしょうか。
誰ですか。	誰でしょうか。

The first sentence is simply asking who the person is. The second sentence is asking who the person is, and also explicitly stating that the speaker is uncertain. People will often use *darou* だろう or *deshou* でしょう like this, simply to express that they are uncertain about the sentence.

Darou だろう or *deshou* でしょう can also be used as a tag question to confirm information:

You like Japanese food, right?	**I spoke to you yesterday, didn't I?**
Nihon no tabemono ga suki, deshou?	*Kinou, anata to hanashita darou?*
にほんのたべものがすきでしょう。	きのう、あなたとはなしただろう。
日本の食べ物が好きでしょう。	昨日、あなたと話しただろう。

Another way to express certainty is *kamoshiremasen* かもしれません(maybe / might). Unlike other certainty words, it will always appear at the end of a sentence. The casual form is *kamoshirenai* かもしれない, and most people shorten this to just *kamo* かも. When used, *da* だ or *desu* です will be dropped.

Some of the vocabulary words today are adjectives and adverbs. A thorough explanation of adjectives and adverbs will be given later in the book. The final word today will have **(Na)** written next to it. Write it on your card, but don't worry about for now.

Day 38 Grammar Cards:

1. unsure / tag question / confirm information	End of sentence *darou / deshou*	End of sentence だろう・でしょう
2. maybe / might	End of sentence *kamoshiremasen* Drop *da* or *desu*	End of sentence かもしれません Drop だ or です

Day 38 Vocabulary:

1. certainly	*zehi*	ぜひ	

People will often say this twice, *zehi zehi* ぜひぜひ. It is not used to modify verbs like *certainly* in English, but rather, as a reply, to say that you will *certainly* do something.

2. sure / certain	*tashika*	たしか	確か

Tashika たしか[確か] is often used with the particle *ni* に.

3. probably	*tabun*	たぶん	多分
4. Of course.	*mochiron*	もちろん	勿論 (UK)
5. exactly	*choudo*	ちょうど	丁度 (UK)

This is used to say an exact amount, as in money or time. In English, *Exactly!* can be used to show your agreement, but this word can not be used in that context.

6. properly / diligently	*chanto*	ちゃんと	

This word is often used with commands to tell someone to do something properly, as in, *give a real effort.*

7. somewhat / a little bit	*chotto*	ちょっと	

This word is used often, and in a lot of contexts. In the expression *chotto matte* ちょっとまって[ちょっと待って] (please wait a minute), *chotto dake* ちょっとだけ (just a little bit). It can be used with adjectives to say something was *somewhat,* or *little bit.* By itself, it can be used in anger or frustration to say something like: *Hey! What are you doing? What's wrong with you?*

8. be sure to / certainly	*kanarazu*	かならず	必ず

This is often used to tell someone to make certain that they do something.

9. not necessarily / not always the case	*kanarazushimo*	かならずしも	必ずしも

This is the opposite of *kanarazu* かならず[必ず].

10. delicate / subtle	*bimyou*	びみょう	微妙 (Na)

This word is often used idiomatically by itself to say: *I'm not entirely certain what your saying is true,* or, *What you just said has raised more questions than answers.* What the speaker is saying, is that the situation has become *delicate,* because it would be impolite to ask certain questions to get the truthful answers.

Day 38 Example Sentences:

1. (Of course) I'll come.

2. Surely you're joking.

3. I will probably decide tomorrow.

4. Will I buy it? Of course!

5. This is exactly 400 yen.

6. Please study diligently.

7. This soup is a bit cold.

8. Be sure to eat your vegetables.

9. Money is not necessarily happiness.

10. This is a delicate problem.

1. ぜひいきます。

2. たしかにふざけている。

3. たぶん、あしたきめます。

4. かいますか。もちろん。

5. これはちょうどよんひゃくえん。

6. ちゃんとべんきょうしてください。

7. このしるはちょっとつめたいです。

8. かならずやさいをたべてください。

9. おかねはかならずしもしあわせじゃない。

10. これはびみょうなもんだいです。

1. *Zehi ikimasu.*

2. *Tashika ni fuzakete iru.*

3. *Tabun, ashita kimemasu.*

4. *Kaimasu ka? Mochiron!*

5. *Kore wa choudo yonhyaku en.*

6. *Chanto benkyou shite kudasai.*

7. *Kono shiru wa chotto tsumetai desu.*

8. *Kanarazu yasai o tabete kudasai.*

9. *Okane wa kanarazushimo shiawase ja nai.*

10. *Kore wa bimyou na mondai desu.*

1. ぜひ行きます。

2. 確かに巫山戯ている。

3. 多分、明日決めます。

4. 買いますか。勿論。

5. これは丁度四百円。

6. ちゃんと勉強して下さい。

7. この汁はちょっと冷たいです。

8. 必ず野菜を食べて下さい。

9. お金は必ずしも幸せじゃない。

10. これは微妙な問題です。

Day 39: Negative Te-Form

The negative Te-Form has two different forms. It is constructed using the Nai-Form, with a few changes. The first negative Te-Form is made by adding *de* で to the Nai-Form. This will be called the NaiDe-Form.

tabenai → tabenaide	たべない → たべないで	食べない → 食べないで
ikanai → ikanaide	いかない → いかないで	行かない → 行かないで

The second negative Te-Form is made by replacing the final *i* い from the Nai-Form with *kute* くて. This will be called the Nakute-Form.

tabenai → tabenakute	たべない → たべなくて	食べない → 食べなくて
ikanai → ikanakute	いかない → いかなくて	行かない → 行かなくて

Both of these are negative Te-Forms, and have various uses. For negative commands, use the NaiDe-Form:

Please <u>don't eat</u> that.
Sore o <u>tabenaide</u> kudasai.
それを<u>たべないで</u>ください。
それを<u>食べないで</u>下さい。

To say that you did something *without doing* something else, or to say you did something *instead of* something else, use the NaiDe-Form:

<u>Without studying</u>, I passed the test.
<u>Benkyou shinaide</u>, shiken o goukaku shita.
<u>べんきょうしないで</u>、しけんをごうかくした。
<u>勉強しないで</u>、試験を合格した。

<u>Instead of studying</u>, I watched TV.
<u>Benkyou shinaide</u>, terebi o mita.
<u>べんきょうしないで</u>、テレビをみた。
<u>勉強しないで</u>、テレビを見た。

Notice, the grammar is the same in both of the previous example sentences, so the context is important for translation. These sentences could have also been translated as, *Instead of studying I passed the test,* and, *Without studying I watched TV,* but those sentences don't make much sense, do they?

There is also a shorter version the NaiDe-Form. Simply add *zuni* ずに to the A-Form. The *ni* に can be dropped. This construction can't be used for commands, but can be used to say *without doing* and *instead of doing*. The two irregular verbs, *suru* する(to do), and *kuru* くる(to come), become *sezu* せず, and *kozu* こず.

Without studying, I passed the test.
Benkyou sezu, shiken o goukaku shita.
べんきょうせず、しけんをごうかくした。
勉強せず、試験を合格した。

There is one more way to say *without doing*. Use *nashi* なし[無し] and the particle *ni* に. This word can only be used with nouns, so change the verb into a noun by adding *koto* こと.

Without studying, I passed the test.
Benkyou suru koto nashi ni, shiken o goukaku shita.
べんきょうすることなしに、しけんをごうかくした。
勉強すること無しに、試験を合格した。

The Nakute-Form is used to say, *not this but that,* and to connect negative sentences with *and.*

I didn't eat sushi, but rather ramen.	**He didn't win and became angry.**
Osushi o tabenakute, raamen o tabemashita.	*Kare wa katenakute, okorimashita.*
おすしをたべなくて、ラーメンをたべました。	かれはかてなくて、おこりました。
お寿司を食べなくて、ラーメンを食べました。	彼は勝てなくて、怒りました。

Day 39 Grammar Cards:

1. Naide-Form *(negative commands, without doing, instead of doing)*	Nai-Form + *de*	Nai-Form + で	
2. Zuni-Form *(without doing, instead of doing)*	A-Form + *zuni*	A-Form ずに	
Zuni-Form of suru / kuru	*sezu / kozu*	せず・こず	
3. without doing	U-Form + *koto* + *nashi ni*	U-Form + こと + なしに	U-Form + こと + 無しに
4. Nakute-Form *(not this but that*, negative sentence *and)*	Nai-Form replace *i* with *kute*	Nai-Form replace い with くて	

Day 39 Vocabulary:

1. friend	*tomodachi*	ともだち	友達
2. problem	*mondai*	もんだい	問題
3. western style clothes	*youfuku*	ようふく	洋服
4. Japanese style clothes	*wafuku*	わふく	和服
5. the sky	*sora*	そら	空
6. intersection	*kousaten*	こうさてん	交差点
7. corner	*kado*	かど	角
8. company	*kaisha*	かいしゃ	会社
9. entrance	*iriguchi*	いりぐち	入口
10. exit	*deguchi*	でぐち	出口

Day 39 Example Sentences:

1. He is not a friend, but an enemy.

2. This is not a problem, but a solution.

3. Instead of wearing western style clothes, I wore a kimono.

4. Instead of wearing Japanese style clothes, I wore an aloha shirt.

5. Without looking into the sky, he shot.

6. Without looking, she walked through the intersection.

7. Instead of turning at the corner, I continued forward.

8. This is not a company, but a government office.

9. This is not an entrance, but rather an exit.

10. This is not an exit, but rather a window.

1. かれはともだちじゃなくて、てきです。

2. これはもんだいじゃなくて、かいとうです。

3. ようふくをきないで、きものをきていた。

4. わふくをきないで、アロハシャツをきていた。

5. そらをみずに、かれはうった。

6. しんごうをみずに、かのじょはこうさてんをわたった。

7. かどをまがらずに、ちょくしんした。

8. これはかいしゃじゃなくて、かんちょうです。

9. これはいりぐちじゃなくて、でぐちです。

10. これはでぐちじゃなくて、まどです。

1. *Kare wa tomodachi ja nakute, teki desu.*

2. *Kore wa mondai ja nakute, kaitou desu.*

3. *Youfuku o kinai de, kimono o kite ita.*

4. *Wafuku o kinai de, aroha shatsu o kite ita.*

5. *Sora o mizuni, kare wa utta.*

6. *Shingou o mizuni, kanojo wa kousaten o watatta.*

7. *Kado o magarazuni, chokushin shita.*

8. *Kore wa kaisha ja nakute, kanchou desu.*

9. *Kore wa iriguchi ja nakute, deguchi desu.*

10. *Kore wa deguchi ja nakute, mado desu.*

1. 彼は友達じゃなくて、敵です。

2. これは問題じゃなくて、解答です。

3. 洋服を着ないで、着物を着ていた。

4. 和服を着ないで、アロハシャツを着ていた。

5. 空を見ずに、彼は撃った。

6. 信号を見ずに、彼女は交差点を渡った。

7. 角を曲がらずに、直進した。

8. これは会社じゃなくて、官庁です。

9. これは入口じゃなくて、出口です。

10. これは出口じゃなくて、窓です。

Day 40: Commands

Most of the ways to give commands have been covered in previous lessons, but there are a few more grammar constructions to learn.

The polite way to give a command is to use the Te-Form + *kudasai* ください.

Please eat this.	**Please sit** here.
Kore o tabete kudasai.	*Koko ni suwatte kudasai.*
これをたべてください。	ここにすわってください。
これを食べてください。	ここに坐って下さい。

To make a negative request, use the NaiDe-Form.

Please don't eat this.	**Please don't sit** here.
Kore o tabenaide kudasai.	*Koko ni suwaranaide kudasai.*
これをたべないでください。	ここにすわらないでください。
これを食べないで下さい。	ここに坐らないで下さい。

The Imperative-Form can be used to give an angry or rude command. Remember, *ichidan* いちだん verbs add *ro* ろ to the E-Form, and *godan* ごだん verbs are the same as the E-Form.

Eat this!	**Sit** here!
Kore o tabero!	*Koko ni suware!*
これをたべろ!	ここにすわれ!
これを食べろ!	ここに坐れ!

To make an angry or rude negative request, don't use the E-Form. Just add *na* な to the U-Form.

Don't eat this!	**Don't sit** here!
Kore o taberuna!	*Koko ni suwaruna!*
これをたべるな!	ここにすわるな!
これを食べるな!	ここに坐るな!

Commands can be given with the I-Form + *nasai* なさい. This grammar is less polite than the Te-Form construction, but not angry like the E-Form. It is an authoritative command, where you are telling someone to do something, not asking them. Actually, you've already used this grammar. When saying *oyasuminasai* おやすみなさい[お休みなさい] (good night), you are actually giving this person a command *to rest*. This doesn't have a negative form.

Eat your vegetables.	**Clean** your room.
Yasai o tabenasai.	*Heya o souji shinasai.*
やさいをたべなさい。	へやをそうじしなさい。
野菜を食べなさい。	部屋を掃除しなさい。

A casual slang version of *nasai* なさい is to use *goran* ごらん with the Te-Form.

Eat your vegetables.	**Clean** your room.
Yasai o tabete goran.	*Heya o souji shite goran.*
やさいをたべてごらん。	へやをそうじしてごらん。
野菜を食べてごらん。	部屋を掃除してごらん。

The Ta-Form + *mae* まえ can be used to give a command. This is a slang version, used only by men.

Eat your vegetables.
Yasai o tabeta mae.
やさいをたべたまえ。
野菜を食べたまえ。

Day 40 Grammar Cards:

1. Polite command	Te-Form + *kudasai*	Te-Form + ください
2. Polite negative command	Naide-Form + *kudasai*	Naide-Form + ください
3. Rude command	E-Form + *ro* (ichidan) E-Form (godan)	E-Form + ろ (ichidan) E-Form (godan)
4. Negative rude command	U-Form + *na*	U-Form + な
5. Authoritative command	I-Form + *nasai* Te-Form + *goran*	I-Form + なさい Te-Form + ごらん
6. slang command (male only)	Ta-Form + *mae*	Ta-Form + まえ

Day 40 Vocabulary:

1. cafeteria / dining hall	*shokudou*	しょくどう	食堂
2. hallway	*rouka*	ろうか	廊下
3. salt	*shio*	しお	塩
4. sugar	*satou*	さとう	砂糖
5. soy sauce	*shouyu*	しょうゆ	醤油
6. trip / travel	*ryokou*	りょこう	旅行

This can be paired with *suru* する to mean *to go on on a trip.*

7. airplane	*hikouki*	ひこうき	飛行機
8. electricity / power	*denki*	でんき	電気

Instead of saying the name of the electric device, many Japanese people will just talk about turning on the electricity of the device. So instead of saying, *Turn on the lights*, they will say *Turn on the electricity.*

9. voice	*koe*	こえ	声
10. magazine	*zasshi*	ざっし	雑誌

Day 40 Example Sentences:

1. Please eat in the cafeteria.

2. Don't run in the hallway!

3. Please don't add salt.

4. Please add sugar.

5. Please use the soy sauce.

6. Please enjoy your trip.

7. Don't touch my airplane!

8. Turn off the power!

9. Please say it out loud.

10. Read this magazine.

1. しょくどうでたべなさい。

2. ろうかをはしるな。

3. しおをたさないでください。

4. さとうをたしてください。

5. しょうゆをつかってください。

6. りょこうをたのしんでください。

7. ぼくのひこうきをさわるな。

8. でんきをけせ。

9. こえをだしてください。

10. このざっしをよんでごらん。

1. *Shokudou de tabenasai.*

2. *Rouka o hashiru na!*

3. *Shio o tasanaide kudasai.*

4. *Satou o tashite kudasai.*

5. *Shouyu o tsukatte kudasai.*

6. *Ryokou o tanoshinde kudasai.*

7. *Boku no hikouki o sawaru na!*

8. *Denki o kese!*

9. *Koe o dashite kudasai.*

10. *Kono zasshi o yonde goran.*

1. 食堂で食べなさい。

2. 廊下を走るな。

3. 塩を足さないで下さい。

4. 砂糖を足して下さい。

5. 醤油を使って下さい。

6. 旅行を楽しんで下さい。

7. 僕の飛行機を触るな。

8. 電気を消せ。

9. 声を出して下さい。

10. この雑誌を読んでごらん。

Day 41: Like, Love, Hate, Need

Some verbs in English aren't used as verbs in Japanese. For example, *suku* すく[好く] (to like). In Japanese, the noun *suki* すき[好き] (like) will be used with *da* だ or *desu* です. The *da* だ or *desu* です is often just dropped from the sentence. This type of sentence is literally saying that the subject *is liked*. Instead of being an object of the verb, the thing being liked is actually the subject of the sentence, and takes the particle *ga* が.

> **I <u>like</u> sushi. (Lit. Sushi is liked.)**
> *Osushi ga <u>suki</u> desu.*
> おすしが<u>すき</u>です。
> お寿司が<u>好き</u>です。

To say that you don't like something, change the *da* だ or *desu* です.

> **I <u>don't like</u> sushi. (Lit. Sushi is not liked.)**
> *Osushi ga <u>suki ja nai</u>.*
> おすしが<u>すきじゃない</u>。
> お寿司が<u>好きじゃない</u>。

To say that you *love* something, use the word *daisuki* だいすき[大好き]. This literally means *big like*.

> **I <u>love</u> sushi.**
> *Osushi ga <u>daisuki</u> desu.*
> おすしが<u>だいすき</u>です。
> お寿司が<u>大好き</u>です。

However, *daisuki* だいすき[大好き] is not romantic love. For that, use the verb *ai suru* あいする[愛する] in the continuous tense.

> **I <u>love</u> you.**
> *Anata o <u>ai shite imasu</u>.*
> あなたを<u>あいしています</u>。
> あなたを<u>愛しています</u>。

The word for *hate* is *kirai* きらい[嫌い], which is derived from the verb *kirau* きらう[嫌う]. Like *suki* すき[好き], *dai* だい[大] can be added to say that you *really hate* something.

> **I <u>really hate</u> sushi.**
> *Osushi ga <u>daikirai</u>.*
> おすしが<u>だいきらい</u>。
> お寿司が<u>大嫌い</u>。

The verb *to need* is *iru* いる[要る]. Don't confuse this with the verb *to exist*. Although it ends in *i-r-u*, this is actually a *godan* ごだん verb.

I don't need sushi.
Osushi wa iranai.
おすしはいらない。
お寿司は要らない。

Similar to *like* and *hate*, people will often use the word *hitsuyou* ひつよう[必要] (necessary), in combination with *da* だ or *desu* です, to say that they need something.

I don't need sushi. (Lit. Sushi is not necessary.)
Osushi wa hitsuyou ja nai.
おすしはひつようじゃない。
お寿司は必要じゃない。

Day 41 Vocabulary:

1. like	suki	すき	好き
really like	daisuki	だいすき	大好き
2. hate	kirai	きらい	嫌い
really hate	daikirai	だいきらい	大嫌い
3. to need	iru	いる	要る (G)
4. necessary	hitsuyou	ひつよう	必要
5. song	uta	うた	歌
6. jacket / overcoat	uwagi	うわぎ	上着
7. vase	kabin	かびん	花瓶
8. tree / wood	ki	き	木
9. sand	suna	すな	砂
10. vegetable store	yaoya	やおや	八百屋

Like the ending for people, *san* さん can be added to this word, as well as other small stores.

Day 41 Example Sentences:

1. I really like Japanese!

2. I hate studying.

3. Do I need a ticket?

4. What is necessary?

5. Do you like this song?

6. I really hate leather jackets.

7. Why don't you like my vase?

8. We need more trees.

9. We need sand for our beach.

10. I really like the vegetable store near my house.

1. にほんごがだいすきだよ。

2. べんきょうすることがきらいです。

3. きっぷはいりますか。

4. なにがひつようですか。

5. このうたがすきですか。

6. かわのうわぎがだいきらいです。

7. なんでわたしのかびんがすきじゃないのですか。

8. もっときがいります。

9. わたしたちのうみのために、すながひつようです。

10. うちのちかくのやおやさんがだいすきです。

1. *Nihongo ga daisuki da yo!*

2. *Benkyou suru koto ga kirai desu.*

3. *Kippu wa irimasu ka?*

4. *Nani ga hitsuyou desu ka?*

5. *Kono uta ga suki desu ka?*

6. *Kawa no uwagi ga daikirai desu.*

7. *Nande watashi no kabin ga suki ja nai no?*

8. *Motto ki ga irimasu.*

9. *Watashitachi no umi no tame ni, suna ga hitsuyou desu.*

10. *Uchi no chikaku no yaoyasan ga daisuki desu.*

1. 日本語が大好きだよ。

2. 勉強することが嫌いです。

3. 切符は要りますか。

4. 何が必要ですか。

5. この歌が好きですか。

6. 革の上着が大嫌いです。

7. 何で私の花瓶が好きじゃないのですか。

8. もっと木が要ります。

9. 私たちの海のために、砂が必要です。

10. 家の近くの八百屋さんが大好きです。

Day 42: Vocabulary Practice

Now that you've learned all the basics of verbs, it's time to review and practice.
Day 42 Vocabulary:

1. to receive / to get / to take a test	*ukeru*	うける	受ける **(I)**

This word's core meaning is *to receive*, but has a lot of uses in this context. It is also used in many compound verbs. It is not usually used for obtaining physical objects, but rather, in sentences like, *The speech was well received.* Giving and receiving is actually a bit more complicated and is covered in detail in Volume Two.

2. to receive / to accept	*uketoru*	うけとる	受け取る

This is a compound verb with *toru* とる[取る] (to take). This verb shows a more active roll on the subject's part, not passively receiving something, but receiving it with intent, just as the verb *to accept* implies that the receiver must be willing.

3. to accept / to agree	*ukeireru*	うけいれる	受け入れる **(I)**

This is paired with *ireru* いれる[入れる] (to enter) to show that you have *taken in* something. It's interchangeable in many contexts with the previous word, but is more often used to show that you *agree* with something, you *accept it as fact.*

4. to accept / to take	*uketsukeru*	うけつける	受け付ける **(I)**

This is paired with *tsukeru* つける[付ける] (to attach) and is usually used for paperwork and information, as in: *accepting applications.* The noun *uketsuke* うけつけ[受け付け] means *reception* or *front desk.*

5. to be in charge of	*ukemotsu*	うけもつ	受け持つ

This is paired with *motsu* もつ[持つ] (to hold). You've taken something in and now you are holding it, you are *in charge of it.* It is most often used as the noun, *ukemochi* うけもち[受け持ち] paired with a person who is in charge.

6. to break	*kowasu*	こわす	壊す

This is the most general form of breaking. The intransitive form is *kowareru* こわれる[壊れる]

7. to fold / to snap / to break	*oru*	おる	折る

The kanji here means *to fold*, and this word is often used to say that something *broke in half.*

8. to break down / to defeat	*taosu*	たおす	倒す

This is often used to say that someone *defeated* someone else, as in a fight. The intransitive version is *taoreru* たおれる[倒れる]

9. to break / to divide / to crack	*waru*	わる	割る

This is the word for mathematical *division.* It can also mean *to split, to cut, to slice.* The kanji for this word has the symbol for a sword on the right, so that may help you remember the meaning.

10. to break / to stop working	*koshou suru*	こしょうする	故障する

This is the word you will use for machines or devices when they stop working.

Day 42 Example Sentences:

1. I will take a test next week.

2. She accepted the documents.

3. I accept your opinion.

4. The university is now accepting applications.

5. He is in charge of that project.

6. You broke my favorite toy.

7. I folded the origami crane.

8. We defeated the enemies.

9. The plate cracked from the earthquake.

10. My car broke down on the freeway.

1. ぼくはらいしゅうしけんをうけます。

2. かのじょはしょるいをうけとりました。

3. あなたのいけんをうけいれる。

4. だいがくはにゅうがくがんしょをうけつけています。

5. かれはそのしごとをうけもっている。

6. あなたはわたしのいちばんすきなオモチャをこわした。

7. おりがみでつるをおりました。

8. わたしたちはてきをたおした。

9. じしんでおさらがわれました。

10. こうそくどうろでおれのくるまはこしょうした。

1. *Boku wa raishuu shiken o ukemasu.*

2. *Kanojo wa shorui o uketorimashita.*

3. *Anata no iken o ukeireru.*

4. *Daigaku wa nyuugakugansho o uketsuketeimasu.*

5. *Kare wa sono shigoto o ukemotte iru.*

6. *Anata wa watashi no ichiban suki na omocha o kowashita.*

7. *Origami de tsuru o orimashita.*

8. *Watashitachi wa teki o taoshita.*

9. *Jishin de osara ga waremashita.*

10. *Kousokudouro de ore no kuruma wa koshou shita.*

1. 僕は来週試験を受けます。

2. 彼女は書類を受け取りました。

3. あなたの意見を受け入れる。

4. 大学は入学願書を受け付けています。

5. 彼はその仕事を受け持っている。

6. あなたは私の一番好きなオモチャを壊した。

7. 折り紙で鶴を折りました。

8. 私たちは敵を倒した。

9. 地震でお皿が割れました。

10. 高速道路で俺の車は故障した。

Day 43: Vocabulary Practice

Today's vocabulary practice will deal with clothing. In Japanese, there are three different ways to say *wear*, one is for your head, one for you body, and one for your legs and feet.

Day 43 Vocabulary:

1. to wear (head)	*kaburu*	かぶる	被る
2. to wear (body)	*kiru*	きる	着る (I)
3. to wear (legs)	*haku*	はく	履く
4. to undress	*nugu*	ぬぐ	脱ぐ
5. clothes	*fuku*	ふく	服
6. hat	*boushi*	ぼうし	帽子
7. pants / trousers	*zubon*	ズボン	
8. shoes	*kutsu*	くつ	靴
9. socks	*kutsushita*	くつした	靴下
10. business suit	*sebiro*	せびろ	背広

Day 43 Example Sentences:

1. Please don't wear hats inside.

2. What are you wearing?

3. I am wearing pants.

4. Take that ugly sweater off.

5. I have a lot of clothes.

6. I don't like hats.

7. These pants are sold out.

8. These shoes are 30,000 yen.

9. My socks have holes.

10. Japanese men like wearing business suits.

1. しつないではぼうしをかぶらないでください。

2. なにをきていますか。

3. わたしはずぼんをはいています。

4. そのみにくいセーターぬいで。

5. わたしはたくさんふくをもっています。

6. ぼうしがすきじゃない。

7. このズボンはかんばいです。

8. このくつはさんまんえんです。

9. ぼくのくつしたはあながある。

10. にほんのだんせいはせびろをきるのがすきです。

1. *Shitsunai de wa boushi o kaburanaide kudasai.*

2. *Nani o kite imasu ka?*

3. *Watashi wa zubon o haite imasu.*

4. *Sono minikui seetaa nuide.*

5. *Watashi wa takusan fuku o motte imasu.*

6. *Boushi ga suki ja nai.*

7. *Kono zubon wa kanbai desu.*

8. *Kono kutsu wa san man en desu.*

9. *Boku no kutsushita wa ana ga aru.*

10. *Nihon no dansei wa sebiro o kiru no ga suki desu.*

1. 室内では帽子を被らないで下さい。

2. 何を着ていますか。

3. 私はズボンを履いています。

4. その醜いセーター脱いで。

5. 私はたくさん服を持っています。

6. 帽子が好きじゃない。

7. このズボンは完売です。

8. この靴は三万円です。

9. 僕の靴下は穴がある。

10. 日本の男性は背広を着るのが好きです。

Day 44: Vocabulary Practice

Today's vocabulary practice deals with food. In Japanese, there are three words for your stomach. The basic word for your stomach is *hara* はら[腹]. Your stomach is in the middle of your body, so an alternate reading of the kanji developed: *onaka* おなか[お腹]. In Japanese, *naka* なか[中] means *middle*, so this word literally means, *our middle.* The stomach organ itself has a different word: *i* い [胃].

To say that you are hungry, you will literally say, *my stomach is empty,* or, *the food in my stomach has decreased.* These verbs are *suku* すく[空く] (to be empty), and *heru* へる[減る] (to decrease). To say that you are hungry, you can use either word for stomach, and either verb conjugated in the past tense. Study the following examples:

I'm hungry. **(Lit. My stomach has emptied.)** *Hara suita.* はらすいた。 腹空いた。	**I'm hungry.** **(Lit. My stomach has emptied.)** *Onaka suita.* おなかすいた。 お腹空いた。
I'm hungry. **(Lit. The food in my stomach has decreased.)** *Hara hetta.* はらへった。 腹減った。	**I'm hungry.** **(Lit. The food in my stomach has decreased.)** *Onaka hetta.* おなかへった。 お腹減った。

Though grammatically possible, *hara suita* はらすいた [腹空いた] is not common and sounds cute or childish to Japanese speakers. The most common are *onaka suita* おなかすいた[お腹空いた] and *hara hetta* はらへった[腹減った].

The same idea works for *full.* There is only one word for *full: ippai* いっぱい. This word means *many*, so we are saying: *there is a lot of food in my stomach.*

I'm full. **(Lit. There is a lot of food in my stomach.)** *Hara ippai desu.* はらいっぱいです。 腹いっぱいです。	**I'm full.** **(Lit. There is a lot of food in my stomach.)** *Onaka ippai desu.* おなかいっぱいです。 お腹いっぱいです。

Day 44 Vocabulary:

1. stomach	hara	はら	腹
stomach (middle)	onaka	おなか	お腹
stomach (organ)	i	い	胃
2. to be empty	suku	すく	空く
3. to decrease / to diminish	heru	へる	減る (G)
4. many / full of	ippai	いっぱい	
5. candy	ame	あめ	飴
6. snacks	okashi	おかし	お菓子

This can also be used for sweet snacks, and is interchangeable with *ame* あめ[飴] in a lot of cases.

7. alcohol	osake	おさけ	お酒

In Western countries, *sake* refers to only rice wine, but in Japan, it refers to any type of alcohol.

8. pig	buta	ぶた	豚

The word *meat* can be added to this to create *pork: butaniku* ぶたにく[豚肉]. This can be done with all animals to talk about the meat from that animal.

9. cow	ushi / gyuu	うし・ぎゅう	牛

For cows, *ushi* うし[牛] is the animal, while *gyuu* ぎゅう[牛] is used to make words like *gyuuniku* ぎゅうにく[牛肉] (beef) and *gyuunyuu* ぎゅうにゅう[牛乳] (milk).

10. animal	doubutsu	どうぶつ	動物

Day 44 Example Sentences:

1. **My stomach hurts.**
2. **The afternoon train is empty.**
3. **I've lost five kilos.**
4. **There was a lot of food.**
5. **Eat vegetables before candy.**
6. **Snacks have no vitamins.**
7. **Do you drink alcohol?**
8. **Bacon is made from pigs.**
9. **The cow says "moo."**
10. **I love animals.**

1. わたしのおなかがいたいです。
2. ごごのでんしゃはすいています。
3. ごキロへりました。
4. たべものがいっぱいあった。
5. あめのまえにやさいをたべて。
6. おかしにはビタミンははいっていない。
7. おさけをのみますか。
8. ベーコンはぶたでできています。
9. うしは[もぉ]となきます。
10. どうぶつがだいすきです。

1. *Watashi no onaka ga itai desu.*
2. *Gogo no densha wa suiteimasu.*
3. *Go kilo herimashita.*
4. *Tabemono ga ippai atta.*
5. *Ame no mae ni yasai o tabete.*
6. *Okashi ni wa bitamin wa haitte inai.*
7. *Osake o nomimasu ka?*
8. *Beekon wa buta de dekite imasu.*
9. *Ushi wa "moo" to nakimasu.*
10. *Doubutsu ga daisuki desu.*

1. 私の腹が痛いです。
2. 午後の電車は空いています。
3. 五キロ減りました。
4. 食べ物がいっぱいあった。
5. 飴の前に野菜を食べて。
6. お菓子にはビタミンは入っていない。
7. お酒を飲みますか。
8. ベーコンは豚で出来ています。
9. 牛は「もぉ」と鳴きます。
10. 動物が大好きです。

Day 45: Vocabulary Practice

You've already learned two vocabulary word for school and students: *gakkou* がっこう[学校 (school) and *gakusei* がくせい[学生] (student). To say elementary, middle, high, and university and the respective types of students, Japanese will literally say *small, middle, high,* and *big*.

For example, the kanji for *small* is 小. In this context it is pronounced *shou* しょう. The word for elementary school is a combination of this word and *school*: *shougakkou* しょうがっこう[小学校]. To say an elementary student, combine *small* with *student*: *shougakusei* しょうがくせい[小学生]. This can be done for all four levels of students.

Day 45 Vocabulary:

1. elementary school	*shougakkou*	しょうがっこう	小学校
elementary school student	*shougakusei*	しょうがくせい	小学生
2. middle school	*chuugakkou*	ちゅうがっこう	中学校
middle school student	*chuugakusei*	ちゅうがくせい	中学生
3. high school	*koukou*	こうこう	高校
high school student student	*koukousei*	こうこうせい	高校生

If you compare the kanji in this word to the others, you can see why it has a different pronunciation. A less common version of this word is *koutougakkou* こうとうがっこう[高等学校]. In this alternate word, that it maintains the *gakkou* pronunciation.

4. university	*daigaku*	だいがく	大学
university student	*daigakusei*	だいがくせい	大学生

Again, compare the kanji in this word to the others for pronunciation.

5. to enter a school	*nyuugaku suru*	にゅうがくする	入学する

The noun *nyuugaku* means *matriculation* or *enrollment*.

6. to graduate	*sotsugyou suru*	そつぎょうする	卒業する

Like the words for school and student, the prefixes can be combined with *sotsu* そつ[卒] to say a graduate of that school. For example, *high school graduate*: *kousotsu* こうそつ[高卒].

7. math	*suugaku*	すうがく	数学
8. science	*kagaku*	かがく	科学
chemistry	*kagaku*	かがく	化学
9. history	*rekishi*	れきし	歴史
10. art	*bijutsu*	びじゅつ	美術

Day 45 Example Sentences:

1. Elementary school students attend elementary school.

2. Middle school students attend middle school.

3. High school students attend high school.

4. University students attend university.

5. I will enter school this spring.

6. I graduated from university. I am a college graduate.

7. I want to study math.

8. I work in a science field.

9. Japan has a long history.

10. Do you like to study art?

1. しょうがくせいはしょうがっこうにかよいます。

2. ちゅうがくせいはちゅうがっこうにかよいます。

3. こうこうせいはこうこうにかよう。

4. だいがくせいはだいがくにかよう。

5. わたしはこのはるににゅうがくします。

6. だいがくをそつぎょうした。わたしはだいそつです。

7. すうがくをべんきょうしたいです。

8. かがくのぶんやにつとめています。

9. にほんはながいれきしがあります。

10. びじゅつをべきょうすることがすきですか。

1. *Shougakusei wa shougakkou ni kayoimasu.*

2. *Chuugakusei wa chuugakkou ni kayoimasu.*

3. *Koukousei wa koukou ni kayou.*

4. *Daigakusei wa daigaku ni kayou.*

5. *Watashi wa kono haru ni nyuugaku shimasu.*

6. *Daigaku o sotsugyou shita. Watashi wa daisotsu desu.*

7. *Suugaku o benkyou shitai desu.*

8. *Kagaku no bunya ni tsutomete imasu.*

9. *Nihon wa nagai rekishi ga arimasu.*

10. *Bijutsu o benkyou suru koto ga suki desu ka?*

1. 小学生は小学校に通います。

2. 中学生は中学校に通います。

3. 高校生は高校に通う。

4. 大学生は大学に通う。

5. 私はこの春に入学します。

6. 大学を卒業した。私は大卒です。

7. 数学を勉強したいです。

8. 科学の分野に勤めています。

9. 日本は長い歴史があります。

10. 美術を勉強することが好きですか。

Day 46: Vocabulary Practice

Day 46 Vocabulary:

1. medicine	*kusuri*	くすり	薬
In English the verb *take* is used with medicine. Japanese uses *nomu* のむ[飲む] (to drink).			
2. cold (sickness)	*kaze*	かぜ	風邪
In English, *get* or *catch* is used. Japanese uses *hiku* ひく[引く] (to pull).			
3. condition / health	*guai*	ぐあい	具合
4. height / stature	*se*	せ	背
This word is used for the height of humans, not buildings or mountains.			
5. length	*tate*	たて	縦
This word can be used for any length, not just humans.			
6. illness	*byouki*	びょうき	病気
To say that you are sick, don't use this word, it is used for more serious diseases, and can be translated to mean that you have an STD. To say that you are sick, say that your *condition is bad,* by using *guai* ぐあい[具合] (condition / health).			
7. household	*katei*	かてい	家庭
8. a large number of people	*oozei*	おおぜい	大勢
9. tooth	*ha*	は	歯
10. to wash clothes	*sentaku suru*	せんたくする	洗濯する
The noun *sentaku* せんたく[洗濯] by itself means *laundry.*			

1. I've taken a lot of medicine.

2. I've caught a cold.

3. I don't feel well.

4. How tall are you?

5. What is the length of this table?

6. I have a serious illness.

7. My household has four members.

8. A large number of people are waiting outside.

9. Please brush your teeth.

10. I have to wash my clothes.

1. たくさんくすりをのみました。

2. かぜをひいた。

3. ぐあいがわるい。

4. せはなんセンチですか。

5. このテーブルのたてはなんセンチ。

6. ひどいびょうきにかかっています。

7. わたしのかていはよにんです。

8. そとにおおぜいがまっています。

9. はをみがいてください。

10. ふくをせんたくしなければいけない。

1. *Takusan kusuri o nomimashita.*

2. *Kaze o hiita.*

3. *Guai ga warui.*

4. *Se wa nan senchi desu ka?*

5. *Kono teeburu no tate wa nan senchi?*

6. *Hidoi byouki ni kakatte imasu.*

7. *Watashi no katei wa yonin desu.*

8. *Soto ni oozei ga matte imasu.*

9. *Ha o migaite kudasai.*

10. *Fuku o sentaku shinakereba ikenai.*

1. たくさん薬を飲みました。

2. 風邪を引いた。

3. 具合が悪い。

4. 背は何センチですか。

5. このテーブルの縦は何センチ。

6. 酷い病気にかかっています。

7. 私の家庭は四人です。

8. 外に大勢が待っています。

9. 歯を研いて下さい。

10. 服を洗濯しなければいけない。

Day 47: Vocabulary Practice

Day 47 Vocabulary:

1. scenery	*keshiki*	けしき	景色
2. address / residence	*juusho*	じゅうしょ	住所
3. shape / form / figure	*katachi*	かたち	形
4. circle	*maru*	まる	丸・○
The second kanji isn't a kanji, it's a circle. It's there because in written Japanese, they often use circles to express the word *correct*.			
5. X	*batsu*	ばつ	×
Again, not a kanji, but a mark used to say *incorrect*.			
6. triangle	*sankaku*	さんかく	三角
Literally this means *three angles.*			
7. square	*shikaku*	しかく	四角
As you can see, the shapes are made by saying a number, and then the word *angle*. So of course, you already know a pentagon is *gokaku* ごかく[五角].			
8. to translate / interpret	*yakusu*	やくす	訳す
Interpreters are different from translators in that their job is to convey the core meaning of the original speakers intent, rather than a word for word translation.			
9. translation	*honyaku*	ほんやく	翻訳
This can be paired with *suru* する to make the verb *to translate*.			
10. goods / things	*shinamono*	しなもの	品物
This usually refers to things being sold, a store's *goods*.			

Day 47 Example Sentences:

1. **Kyoto has beautiful scenery.**

2. **Please write your address here.**

3. **The vase has a beautiful shape.**

4. **He drew a perfect circle.**

5. **Please circle X.**

6. **A triangle is my favorite shape.**

7. **The angles of a square are ninety degrees.**

8. **Please interpret this sentence.**

9. **I can't translate this report.**

10. **This store's goods are expensive.**

1. きょうとはうつくしいけしきがある。

2. ここにじゅうしょをかいてください。

3. かびんはきれいなかたちです。

4. かれはかんぺきなまるをえがいた。

5. ばつをまるでかこんでください。

6. さんかくはわたしのいちばんすきなかたちです。

7. しかくのかくはきゅうじゅうどです。

8. このぶんをやくしてください。

9. このほうこくをほんやくすることができません。

10. このみせのしなもののねだん。

1. *Kyouto wa utsukushii keshiki ga aru.*

2. *Koko ni juusho o kaite kudasai.*

3. *Kabin wa kirei na katachi desu.*

4. *Kare wa kanpeki na maru o egaita.*

5. *Batsu o maru de kakonde kudasai.*

6. *Sankaku wa watashi no ichiban suki na katachi desu.*

7. *Shikaku no kaku wa kyuujuu do desu.*

8. *Kono bun o yakushite kudasai.*

9. *Kono houkoku o honyaku suru koto ga dekimasen.*

10. *Kono mise no shinamono no nedan ga takai.*

1. 京都は美しい景色がある。

2. ここに住所を書いて下さい。

3. 花瓶は綺麗な形です。

4. 彼は完璧な丸を描いた。

5. ばつを丸で囲んで下さい。

6. 三角は私の一番好きな形です。

7. 四角の角は九十度です。

8. この文を訳して下さい。

9. この報告を翻訳することができません。

10. この店の品物の値段が高い。

There are three ways to say *want* in Japanese, depending on if you want a noun, want to do a verb, or want someone else to do a verb.

If you want a noun, simply add *hoshii* ほしい, just like you did with *like, hate,* and *need.*

I <u>want</u> money.	I <u>want</u> a car.
Okane ga <u>hoshii</u>.	*Kuruma ga hoshii.*
おかねが<u>ほしい</u>。	くるまが<u>ほしい</u>。
お金が<u>欲しい</u>。	車が<u>欲しい</u>。

To make past and negative sentences with *hoshii* ほしい[欲しい], conjugate it like an adjective. The final *i* い is dropped in the past tense, and changes to *ku* く in the negative, and negative past tense forms. Adjectives aren't covered until later, but for now, study the following list:

Want	*hoshii*	ほしい	欲しい
Don't want	*hoshikunai*	ほしくない	欲しくない
Wanted	*hoshikatta*	ほしかった	欲しかった
Didn't want	*hoshikunakatta*	ほしくなかった	欲しくなかった

To say that you *want to do something*, use the I-Form + *tai* たい.

I <u>want to drink</u> beer.	I <u>want to go</u> to Japan.
Biiru o <u>nomitai</u>.	*Nihon ni <u>ikitai</u>.*
ビールを<u>のみたい</u>。	にほんに<u>いきたい</u>。
ビールを<u>飲みたい</u>。	日本に<u>行きたい</u>。

This *tai* たい ending also conjugates like an adjective:

Want to go	*ikitai*	いきたい	行きたい
Don't want to go	*ikitakunai*	いきたくない	行きたくない
Wanted to go	*ikitakatta*	いきたかった	行きたかった
Didn't want to go	*ikitakunakatta*	いきたくなかった	行きたくなかった

To say that you want *someone else* to do something, use the Te-Form + *hoshii* ほしい.

I <u>want you to work hard</u>.	I <u>want you to come</u>.
<u>Hataraite hoshii.</u>	*<u>Kite hoshii</u>.*
<u>はたらいてほしい</u>。	<u>きてほしい</u>。
<u>働いてほしい</u>。	<u>来てほしい</u>。

Day 48 Grammar Cards:

1. (noun) want	(noun) + *hoshii*	(noun) ＋ほしい	(noun) ＋ 欲しい
don't want	(noun) + *hoshikunai*	(noun) ＋ほしくない	(noun) ＋ 欲しくない
wanted	(noun) + *hoshikatta*	(noun) ＋ほしかった	(noun) ＋ 欲しかった
didn't want	(noun) +*hoshikunakatta*	(noun) ＋ほしくなかった	(noun) ＋ 欲しくなかった
2. (verb) want to	I-Form + *tai*	I-Form ＋ たい	
don't want to	I-Form + *takunai*	I-Form ＋ たくない	
wanted to	I-Form + *takatta*	I-Form ＋ たかった	
didn't want to	I-Form + *takunakatta*	I-Form ＋ たくなかった	
3. (verb) want someone else to	Te-Form + *hoshii*	Te-Form ＋ ほしい	Te-Form ＋ 欲しい

Day 48 Vocabulary:

1. **to show**	*miseru*	みせる	見せる **(I)**
2. **to go out / to vanish**	*kieru*	きえる	消える **(I)**

This doesn't mean *to go outside*, but rather *to go off*, as in, the lights. This verb is intransitive.

3. **meaning**	*imi*	いみ	意味
4. **color**	*iro*	いろ	色
5. **birthday**	*tanjoubi*	たんじょうび	誕生日

To say *happy birthday,* add *omedetou gozaimasu* おめでとうございます to the end.

6. **bookshelf**	*hondana*	ほんだな	本棚
book case	*honbako*	ほんばこ	本箱

I bet you don't know the difference between a book shelf and a book case! Don't worry, no one knows in Japanese either. If we deconstruct the kanji, *bookshelf* literally means *book ledge,* and *book case* literally means *book box.*

7. **to touch**	*sawaru*	さわる	触る
8. **to attach / to join / to add**	*tsukeru*	つける	付ける **(I)**

This verb can be used in many contexts where you are attaching or joining things together. It is used often in compound verbs as well. We previously learned three different verbs for *to wear,* this is yet another, for jewelry, glasses, or anything you attach to yourself.

9. **to fish**	*tsuru*	つる	釣る
10. **to cry**	*naku*	なく	泣く

Day 48 Example Sentences:

1. **I want you to show me.**   1. みせてほしいです。

2. **He wanted the lights to go out.**   2. かれはでんきがきえてほしかった。

3. **I want to know the meaning of this word.**   3. このたんごのいみをしりたいです。

4. **What color do you want?**   4. なにいろがほしいですか。

5. **What do you want to do for your birthday?**   5. たんじょうびはなにがしたいの。

6. **I want you to put this on the bookshelf.**   6. これをほんだなにおいてほしい。

7. **I don't want to touch the animals.**   7. どうぶつをさわりたくない。

8. **I want to attach the license plate to my car.**   8. くるまにナンバープレートをつけたいです。

9. **Do you want to fish?**   9. つりたいですか。

10. **I don't want you to cry.**   10. ないてほしくない。

1. *Misete hoshii desu.*   1. 見せて欲しいです。

2. *Kare wa denki ga kiete hoshikatta.*   2. 彼は電気が消えて欲しかった。

3. *Kono tango no imi o shiritai desu.*   3. この単語の意味を知りたいです。

4. *Nani iro ga hoshii desu ka?*   4. 何色が欲しいですか。

5. *Tanjoubi wa nani ga shitai no?*   5. 誕生日は何がしたいの。

6. *Kore o hondana ni oite hoshii.*   6. これを本棚に置いて欲しい。

7. *Doubutsu o sawaritakunai.*   7. 動物を触りたくない。

8. *Kuruma ni nanbaapureeto o tsuketai desu.*   8. 車にナンバープレートを付けたいです。

9. *Tsuritai desu ka?*   9. 釣りたいですか。

10. *Naite hoshikunai.*   10. 泣いて欲しくない。

Day 49: Invitations

In English, when inviting someone to do something, you usually ask the person: *Do you want to?*
In Japanese, they don't use *want to* like this. Instead, they will use a negative question for
invitations. This can be done in English too. Instead of saying, *Do you want to come?* You can say,
Won't you come?

Do you <u>want to come</u>? **(Lit. Won't you come?)**	**Do you <u>want to participate</u>?** **(Lit. Won't you participate?)**
Kimasen ka? きませんか。 来ませんか。	*Sanka shimasen* ka? さんかしませんか。 参加しませんか。

In English, the phrase *Shall we* can also be used for invitations. In Japanese, this can be done by
asking a question with the O-Form. It's best to use the Masu-Form as well, to make your
invitations polite.

<u>Shall we go out</u> to eat?
Tabe ni <u>ikimashou ka</u>? たべに<u>いきましょうか</u>。 食べに<u>行きましょうか</u>。

Day 49 Grammar Card:

1. Invitations	Negative Question / O-Form + Masu-Form Question

Day 49 Vocabulary:

1. bridge	*hashi*	はし	橋
2. garden	*niwa*	にわ	庭
3. street	*michi*	みち	道
4. area	*hen*	へん	辺
5. free time	*hima*	ひま	暇
6. pond	*ike*	いけ	池
7. beach / sea	*umi*	うみ	海

This word refers to the water, not the sand. In English to say *Let's go to the beach* in Japanese
will be *Let's go to the sea*.

8. tea lounge / coffee shop	*kissaten*	きっさてん	喫茶店
9. invitation	*shoutai*	しょうたい	招待

This can be used with *suru* する to say *to invite*.

10. to invite	*sasou*	さそう	誘う

Day 49 Example Sentences:

1. Shall we walk over the bridge?

2. Won't you come to my garden?

3. How about meeting near the street?

4. How about walking around this area?

5. Shall we meet during our free time?

6. How about talking by the pond?

7. Want to come to the beach with me?

8. How about going to a tea shop?

9. Won't you give him an invitation?

10. Shall we invite our friends?

1. はしをわたりましょうか。

2. わたしのにわにきませんか。

3. みちのちかくであいませんか。

4. このへんをあるきませんか。

5. ひまなときにあいませんか。

6. いけのとなりではなしあいましょうか。

7. いっしょにうみにいきませんか。

8. きっさてんにいきましょうか。

9. かれをしょうたいしませんか。

10. ともだちをさそいましょうか。

1. *Hashi o watarimashou ka?*

2. *Watashi no niwa ni kimasen ka?*

3. *Michi no chikaku de aimasen ka?*

4. *Kono hen o arukimasen ka?*

5. *Hima na toki ni aimasen ka?*

6. *Ike no tonari de hanashiaimashou ka?*

7. *Issho ni umi ni ikimasen ka?*

8. *Kissaten ni ikimashou ka?*

9. *Kare o shoutai shimasen ka?*

10. *Tomodachi o sasoimashou ka?*

1. 橋を渡りましょうか。

2. 私の庭に来ませんか。

3. 道の近くで会いませんか。

4. この辺を歩きませんか。

5. 暇な時に会いませんか。

6. 池の隣で話し合いましょうか。

7. 一緒に海に行きませんか。

8. 喫茶店に行きましょうか。

9. 彼を招待しませんか。

10. 友達を誘いましょうか。

Day 50: Can

There are two ways to say *can* in Japanese. The verb *can do* is *dekiru* できる. To be polite, use its Masu-Form: *dekimasu* できます. However, it is not enough just to say a verb and add *dekiru* できる, *koto* こと must also be added to the main verb. Study the following examples:

I <u>can</u> eat.	**I <u>can</u> sit.**
Taberukoto ga dekiru.	*Suwarukoto ga dekiru.*
たべることができる。	すわることができる。
食べることが出来る。	座ることが出来る。

Remember, by adding *koto* こと to a verb, it turns the verb into an intangible noun. This is why *ga* が must also be added. This verb has now become a noun, which is the subject of the sentence. The previous examples are literally saying: *The eating thing, I can do it. The sitting thing, I can do it.*

The second way to say can is to use the E-Form plus *rareru* られる for *ichidan* いちだん verbs, and *ru* る for *godan* ごだん verbs. This will be called the Can-Form.

Ichidan いちだん verbs

tabe → taberareru	たべ → たべられる	食べ → 食べられる

The passive voice will be covered in Volume Two, however, for ichidan いちだん verbs, this form is exactly the same as the passive voice. Because of this, some speakers will drop the *ra* ら to avoid confusion.

Godan ごだん verbs

kae → kaeru	かえ → かえる	買え → 買える
mate → materu	まて → まてる	待て → 待てる
kaere → kaereru	かえれ → かえれる	帰れ → 帰れる
yome → yomeru	よめ → よめる	読め → 読める
asobe → asoberu	あそべ → あそべる	遊べ → 遊べる
hatarake → hatarakeru	はたらけ → はたらける	働け → 働ける
isoge → isogeru	いそげ → いそげる	急げ → 急げる
hanase → hanaseru	はなせ → はなせる	話せ → 話せる

Special verbs

suru → dekiru	する → できる	
kuru → koreru	くる → これる	来る → 来れる

There are two more special verbs in this form:

| miru → mieru | みる → みえる | 見る → 見える |
| kiku → kikoeru | きく → きこえる | 聞く → 聞こえる |

As you may have noticed, this can create some confusion with some verbs, as this creates a lot of new homonyms. For example *kaeru* かえる[買える] (can buy), sounds just like *kaeru* かえる[帰る] (to return), or *kaeru* かえる[変える] (to change). To avoid confusion with homonyms like this, many people will use the *koto ga dekiru* ことができる construction. However, from context alone, you should be able to determine what the speaker is saying.

Day 50 Grammar Cards:

1. Can	U-Form + *koto ga dekiru*	U-Form + ことができる	
	E-Form + *rareru / reru* (ichidan)	E-Form +られる・れる (ichidan)	
	E-Form + *ru* (godan)	E-Form + る(godan)	
2. Can: *suru*	*dekiru*	できる	出来る
kuru	*koreru*	これる	来れる
miru	*mieru*	みえる	見える
kiku	*kikoeru*	きこえる	聞こえる

Day 50 Vocabulary:

1. to escape	*nigeru*	にげる	逃げる **(I)**
2. to become fat	*futoru*	ふとる	太る
3. to become thin	*yaseru*	やせる	痩せる **(I)**
4. to win	*katsu*	かつ	勝つ
5. to lose / to be defeated	*makeru*	まける	負ける **(I)**
6. to discover / to find	*mitsukeru*	みつける	見つける **(I)**
7. to laugh	*warau*	わらう	笑う
The kanji is also used in cyberspace language to mean LOL.
8. to live / to be alive	*ikiru*	いきる	生きる **(I)**
9. to think / to opine	*omou*	おもう	思う
The word *opine* is not often used in English, but this verb is used to give your *opinion*.
10. to think / to consider	*kangaeru*	かんがえる	考える **(I)**
Use this verb to say *think about*.

Day 50 Example Sentences:

1. **You can't escape!**

2. **That guy can never get fat.**

3. **If I diet, can I get thin?**

4. **I wonder if we can win.**

5. **I can never lose!**

6. **I couldn't find it.**

7. **She has a problem. She can't laugh.**

8. **I can't live without you!**

9. **I can't think of you.**

10. **I can't think about such things.**

1. あなたはにげられないよ。

2. あのかれはけっしてふとれない。

3. ダイエットしたら、やせることができますか。

4. かてるかな。

5. わたしはけっしてまけられないよ。

6. みつけられなかった。

7. かのじょはもんだいがある。わらうことができない。

8. あなたなしにいきられないよ。

9. あなたをおもうことができません。

10. そんなことをかんがえられない。

1. *Anata wa nigerarenai yo!*

2. *Ano kare wa kesshite futorenai.*

3. *Daietto shitara, yaseru koto ga dekimasu?*

4. *Kateru ka na.*

5. *Watashi wa kesshite makerarenai yo!*

6. *Mitsukerarenakatta.*

7. *Kanojo wa mondai ga aru. Warau koto ga dekinai.*

8. *Anata nashi ni ikirarenai yo!*

9. *Anata o omou koto ga dekimasen.*

10. *Sonna koto o kangaerarenai.*

1. あなたは逃げられないよ。

2. あの彼は決して太れない。

3. ダイエットしたら、痩せることが出来ますか。

4. 勝てるかな。

5. 私は決して負けられないよ。

6. 見つけられなかった。

7. 彼女は問題がある。笑うことが出来ない。

8. あなた無しに生きられないよ。

9. あなたを思うことが出来ません。

10. そんなことを考えられない。

Day 51: Transitive and Intransitive Verbs

There is one more point of confusion that needs to be cleared up that links with yesterday's lesson. In Japanese, verbs that can be transitive or intransitive have two different forms. That is, verbs that can have an object have different forms. Take for example the following sentences:

1. The door opens.
2. I open the door.

In sentence one, the verb *open* has no object, however, in sentence two, *door* is the object of the verb. In English, most verbs are the same whether they are transitive or not, *open* is still *open* in both sentences. Some exceptions of this are verbs like *to raise* and *to rise*, and *to wake* and *to awake*. In Japanese, transitive and intransitive verbs have different versions.

(intransitive) to open	*aku*	あく	開く
(transitive) to open	*akeru*	あける	開ける

The door <u>opens</u>.	I <u>open</u> the door.
Doa ga <u>akimasu</u>.	*Doa o <u>akemasu</u>.*
ドアがあきます。	ドアをあけます。
ドアが<u>開き</u>ます。	ドアを<u>開け</u>ます。

In the second sentence, the transitive form of the verb was used, and the particle changed as well. Very often, you may see a transitive verb like this, and think that it means *can open*, but that is incorrect. It is simply the transitive form of the verb. So please be careful. Also note, the transitive versions will always be *ichidan* いちだん verbs.

There are a few more transitive or intransitive verb rules to learn for verbs that end in *ru* る. Some of them have the opposite rule that you just learned. Study the following example:

(transitive) to crack	*waru*	わる	割る
(intransitive) to crack	*wareru*	われる	割れる

I <u>cracked</u> the dish.	The plate <u>cracked</u>.
Osara o <u>watta</u>.	*Osara ga <u>wareta</u>.*
おさらをわった。	おさらがわれた。
お皿を<u>割っ</u>た。	お皿が<u>割れ</u>た。

If you notice, the rule is opposite, the *ichidan* いちだん verb is intransitive, while the *godan* ごだん verb is transitive. This can be very confusing. Just remember that the rule is opposite with verbs that end in *ru* る. In addition, many verbs that end in *ru* る will have a companion version ending in *su* す. The *su* す version will be the subject doing the action to an object, and the *ru* る version will be the subject itself doing the action. Study the following examples:

to hand over	*watasu*	わたす	渡す
to cross over	*wataru*	わたる	渡る

I handed in the report.	**I crossed over the bridge.**
Houkokusho o watashimashita.	*Watashi wa hashi o watarimashita.*
ほうこくしょをわたしました。	わたしははしをわたりました。
報告書を渡しました。	私は橋を渡りました。

In the first example, you performed the action onto an object, whereas in the second example, you yourself were doing the action. Study an additional example:

to give back	*kaesu*	かえす	返す
to come back	*kaeru*	かえる	返る

He gave the phone back.	**My strength has come back.**
Kare wa denwa o kaeshita.	*Boku no chikara ga kaerimashita.*
かれはでんわをかえした。	ぼくのちからがかえりました。
彼は電話を返した。	僕の力が返りました。

Usually, the only difference between the versions is *su* す or *ru* る, however, some verbs have bigger changes when they are transitive or intransitive.

In today's lesson both versions of the verbs will be written to help you get used to seeing both forms. You've actually learned a few verbs in the previous lessons that also have multiple versions. Just remember, if a verb has an *a* あ or *e* え sound before the final kana, or ends in *ru* る or *su* す, it is highly likely that there are transitive and intransitive versions of that verb. Go back and look through your cards to see if you can find them.

Day 51 Vocabulary:

1. to open	*aku / akeru*	あく・あける	開く・開ける
2. to close	*shimaru / shimeru*	しまる・しめる	閉まる・閉める
3. to begin	*hajimaru / hajimeru*	はじまる・はじめる	始まる・始める

This verb has some idiomatic usages. *Hajime* はじめ[始め] is a noun that means *beginning*. *Hajimete* はじめて[初めて] means *for the first time*. Notice the different kanji. This is often combined with the Te-Form to say that you are doing something for the first time.

4. to stop (moving)	*tomaru / tomeru*	とまる・とめる	止まる・止める
5. to line up	*narabu / naraberu*	ならぶ・ならべる	並ぶ・並べる
6. to turn / to bend	*magaru / magareru*	まがる・まがれる	曲がる・曲がれる
7. to rise/ to raise	*agaru / ageru*	あがる・あげる	上がる・上げる

The more common meaning of *ageru* あげる[上げる] is actually *to give*. This word comes from someone kneeling and offering something up to someone.

8. to be born / to give birth	*umareru / umu*	うまれる・うむ	生まれる・生む

This verb is a bit special, because *to be born* is the passive form of to give birth.

9. to hand over / to cross over	*watasu / wataru*	わたす・わたる	渡す・渡る
10. to give back / to come back	*kaesu / kaeru*	かえす・かえる	返す・返る

Note that this verb can also be translated as *to return*.

Day 51 Example Sentences:

1. **Open the door please.**

2. **Close the window please.**

3. **Let's begin the class.**

4. **This train never stops.**

5. **Let's line up over there.**

6. **Turn left at the next corner.**

7. **If you have a question, please raise your hand.**

8. **She gave birth to a girl.**

9. **We crossed over the bridge.**

10. **I gave him back his pencil.**

1. ドアをあけてください。

2. まどをしめてください。

3. じゅぎょうをはじめましょう。

4. このでんしゃはけっしてとまらない。

5. あそこにならびましょう。

6. つぎのかどをひだりにまがってください。

7. しつもんがあったら、てをあげてください。

8. かのじょはおんなのあかちゃんをうんだ。

9. わたしたちははしをわたりました。

10. かれのえんぴつをかえした。

1. *Doa o akete kudasai.*

2. *Mado o shimete kudasai.*

3. *Jugyou o hajimemashou.*

4. *Kono densha wa kesshite tomaranai.*

5. *Asoko ni narabimashou.*

6. *Tsugi no kado o hidari ni magatte kudasai.*

7. *Shitsumon ga attara, te o agete kudasai.*

8. *Kanojo wa onna no akachan o unda.*

9. *Watashitachi wa hashi o watarimashita.*

10. *Kare no enpitsu o kaeshita.*

1. ドアを開けて下さい。

2. 窓を閉めて下さい。

3. 授業を始めましょう。

4. この電車は決して止まらない。

5. あそこに並びましょう。

6. 次の角を左に曲がって下さい。

7. 質問があったら、手を上げて下さい。

8. 彼女は女の赤ちゃんを生んだ。

9. 私たちは橋を渡りました。

10. 彼の鉛筆を返した。

Day 52: かかる and かける

This lesson will cover the verb *kakaru* かかる[掛かる] and its transitive equivalent *kakeru* かける[掛ける]. This verb earns the award for having the most meanings ever! It has about thirty different translations depending on the context. However, there are three core meanings from which you can derive the others. The core meanings are *hang, splash,* and *require.*

This verb can be used to say *hang,* be it a picture, clothing, or glasses on your face. But it can also be used to mean *hang on to,* or *lean against.* From this, you can derive another meaning *to cover,* as in, a table covered with a cloth. It can be used emotionally as well, to say that you *pity* or have *hope* for someone - your emotion is *hanging on them.* It can also mean *to burden* someone - your problems are *hanging* on them. In English, you can say *hold a play,* or *hold a festival*, so imagine you are literally *holding* a play, it is *hanging* from your hand.

The next meaning, *splash*, has an idea of something moving outward. This is used very similarly to *dasu* だす[出す]. It can be used to say *pour* liquids, or *sprinkle* salt. It can be used to say that you *began* something, but haven't finished it yet - you *set out to do* something. It can be used to say you turned on something, some device that has an *output.* It can mean *to argue in court, to deliberate, to present* - words are coming *out* of your mouth. It can be used to say, *make a phone call* - your call is going *outward* toward the other person. It can mean, *to apply for* - your application is going *out* to the company.

The final meaning, *require* can be a bit abstract. It is most often used to say that something *takes time* or *money.* It *requires* time or money. It can be used to say, *to come under* contracts or tax laws - they *require* you to behave in a certain way. It can be used to say, *to deal with, to attend, to handle* - something *requires* your attention. It can mean to *fasten* or *secure,* as in seat belts. This one is a bit tough to imagine, but if you remember that seat belts are *required*, it's easier. It can mean *to catch* or *be caught* in a trap - it *requires* you to escape. It can mean *to depend on* - the other person is *required.*

Now, it's probably going to take you some time to remember all these, and an even greater time to use the verb correctly. However, if you keep in mind the three core meanings, *hang, splash, require*, it will be easier to understand sentences using this verb. From context alone, it is usually obvious which meaning it is.

There are also a lot of homonyms that sound like *kakaru* or *kakeru.* But most of them aren't very common words. Of course, the kanji in these words are different. In writing it won't be confusing, but in conversation you have to pay close attention! There are also a lot of compound verbs that are formed using *kakeru* かける[掛ける]. In all of these words, the *kakeru* part will be written with kana only.

Day 52 Vocabulary:

1. to hang / to splash / to require	*kakaru / kakeru*	かかる・かける	掛かる・掛ける **(UK)**
2. to bet / to risk	*kakeru*	かける	賭ける **(I)**
3. to suffer from	*kakaru*	かかる	罹る **(UK)**
4. to be the work of / to be the result of / to be done by	*kakaru*	かかる	係る
5. to be chipped	*kakeru*	かける	欠ける **(I)**
6. to go out	*dekakeru*	でかける	出かける **(I)**
7. to begin to ask	*toikakeru*	といかける	問い掛ける **(I)**
8. to be worried about	*ki ni kakaru*	きにかかる	気に掛かる **(UK)**

This is an idiomatic phrase.

9. to set about / to start	*torikakaru*	とりかかる	取り掛かる **(UK)**

This is often paired with *shigoto* しごと[仕事] in the phrase: *get to work*.

10. to approach and talk	*hanashikakeru*	はなしかける	話し掛ける

This usually just translates to *talk*, but has the implied meaning that you went up to someone and started talking to them.

1. It takes a lot of money to live in Tokyo.

2. She bet 10,000 yen.

3. I suffer from asthma.

4. Our success is a result of the boss's hard work.

5. My favorite plate chipped.

6. I won't go out today.

7. Please question yourself.

8. I'm worried about tomorrow.

9. Stop taking a break, let's get to work.

10. Why don't you go talk to her?

1. とうきょうにすむのにたくさんのおかねがかかります。

2. かのじょはいちまんえんかけた。

3. ぜんそくにかかります。

4. せいこうはじょうしのどりょくにかかっている。

5. いちばんすきなおさらがかけた。

6. きょうはでかけない。

7. じぶんじしんにといかけてください。

8. あしたのことがきにかかる。

9. きゅうけいはやめてしごとにとりかかりましょう。

10. なぜかのじょにはなしかけないのですか。

1. *Toukyou ni sumu no ni takusan no okane ga kakarimasu.*

2. *Kanojo wa ichi man en kaketa.*

3. *Zensoku ni kakarimasu.*

4. *Seikou wa joushi no doryoku ni kakatte iru.*

5. *Ichiban suki na osara ga kaketa.*

6. *Kyou wa dekakenai.*

7. *Jibun jishin ni toikakete kudsai.*

8. *Ashita no koto ga ki ni kakaru.*

9. *Kyuukei wa yamete, shigoto ni torikakarimashou.*

10. *Naze kanojo ni hanashikakenai no desu ka?*

1. 東京に住むのにたくさんのお金がかかります。

2. 彼女は一万円賭けた。

3. 喘息に罹ります。

4. 成功は上司の努力に係っている。

5. 一番好きなお皿が欠けた。

6. 今日は出かけない。

7. 自分自身に問い掛けてください。

8. 明日のことが気に掛かる。

9. 休憩は止めて仕事に取り掛かりましょう。

10. なぜ彼女に話し掛けないのですか。

Day 53: Should

There are a few ways to say *should* in Japanese, the easiest of which is to simply add *beki* べき to the U-Form:

I should study every day.	**You should speak Japanese.**
Watashi wa mainichi benkyou suru beki.	*Anata wa nihongo o hanasu beki.*
わたしはまいにちべんきょうするべき。	あなたはにほんごをはなすべき。
私は毎日勉強するべき。	あなたは日本語を話すべき。

Using *beki* べき is casual, and not just that, but a little direct and abrupt. Remember, in Japanese, people prefer to speak vaguely, and it is a bit impolite to simply tell someone directly that they should do something. That's why there is another more polite way. Suggestions can also be made by using the the Ta-Form + *hou ga ii* ほうがいい. This literally translates to *It is better to:*

I should study every day.	**You should speak Japanese.**
(Lit: It is better that I study everyday).	**(Lit: It is better that you speak Japanese).**
Watashi wa mainichi benkyou shita hou ga ii.	*Anata wa nihongo o hanashita hou ga ii.*
わたしはまいにちべんきょうしたほうがいい。	あなたはにほんごをはなしたほうがいい。
私は毎日勉強したほうがいい。	あなたは日本語を話したほうがいい。

In English *should* can also be used to indicate our expectation that something took place, as in: *He should have come here by now.* This phrase shows our expectations, and is not the same definition as saying that someone *should do something*. To express expectations in Japanese, place the word *hazu* はず at the end of a sentence, to show what was expected to happen.

He should have been here by now.
Kare wa ima made koko ni ita hazu.
かれはいままでここにいたはず。
彼は今までここにいたはず。

Day 53 Grammar Cards:

1. Should (casual)	U-Form + *beki*	U-Form + べき	
2. Should (polite)	Ta-Form + *hou ga ii*	Ta-Form + ほうがいい	Ta-Form + 方が良い
3. Should (expectations)	End of sentence *hazu*	End of sentence はず	

Day 53 Vocabulary:

1. to fix	*naosu*	なおす	直す
to heal	*naosu*	なおす	治す
Note that these verbs are transitive.			
2. to tidy up / to put in order	*katazukeru*	かたづける	片付ける (I)
3. to bite / to chew	*kamu*	かむ	噛む
4. to compare	*kuraberu*	くらべる	比べる (I)
5. to report	*tsutaeru*	つたえる	伝える (I)
6. to wrap	*tsutsumu*	つつむ	包む
7. to help	*tasukeru*	たすける	助ける
8. to assist	*tetsudau*	てつだう	手伝う
The phrase, *How may I help you,* will use this verb, not *tasukeru* たすける[助ける] (to help).			
9. to get used to / to grow accustomed to	*nareru*	なれる	慣れる
10. to steal	*nusumu*	ぬすむ	盗む

1. This should heal soon.

2. It's better to tidy up your room every day.

3. You should chew your food!

4. We should compare it to the other result.

5. I should report this to my boss.

6. It's better to wrap it, right?

7. You should help too!

8. Should I assist him?

9. You should get used to it soon.

10. We should steal this!

1. これはすぐになおすべきだ。

2. まいにちへやをかたづけたほうがいいです。

3. たべものをかむべきだよ。

4. ほかのけっかとくらべるべきです。

5. これをじょうしにつたえるべき。

6. つつんだほうがいいでしょう。

7. あなたもたすけるべきだよ。

8. かれをてつだうべきですか。

9. そろそろなれるはず。

10. これをぬすむべきだ。

1. *Kore wa sugu ni naosu beki da.*

2. *Mainichi heya o katazuketa hou ga ii desu.*

3. *Tabemono o kamu beki da yo!*

4. *Hoka no kekka to kuraberu beki desu.*

5. *Kore o joushi ni tsutaeru beki.*

6. *Tsutsunda hou ga ii, deshou?*

7. *Anata mo tasukeru beki da yo!*

8. *Kare o tetsudau beki desu ka?*

9. *Sorosoro nareru hazu.*

10. *Kore o nusumu beki da!*

1. これはすぐに治すべきだ。

2. 毎日部屋を片付けた方が良いです。

3. 食べ物を噛むべきだよ。

4. 他の結果と比べるべきです。

5. これを上司に伝えるべき。

6. 包んだ方が良いでしょう。

7. あなたも助けるべきだよ。

8. 彼を手伝うべきですか。

9. そろそろ慣れるはず。

10. これを盗むべきだ。

Day 54: Have To, Must

There are many different ways to say that *you have to do something*, and how to say it is totally different than in English. Basically, the literal translation of *have to* is: *if I don't do something, then something bad will happen,* or, *if I don't do something, it won't be good.*

To say *have to*, use the A-Form + *nakereba* なければ, plus the negative of the verb *naru* なる[成る] (to become).

I **have to go**. (casual)	I **have to go**. (polite)
Ikanakereba naranai.	*Ikanakereba narimasen*.
いかなければならない。	いかなければなりません。
行かなければならない。	行かなければなりません。

Nakereba なければ can be translated as something like, *if it were not so*. Literally, you are saying: *if it were so that I don't go, then it won't become, w*hich translates to: *I have to go.*

Other words can be substituted for *naru* なる, such as *ikenai* いけない, *ikemasen* いけません, or *dame* だめ.

I **have to go**. (casual)	I **have to go**. (polite)
Ikanakerba dame desu.	*Ikanakereba ikemasen.*
いかなければだめです。	いかなければいけません。
行かなければだめです。	行かなければいけません。

Using *naranai* ならない, *ikenai* いけない, or *dame* だめ is entirely up to the speaker. *Ikenai* いけない and *dame* だめ are also used to say that something is not allowed, something is prohibited.

Another way to say *have to* is the Nakute-Form followed by *wa* は, however, the *wa* は is often omitted.

I **have to go**. (casual)
Ikanakute wa dame desu.
いかなくてはだめです。
行かなくてはだめです。

We have many options! It might seem a bit overwhelming at first, but take a look at this to help you:

Choose One:

| 1. A-Form + *nakereba* | A-Form + なければ |
| 2. Nakute-Form + optional *wa* | Nakute-Form + optional は |

Choose one ending:

1. *naranai / narimasen*	ならない・なりません
2. *ikenai / ikemasen*	いけない・いけません
3. *dame desu*	だめです

That's not too bad, right? Of course, you may have noticed, that it takes a lot of syllables to say *have to*! Luckily there are very short, casual versions. The entire second word can be dropped, and *nakereba* なければ can change to *nakya* なきゃ or *nakucha* なくちゃ. These forms are casual, and shouldn't be used with strangers or at work.

I <u>have to go</u>. (casual)	**I <u>have to go</u>.** (casual)
Ikanakya.	*Ikanakucha.*
いかなきゃ。	いかなくちゃ。
行かなきゃ。	行かなくちゃ。

Day 54 Grammar Cards:

1. **Have to / must** Choose One:	1. A-Form + *nakereba* 2. Nakute-Form + optional *wa*	1. A-Form + なければ 2. Nakute-Form + optional は
Choose one ending:	1. *naranai / narimasen* 2. *ikenai / ikemasen* 3. *dame desu*	1. ならない・なりません 2. いけない・いけません 3. だめです
2. **have to / must (casual)**	A-Form + *nakya / nakucha*	A-Form + なきゃ・なくちゃ

Day 54 Vocabulary:

1. **to transfer (train / bus)**	*norikaeru*	のりかえる	乗り換える (I)
2. **to transfer location**	*utsuru*	うつる	移る
This is used for transferring residential locations as well as job locations, or job departments within a company. It can also mean to *shift* as is *shifting topics,* or *spread / be contagious.*			
3. **to move (residence)**	*hikkosu*	ひっこす	引っ越す
4. **to send**	*okuru*	おくる	送る
5. **to descend**	*oriru*	おりる	下りる (I)
to get off	*oriru*	おりる	降りる (I)
6. **to change / to convert**	*kawaru / kaeru*	かわる・かえる	変わる・変える (I)
This intransitive / transitive pair is a bit irregular. *Kaeru* かえる[変える] is the transitive version. This word has a sense of changing completely.			
7. **to change / to modify**	*henka suru*	へんかする	変化する
This verb is different in that it has a sense of not changing something completely, but merely making modifications or alterations to it.			
8. **to change / to revise**	*aratameru*	あらためる	改める (I)
This verb has a sense of a new version, replacing something or revising an old thing with something new. The core meaning of the kanji is to *reform.*			
9. **to decide**	*kimeru*	きめる	決める (I)
10. **to advance / to make progress**	*susumu*	すすむ	進む

Day 54 Example Sentences:

1. I have to transfer at the next station.

2. I have to transfer to Tokyo.

3. I have to move on Sunday.

4. I have to send this letter by tomorrow.

5. I have to get off at this station.

6. I have to convert this file.

7. I have to modify this report.

8. I have to revise my thesis.

9. You must decide now!

10. Society must advance quickly.

1. つぎのえきでのりかえなければなりません。

2. とうきょうにうつらなければならない。

3. にちようびにひっこさなくちゃ。

4. あしたまでにこのてがみをおくらなきゃ。

5. このえきでおりなければだめです。

6. このファイルをかえなければいけません。

7. このほうこくをへんかしなきゃ。

8. わたしのろんぶんをあらためなければなりません。

9. いまからきめなくちゃよ。

10. しゃかいははやくすすまなければだめです。

1. *Tsugi no eki de norikaenakereba narimasen.*

2. *Toukyou ni utsuranakereba naranai.*

3. *Nichiyoubi ni hikkosanakucha.*

4. *Ashita made ni kono tegami o okuranakya.*

5. *Kono eki de orinakereba dame desu.*

6. *Kono fairu o kaenakereba ikemasen.*

7. *Kono houkoku o henka shinakya.*

8. *Watashi no ronbun o aratamenakereba narimasen.*

9. *Ima kara kimenakucha yo!*

10. *Shakai wa hayaku susumanakereba dame desu.*

1. 次の駅で乗り換えなければなりません。

2. 東京に移らなければならない。

3. 日曜日に引っ越さなくちゃ。

4. 明日までにこの手紙を送らなきゃ。

5. この駅で降りなければだめです。

6. このファイルを変えなければ行けません。

7. この報告を変化しなきゃ。

8. 私の論文を改めなければなりません。

9. 今から決めなくちゃよ。

10. 社会は早く進まなければだめです。

Day 55: Have to, Must, Part 2

There is actually one more way to say *have to*, but don't worry, it's much simpler than the forms learned yesterday. Do you remember that when you say *have to* in Japanese, you are actually making an *if* sentence, and saying that if you don't do something, the result will turn out bad? Because of this, there is another way to say *have to,* using an *if* sentence. The grammar for *if* sentences is found in Volume Two, but for now, study this easy way to make a *have to* sentence.

To make the most simple *have to* sentence, use the Nai-Form + *to* と:

I <u>have to</u> go.
Ika<u>nai to</u>.
いか<u>ないと</u>。
行か<u>ないと</u>。

What you are literally saying in this sentence is: *if I don't go*. This is very simple, isn't it? Because of its simplicity, you'd think all speakers prefer this grammar over the ones we learned yesterday. However, because this sentence can also mean *if I don't go*, speakers will only use it when the context is clear that they are not making an *if* sentence.

To say *don't have to,* use the Nakute-Form + *moii* もいい. This translates to: *It's okay not to*.

You <u>don't have to eat</u> this.	**You <u>don't have to sit</u> here.**
(Lit. It's okay not to eat this.)	**(Lit. It's okay not to sit here.)**
Kore o <u>tabenakute mo ii</u>.	*Koko ni <u>suwaranakute mo ii</u>.*
これを<u>たべなくてもいい</u>。	ここに<u>すわらなくてもいい</u>。
これを<u>食べなくてもいい</u>。	ここに<u>坐らなくてもいい</u>。

Many speakers will drop *mo* も and just say *ii* いい.

You <u>don't have to eat</u> this.
Kore o <u>tabenakute ii</u>.
これを<u>たべなくていい</u>。
これを<u>食べなくていい</u>。

Day 55 Grammar Cards:

| 1. **Have to / must (if version)** | Nai-Form + *to* | Nai-Form + と |
| 2. **Don't have to** | Nakute-Form + *mo ii* | Nakute-Form + もいい |

Today's vocabulary will cover the titles of people around the office. Like many other titles, use these instead of the person's name. If you plan to work in an office, it's important to get these right, because it can be quite a faux pas to call someone by the wrong title.

Day 55 Vocabulary:

1. **meeting**	*kaigi*	かいぎ	会議
2. **report**	*houkoku*	ほうこく	報告

For a printed out paper report, add *sho* しょ[書]: *houkokusho* ほうこく[報告書].

3. **boss**	*joushi*	じょうし	上司
4. **subordinate**	*buka*	ぶか	部下
5. **section manager**	*kachou*	かちょう	課長

This word along with the rest of the words today all have the suffix *chou* ちょう[長] which in this context means *leader*. The words can sometimes be confused with each other, so it's important to emphasize the first kanji's meaning. In this word, the kanji 課 means *chapter* or *section*.

6. **division manager**	*buchou*	ぶちょう	部長

The kanji 部 means *section* or *division*.

7. **chief**	*shochou*	しょうちょ	所長

The kanji 所 means *place*.

8. **bureau director**	*kyokuchou*	きょくちょう	局長

The kanji 局 means *bureau*.

9. **company president**	*shachou*	しゃちょう	社長

The kanji 社 means *company*.

10. **company vice president**	*fukushachou*	ふくしゃちょう	副社長

The kanji 副 means *vice*.

Day 55 Example Sentences:

1. **You don't have to come to the meeting.**

2. **I have to write a report.**

3. **You don't have to tell the boss.**

4. **You have to tell your subordinates.**

5. **I have to buy a souvenir for the section manager.**

6. **I don't have to meet with the division manager.**

7. **I have to eat dinner with the chief.**

8. **I have to call the bureau director.**

9. **I don't have to become president to be happy.**

10. **I have to become vice president to be happy.**

1. かいぎにこなくてもいいです。

2. ほうこくしょをかかないと。

3. じょうしにいわなくてもいいです。

4. あなたのぶかにいわないと。

5. かちょうにおみやげをかわないと。

6. ぶちょうとあわなくてもいいです。

7. しょちょうといっしょにゆうしょくをたべないと。

8. きょくちょうにでんわしないと。

9. しあわせのためにはしゃちょうにならなくてもいいです。

10. しあわせのためにはふくしゃちょうにならないと。

1. *Kaigi ni konakute mo ii desu.*

2. *Houkokusho o kakanai to.*

3. *Joushi ni iwanakute mo ii desu.*

4. *Anata no buka ni iwanai to.*

5. *Kachou ni omiyage o kawanai to.*

6. *Buchou to awanakute mo ii desu.*

7. *Shochou to issho ni yuushoku o tabenai to.*

8. *Kyokuchou ni denwa shinai to.*

9. *Shiawase no tame ni wa shachou ni naranakute mo ii desu.*

10. *Shiawase no tame ni wa fukushachou ni naranai to.*

1. 会議に来なくても良いです。

2. 報告書を書かないと。

3. 上司に言わなくても良いです。

4. あなたの部下に言わないと。

5. 課長にお土産を買わないと。

6. 部長と会わなくても良いです。

7. 所長と一緒に夕食を食べないと。

8. 局長に電話しないと。

9. 幸せのためには社長にならなくても良いです。

10. 幸せのためには副社長にならないと。

Day 56: May

Many people have forgotten how to ask for permission in English. You are supposed to say *may* and not *can*. But after such a long time of making this mistake, English has evolved and you almost never hear people say *may* anymore. Japanese isn't like that, don't use *can* when you want to ask for permission, use *may*.

To ask for permission, use the Te-Form + *moii* もいい. This actually means, *Is it okay to?* You may have noticed, this is similar to the grammar for *don't have to*. In fact, it is the same, but with the Te-Form instead of the Nakute-Form.

May I eat this? (polite) **(Lit. Is it okay to eat this?)** *Kore o tabete mo ii desu ka?* これを<u>たべてもいい</u>ですか。 これを<u>食べてもいい</u>ですか。	**May I sit here? (polite)** **(Lit. Is it okay to sit here?)** *Koko ni suwatte mo ii desu ka?* ここに<u>すわってもいい</u>ですか。 ここに<u>坐ってもいい</u>ですか。

In casual speech, many speakers will drop *mo* も and use their voice inflection to show that they are asking a question:

May I eat this? (casual)   *Kore o tabete ii?*   これを<u>たべていい</u>。   これを<u>食べていい</u>。

To give permission, the sentences are exactly the same, the only difference is your vocal intonation.

You may eat this. (polite) *Kore o tabete mo ii desu.* これを<u>たべてもいい</u>です。 これを<u>食べてもいい</u>です。	**You may sit here. (polite)** *Koko ni suwatte mo ii desu.* ここに<u>すわってもいい</u>です。 ここに<u>坐ってもいい</u>です。

To not give someone permission, to say that they *aren't allowed to do something*, use the Te-Form + *wa* は + *narimasen* なりません, or *ikemasen* いけません, or the casual *dame* だめ. Again, notice that this is the grammar for *have to* but using the Te-Form instead of the Nakute-Form. Try not to confuse these two. It really helps to think of the literal meaning when using this grammar.

You <u>may not eat</u> this.	**You <u>may not sit</u> here.**	**You <u>may not go</u>.**
Kore o <u>tabete wa narimasen</u>.	*Koko ni <u>suwatte wa ikemasen</u>.*	*<u>Itte wa dame</u>.*
これを<u>たべてはなりません</u>。	ここに<u>すわってはいけません</u>。	<u>いってはだめ</u>。
これを<u>食べてはなりません</u>。	ここに<u>坐ってはいけません</u>。	<u>行ってはだめ</u>。

To review the differences between *have to* and *may*, study the following examples one more time:

You <u>have to eat</u> this.	**You <u>don't have to eat</u> this.**
Kore o <u>tabenakereba narimasen</u>.	*Kore o <u>tabenakute mo ii</u>.*
これを<u>たべなければなりません</u>。	これを<u>たべなくてもいい</u>。
これを<u>食べなければなりません</u>。	これを<u>食べなくてもいい</u>。
You <u>may eat</u> this.	**You <u>may not eat</u> this.**
Kore o <u>tabete mo ii</u>.	*Kore o <u>tabete wa narimasen</u>.*
これを<u>たべてもいい</u>。	これを<u>たべてはなりません</u>。
これを<u>食べてもいい</u>。	これを<u>食べてはなりません</u>。
You <u>have to sit</u> here.	**You <u>don't have to sit</u> here.**
Koko ni <u>suwaranakereba ikemasen</u>.	*Koko ni <u>suwaranakute mo ii</u>.*
ここに<u>すわらなければいけません</u>。	ここに<u>すわらなくてもいい</u>。
ここに<u>坐らなければいけません</u>。	ここに<u>坐らなくてもいい</u>。
You <u>may sit</u> here.	**You <u>may not sit</u> here.**
Koko ni <u>suwatte mo ii</u>.	*Koko ni <u>suwatte wa dame</u>.*
ここに<u>すわってもいい</u>。	ここに<u>すわってはだめ</u>。
ここに<u>坐ってもいい</u>。	ここに<u>坐ってはだめ</u>。

Day 56 Grammar Cards:

1. May	Te-Form + *mo ii*	Te-Form + もいい
2. May not	Te-Form + *wa* + *narimasen / ikemasen / dame*	Te-Form + は + なりません・いけません・だめ

Day 56 Vocabulary:

1. to grow (plants)	*ueru*	うえる	植える
2. flavor	*aji*	あじ	味
3. to bake / to grill / to roast / to burn	*yaku*	やく	焼く
4. to boil	*waku*	わく	沸く

This word can also be used to say that you yourself are getting hot or excited. The transitive version of this verb is *wakasu* わかす[沸かす]

5. groceries	*shokuryouhin*	しょくりょうひん	食料品
6. apple	*ringo*	リンゴ	
7. grape	*budou*	ぶどう	葡萄

This refers to purple grapes. Green (muscat) grapes are called *masukatto* マスカット.

8. carrot	*ninjin*	にんじん	人参 (UK)
9. potato	*jagaimo*	ジャガイモ	

The word *poteto* ポテト in Japanese means *french fries*.

10. onion	*tamanegi*	たまねぎ	玉ねぎ

This word literally means *ball onion*. What are usually referred to in English as green onions or scallions are simply called *negi* ねぎ.

Day 56 Example Sentences:

1. You may grow plants in the garden.

2. You may not tell anyone the secret recipe of this flavor.

3. You may cook that outside.

4. You may not boil this water.

5. You may not buy groceries with my money.

6. You may eat this apple.

7. You may not use my grapes.

8. You may take three carrots.

9. You may bake the potatoes now.

10. May I cut the onions?

1. *Niwa ni wa shokubutsu o uete mo ii desu.*

2. *Darenimo kono aji no hiketsu o itte wa dame desu.*

3. *Sore o soto de yaite mo ii desu.*

4. *Kono mizu o wakashite wa dame desu.*

5. *Watashi no okane de shokuryouhin o katte wa narimasen.*

6. *Kono ringo o tabete mo ii desu.*

7. *Watashi no budou wa tsukatte wa dame desu.*

8. *Sanbon ninjin o totte mo ii desu.*

9. *Ima kara jagaimo o yaite mo ii desu.*

10. *Tamanegi o kitte mo ii desu ka?*

1. にわにはしょくぶつをうえてもいいです。

2. だれにもこのあじのひけつをいってはだめです。

3. それをそとでやいてもいいです。

4. このみずをわかしてはだめです。

5. わたしのおかねでしょくりょうひんをかってはなりません。

6. このリンゴをたべてもいいです。

7. わたしのぶどうはつかってはだめです。

8. さんぼんにんじんをとってもいいです。

9. いまからジャガイモをやいてもいいです。

10. たまねぎをきってもいいですか。

1. 庭には植物を植えても良いです。

2. 誰にもこの味の秘訣を言ってはだめです。

3. それを外で焼いても良いです。

4. この水を沸かしてはだめです。

5. 私のお金で食料品を買ってはなりません。

6. このリンゴを食べても良いです。

7. 私の葡萄は使ってはだめです。

8. 三本人参を取ってもいいです。

9. 今からジャガイモを焼いてもいいです。

10. 玉ねぎを切ってもいいですか。

Day 57: And

There are many ways to say *and* in Japanese! Today's lesson, covers using *and* with nouns. The most simple way to say *and* is *to* と. This is only used to connect nouns.

> **I like eggs <u>and</u> bacon.**
> *Watashi wa tamago <u>to</u> beekon ga suki.*
> わたしはたまご<u>と</u>ベーコンがすき。
> 私は卵<u>と</u>ベーコンが好き。

Of all the breakfast items you like to eat, do you only like eggs and bacon? Do you sometimes eat cereal, or perhaps pancakes? If that is the case, you want to use a word that is a bit more vague: *toka* とか. *Toka* とか also means *and,* but is used in a long list of things, to let the listener know that the items mentioned are not the only things on the list, similar to *etc.* In this way, *toka* とか can be translated as *things like...*

> **I like <u>things like</u> eggs <u>and</u> bacon, <u>etc</u>.**
> *Watashi wa tamago <u>toka</u> beekon ga suki.*
> わたしはたまご<u>とか</u>ベーコンがすき。
> 私は卵<u>とか</u>ベーコンが好き。

Another way to say *and* with nouns is *ya* や. *Ya* や has the same meaning as *toka* とか, but is more formal, more likely used in writing rather than conversation.

> **I like <u>things like</u> eggs <u>and</u> bacon, <u>etc</u>.**
> *Watashi wa tamako <u>ya</u> beekon ga suki.*
> わたしはたまご<u>や</u>ベーコンがすき。
> 私は卵<u>や</u>ベーコンが好き。

Similar to *toka* とか and *ya* や, *ri* り can be added to the Ta-Form to say that you did many things, etc. This will also add *suru* する to the end of the sentence, which can be dropped in conversation.

> **Yesterday I slept in <u>and</u> read a book, <u>things like that</u>.**
> *Kinou nebou shi<u>tari</u>, hon o yon<u>dari shita</u>.*
> きのうねぼうし<u>たり</u>、ほんをよん<u>だりした</u>。
> 昨日寝坊し<u>たり</u>、本を読ん<u>だりした</u>。

Day 57 Grammar Cards:

1. and (nouns)	to	と
2. and etc. (nouns)	toka / ya	とか・や
3. did ~ and etc.	Ta-Form ＋ ri + suru	Ta-Form ＋ り ＋ する

Day 57 Vocabulary:

1. etc.	nado	など	
2. to gather / to collect	atsumaru	あつまる	集まる
3. stone	ishi	いし	石
4. receipt	reshiito	レシート	
5. bill (money)	okaikei	おかいけい	お会計
6. change (from a bill)	otsuri	おつり	お釣り
7. gift	okurimono	おくりもの	贈り物
8. closet	oshiire	おしいれ	押入れ
9. festival	matsuri	まつり	祭り
10. souvenir	omiyage	おみやげ	お土産

On a cultural note, most Japanese people will buy snacks as souvenirs whenever they travel somewhere, for their friends, family, or co-workers. If you are going to Japan and plan on staying with someone, be sure to bring them a souvenir from your home country. They will really appreciate it!

Day 57 Example Sentences:

1. **I like apples and oranges, etc.**

2. **I collect stamps and postcards.**

3. **Things like sticks and stones can hurt you.**

4. **This prints receipts and bills and other things.**

5. **I requested the bill and some water.**

6. **I received a ten yen and five yen coin for my change.**

7. **I bought things like cheese and wine for gifts.**

8. **In my closet there are things like shirts and socks.**

9. **We went to the festival and ate food, things like that.**

10. **I went traveling and bought souvenirs, things like that.**

1. リンゴとかオレンジなどすきです。

2. きってとはがきをあつめます。

3. ぼうやいしでけがをする。

4. これはレシートとかおかいけいをいんさつします。

5. みずとおかいけいをたのみました。

6. おつりはじゅうえんとごえんこうかをもらいました。

7. おくりものはチーズとかワインをかった。

8. おしいれにはシャツやくつしたがあります。

9. わたしたちはまつりにいったりたべものをたべました。

10. りょこうしたりおみやげをかった。

1. *Ringo toka orenji nado suki desu.*

2. *Kitte to hagaki o atsumemasu.*

3. *Bou ya ishi de kega o suru.*

4. *Kore wa reshiito toka okaikei o insatsu shimasu.*

5. *Mizu to okaikei o tanomimashita.*

6. *Otsuri wa juu en to go en kouka o moraimashita.*

7. *Okurimono wa chiizu toka wain o katta.*

8. *Oshiire ni wa shatsu ya kutsushita ga arimasu.*

9. *Watashitachi wa matsuri ni ittari tabemono o tabemashita.*

10. *Ryokou shitari omiyage o katta.*

1. リンゴとかオレンジなど好きです。

2. 切手と葉書を集めます。

3. 棒や石で怪我をする。

4. これはレシートとかお会計を印刷します。

5. 水とお会計を頼みました。

6. お釣りは十円と五円硬貨をもらいました。

7. 贈り物はチーズとかワインを買った。

8. 押入れにはシャツや靴下があります。

9. 私たちは祭りに行ったり食べ物を食べました。

10. 旅行したりお土産を買った。

Day 58: And, Part 2

Today's lesson will cover using *and* with verbs connecting sentences. To connect a sentence with *and,* use the Te-Form. Only the final verb in the sentence will be conjugated to show the tense. This is only used when the ideas in the two sentences are related. If the ideas are not related, a different conjunction will be used, which is covered later. Study the following example:

I <u>went</u> to the supermarket, <u>and bought</u> milk, <u>and came home.</u>
Suupaa ni <u>itte</u>, gyuunyuu o <u>katte</u>, ie ni kaerimashita.
スーパーに<u>いって</u>、ぎゅうにゅうを<u>かって</u>、いえにかえりました。
スーパーに<u>行って</u>、牛乳を<u>買って</u>、家に帰りました。

Notice, only the final verb in the sentence is conjugated, which changes the tense of all the previous verbs. To make one of the verbs negative in these sentences, use the Naide-Form:

I went to the supermarket, <u>and didn't buy</u> milk, and came home.
Suupaa ni itte, gyuunyuu o <u>kawanaide</u>, ie ni kaerimashita.
スーパーにいって、ぎゅうにゅうを<u>かわないで</u>、いえにかえりました。
スーパーに行って、牛乳を<u>買わないで</u>、家に帰りました。

Remember, this could also be translated as *without buying milk,* or *instead of buying milk,* so pay attention to the context. Sometimes Japanese speakers will use the Te-Form to simply connect two ideas, and when translated, *then* or *because* is more appropriate.

I <u>went</u> to work, <u>then</u> I read my email. *Shigoto ni <u>itte</u>, meeru o yonda.* しごとに<u>いって</u>、メールをよんだ。 仕事に<u>行って</u>、メールを読んだ。	**I was in trouble <u>because</u> I <u>dropped</u> my ticket!** *Kippu o <u>otoshite</u>, komarimashita!* きっぷを<u>おとして</u>、こまりました。 切符を<u>落として</u>、困りました。

The I-Form can also be used instead of the Te-Form, but this is less common and used more often in written Japanese. In conversation, the *i* い syllable is stressed.

I <u>went</u> to the supermarket, <u>and bought</u> milk, <u>and came home.</u>
Suupaa ni <u>iki</u>, gyuunyuu o <u>kai</u>, ie ni <u>kaerimashita</u>.
スーパーに<u>いき</u>、ぎゅうにゅうを<u>かい</u>、いえに<u>かえりました</u>。
スーパーに<u>行き</u>、牛乳を買い、家に<u>帰りました</u>。

The word *soshite* そして at the beginning of a sentence can be used to connect two unrelated sentences. This is often used when telling a story and a pause is necessary. It can also be translated as *and then, thus, and now.*

> **I went to the supermarket, <u>and uhh</u>, I saw my friend.**
> *Suupaa ni itta. <u>Soshite</u>, tomodachi o mita.*
> スーパーにいった。<u>そして</u>、ともだちをみた。
> スーパーに行った。<u>そして</u>、友達を見た。

Day 58 Grammar Cards:

1. (verb) *and...*	Te-Form...	
	I-Form...	
2. and uhh / and then / thus / and now	*soshite*	そして

Day 58 Vocabulary:

1. mirror	*kagami*	かがみ	鏡
2. air conditioning	*reibou*	れいぼう	冷房

The air conditioning machine itself is just called an *eakon* エアコン. This word refers to the idea or process.

3. heating	*danbou*	だんぼう	暖房

This kanji as well as the previous ones are important to learn if you ever hope to operate the controls of a Japanese air conditioner.

4. roof	*yane*	やね	屋根
5. ceiling	*tenjou*	てんじょう	天井
6. floor	*yuka*	ゆか	床
7. wall	*kabe*	かべ	壁
8. fire	*kaji*	かじ	火事

This word refers to the physical flame or a fire disaster. The idea of a *fire* is *hi* ひ[火].

9. TV show	*bangumi*	ばんぐみ	番組
10. diary / journal	*nikki*	にっき	日記

Day 58 Example Sentences:

1. I looked in the mirror and was surprised.

2. She turned on the air conditioner and it became cool.

3. He broke the heating and it got cold.

4. I am standing on the roof. And uhh, I can see you.

5. I hung a lamp from my ceiling and it fell.

6. I swept my floor and you made it dirty!

7. I painted my wall green and then I was happy.

8. The fire burned my house and then went out.

9. I watched a TV show and then went to sleep.

10. I wrote in my journal then went out.

1. かがみをみておどろいた。

2. かのじょはれいぼうをつけてすずしくなりました。

3. かれはだんぼうをこわしてさむくなった。

4. やねにたっています。そして、あなたみえます。

5. てんじょうからひをかけておちた。

6. ゆかをはいてあなたはよごしたよ。

7. かべをみどりにぬってしあわせだった。

8. かじはわたしのいえをやいてきえた。

9. ばんぐみをみてねました。

10. にっきにかいてでかけた。

1. *Kagami o mite odoroita.*

2. *Kanojo wa reibou o tsukete suzushiku narimashita.*

3. *Kare wa danbou o kowashite samuku natta.*

4. *Yane ni tatte imasu. Soshite, anata miemasu.*

5. *Tenjou kara hi o kakete, ochita.*

6. *Yuka o haite anata wa yogoshita yo!*

7. *Kabe o midori ni nutte shiawase datta.*

8. *Kaji wa watashi no ie o yaite kieta.*

9. *Bangumi o mite nemashita.*

10. *Nikki in kaite dekaketa.*

1. 鏡を見て驚いた。

2. 彼女は冷房を点けて涼しくなりました。

3. 彼は暖房を壊して寒くなった。

4. 屋根に立っています。そして、あなた見えます。

5. 天井から灯を掛けて落ちた。

6. 床を掃いてあなたは汚したよ。

7. 壁を緑に塗って幸せだった。

8. 火事は私の家を焼いて消えた。

9. 番組を見て寝ました。

10. 日記に書いて出かけた。

Day 59: But

Like *and*, there are many ways to say *but*. The most common word is *kedo* けど. Notice the placement of the word in the following example:

I want to go, <u>but</u> I can't.
Ikitai <u>kedo</u>, dekinai.
いきたい<u>けど</u>、できない。
行きたい<u>けど</u>、出来ない。

The more polite versions of *kedo* けど are *keredo* けれど, and *keredomo* けれども. There is also *dakedo* だけど, used at the beginning of sentences. This is actually just a combination of *da* だ and *kedo* けど. It is usually used in response to what someone said, and can be translated as something like: *Yes, but...*

Another way is to add *ga* が to the end of a clause.

I like strawberries, <u>but</u> I don't want to eat now.
Ichigo ga suki desu <u>ga</u>, ima tabetakunai.
いちごがすきです<u>が</u>、いま、たべたくない。
苺が好きです<u>が</u>、今、食べたくない。

Some speakers, especially women, will add *kedo* けど or *ga* が to the end of their sentences to increase the politeness level. In this usage it is not translated.

Yet another word is *demo* でも. This is usually used with a pause between sentences, when you want to think and add more information. If you think about *demo* でも as the two particles *de* で and *mo* も, you can think of it as literally saying, *with that, also...* Because of this, it is not always translated as *but,* and can simply be used to add more information about your previous sentence.

I like strawberries, <u>but</u> I don't want to eat now.
Ichigo ga suki desu. <u>Demo</u>, ima tabetakunai.
いちごがすきです。<u>でも</u>、いま、たべたくない。
苺が好きです。<u>でも</u>、今、食べたくない。

Shikashi しかし is another way to say *but*, and can be translated as *however*.

I want to go, <u>however</u>, I can't.
Ikitai, <u>shikashi</u>, dekinai.
いきたい、<u>しかし</u>、できない。
行きたい、<u>しかし</u>、出来ない。

To say *not this, but (rather) that*, use the Nakute-Form:

> **Not** this one, **but** that one by you.
> *Kore janakute, sore desu.*
> これじゃなくて、それです。

To combine the Tai-Form with *nakute* なくて, replace the final *i* い in *tai* たい with *ku* く, and then add *nakute* なくて:

> **I don't want to go to France, I want to go to Italy.**
> *Furansu ni ikitakunakute, Itaria ni ikitai desu.*
> フランスにいきたくなくて、イタリアにいきたいです。
> フランスに行きたくなくて、イタリアに行きたいです。

Day 59 Grammar Cards:

1. but	kedo / keredo / keredomo / ga / demo	けど・けれど・けれども・が・でも
2. but / however	shikashi	しかし
3. Tai-Form + Nakute-Form	replace *i* in Tai-Form with *ku*	replace い in Tai-Form with く

Day 59 Vocabulary:

1. interest	kyoumi	きょうみ	興味

This is not economic interest, but rather, your desire. To say that you are interested in something you will say that *interest exists: Kyoumi ga aru* きょうみがある[興味がある].

2. hobby	shumi	しゅみ	趣味
3. office	jimusho	じむしょ	事務所
4. toy	omocha	おもちゃ	玩具 (UK)
5. novel	shousetsu	しょうせつ	小説
6. ship	fune	ふね	船
7. insect	mushi	むし	虫
8. customer	kyaku	きゃく	客

Because businesses are always trying to be polite to their customers, this will be said as *okyakusama* おきゃくさま[お客様].

9. pronunciation	hatsuon	はつおん	発音
10. enjoyment	tanoshimi	たのしみ	楽しみ

This word is most often used to say that you are *looking forward* to something, using either *tanoshimi desu* たのしみです[楽しみです] or *tanoshimi ni suru* たのしみにする[楽しみにする].

1. I'm not interested in that, but I'll participate.

2. It's not a hobby, it's my job.

3. I went to the office, but no one was there.

4. I bought this toy, but she didn't like it.

5. I have your novel. But I haven't read it yet.

6. The ship is new, but the equipment is old.

7. This is an insect, but it won't bother you.

8. I don't want to talk with the clerk, but the customers.

9. This pronunciation is difficult, but you can say it.

10. I'm looking forward to it, however, I still have doubts.

1. それはきょうみがないけど、さんかします。

2. しゅみじゃなくて、しごとです。

3. じむしょにいきました。しかし、だれもいませんでした。

4. このおもちゃをかいましたが、かのじょはすきではありませんでした。

5. あなたのしょうせつがある。でも、まだよまなかった。

6. ふねはあたらしですけれども、そうちはふるいです。

7. これはむしだが、めいわくしない。

8. てんいんとはなしたくなくて、おきゃくとはなしたい。

9. このはつおんはむずかしいけれど、いえます。

10. たのしみです。しかし、まだうたがいがあります。

1. *Sore wa kyoumi ga nai kedo, sanka shimasu.*

2. *Shumi ja nakute, shigoto desu.*

3. *Jimusho ni ikimashita. Shikashi, daremo imasen deshita.*

4. *Kono omocha o kaimashita ga, kanojo wa suki dewa arimasen deshtia.*

5. *Anata no shousetsu ga aru. Demo, mada yomanakatta.*

6. *Fune wa atarashi desu keredomo, souchi wa furui desu.*

7. *Kore wa mushi da ga, meiwaku shinai.*

8. *Tenin to hanashitakunakute, okyaku to hanashitai.*

9. *Kono hatsuon wa muzukashii da kedo, iemasu.*

10. *Tanoshimi desu. Shikashi, mada utagai ga arimasu.*

1. それは興味がないけど、参加します。

2. 趣味じゃなくて、仕事です。

3. 事務所に行きました。しかし、誰もいませんでした。

4. このおもちゃを買いましたが、彼女は好きではありませんでした。

5. あなたの小説がある。でも、まだ読まなかった。

6. 船は新しいですけれども、装置は古いです。

7. これは虫だが、迷惑しない。

8. 店員と話したくなくて、お客と話したい。

9. この発音は難しいけれど、言えます。

10. 楽しみです。しかし、まだ疑いがあります。

Day 60: Because

Study the following English sentence using because:

I will go, because I want to see him.

The first clause is the action, the second clause, beginning with *because,* is the reason. In Japanese, the reason comes first, and *because* is placed at the end of that reason. Study this same sentence using Japanese style grammar:

I want to see him because, I will go.

There are two words for *because*: *kara* から and *node* ので. Sentences with *kara* から indicate the specific reason why something has happened, whereas *node* ので is more vague, and indicates that the reason may not be the only one. Study the following examples:

I will go, <u>because</u> I want to see him.	I will go, <u>because</u> I want to see him.
Kare o mitai <u>kara</u>, ikimasu.	*Kare o mitai <u>node</u>, ikimasu.*
かれをみたい<u>から</u>、いきます。	かれをみたい<u>ので</u>、いきます。
彼を見たい<u>から</u>、行きます。	彼を見たい<u>ので</u>、行きます。

In the second sentence, *node* ので was used, which indicates that this might not be the main reason for going. It might not be the only reason we are going. It makes the sentence a bit more vague. Remember, in Japanese, it's more polite to be vague, so this construction is also used to sound more polite.

Sentences using *node* ので with *da* だ or *desu* です will replace them with *na* な.

I'm not going <u>because</u> it <u>is</u> a hot day.
Atsui hi <u>nanode</u>, ikanai.
あつい日<u>なので</u>、いかない。
暑い日<u>なので</u>、行かない。

Day 60 Grammar Cards:

1. because	reason (*kara / node*), action	reason (から・ので), action
2. (*da* だ / *desu* です) + *node* ので	*nanode*	なので

Day 60 Vocabulary:

1. heart / core	*kokoro*	こころしんぞう心臓	心

This refers to your metaphorical heart, not your physical one. The physical heart is called *shinzou* しんぞう[心臓].

2. mood	*kibun*	きぶん	気分
3. feeling	*kimochi*	きもち	気持ち

Said by itself, this word means *good feeling*. When paired with *warui* わるい[悪い] (bad), this has a very negative meaning. It has many translations in this negative context, some of them being: *sick, grossed out, creeped out*, etc.

4. opinion	*iken*	いけん	意見
5. sound / note	*oto*	おと	音
6. conversation	*kaiwa*	かいわ	会話
7. dream	*yume*	ゆめ	夢
8. reason	*riyuu*	りゆう	理由
9. price	*nedan*	ねだん	値段
10. relationship	*kankei*	かんけい	関係

This word can also be used in phrases like, *I have nothing to do with that*, by saying that the relationship doesn't exist: *kankei ga nai* かんけいがない[関係がない].

Day 60 Example Sentences:

1. He is cruel because he has no heart.

2. I'm in a good mood because I met my friend.

3. I won't go because I have a bad feeling.

4. I want to hear your opinion because you are smart.

5. I can't hear because that sound is loud.

6. I couldn't understand the conversation because it was too fast.

7. I didn't dream because I drank too much alcohol.

8. I won't get married because there is no reason to.

9. I won't buy this because the price is high.

10. I have nothing to do with that because I wasn't there.

1. こころないから、かれはざんこくです。

2. ともだちとあったので、きぶんがいい。

3. きもちわるいので、いきません。

4. あたまがいいから、あなたのいけんをききたいです。

5. あのおとはうるさいから、きこえません。

6. はやすぎるから、かいわがわからなかった。

7. おさけをのみすぎたので、ゆめをみませんでした。

8. りゆうがないから、けっこんしません。

9. ねだんがたかいので、かいません。

10. いなかったから、それはかんけいない。

1. *Kokoro nai kara, kare wa zankoku desu.*

2. *Tomodachi to atta node, kibun ga ii.*

3. *Kimochi warui node, ikimasen.*

4. *Atama ga ii kara, anata no iken o kikitai desu.*

5. *Ano oto wa urusai kara, kikoemasen.*

6. *Hayasugiru kara, kaiwa ga wakaranakatta.*

7. *Osake o nomisugita node, yume o mimasen deshita.*

8. *Riyuu ga nai kara, kekkon shimasen.*

9. *Nedan ga takai node, kaimasen.*

10. *Inakatta kara, sore wa kankei nai.*

1. 心ないから、彼は残酷です。

2. 友達と会ったので、気分がいい。

3. 気持ち悪いので、行きません。

4. 頭が良いから、あなたの意見を聞きたいです。

5. あの音は煩いから、聞こえません。

6. 早過ぎるから、会話が分からなかった。

7. お酒を飲み過ぎたので、夢を見ませんでした。

8. 理由がないから、結婚しません。

9. 値段が高いので、買いません。

10. いなかったから、それは関係ない。

Day 61: How to, Difficult to, Easy To, Too much

Today's lesson covers different grammar structures that all use the I-Form.

To ask *how to* do something, use the I-Form + *kata* かた[方]. An alternate translation for *kata* かた [方] is *way* or *method*.

Do you know <u>how to make</u> this dish?	**What is a good <u>way to make</u> this dish?**
Kono ryouri no <u>tsukurikata</u> ga wakarimasu ka?	*Kono ryouri no <u>tsukurikata</u> wa nani ga ii?*
このりょうりの<u>つくりかた</u>がわかりますか。	このりょうりの<u>つくりかた</u>はなにがいい。
この料理の<u>作り方</u>が分かりますか。	この料理の<u>作り方</u>は何がいい。

Combining *suru* する and *kata* かた makes the noun *shikata* しかた[仕方] (way / method), which uses kanji. When using Suru-Verbs with this grammar, add *no* の to the first part of the Suru-Verbs. Study the following example:

to reply	*henji suru*	へんじする	返事する
how to reply	*henji no shikata*	へんじのしかた	返事の仕方

To say that something is difficult to do, use the I-Form + *nikui* にくい.

It is <u>difficult to read</u> kanji.
Kanji wa <u>yominikui</u>.
かんじは<u>よみにくい</u>。
漢字は<u>読みにくい</u>。

To say that something is easy to do, use the I-Form + *yasui* やすい.

It is <u>easy to read</u> English words.
Eitango wa <u>yomiyasui</u>.
えいたんごは<u>よみやすい</u>。
英単語は<u>読みやすい</u>。

To say that you have done something too much, a compound verb is necessary. Use the I-Form of the main verb and add *sugiru* すぎる[過ぎる] (to pass / exceed).

I <u>ate too much</u>.
<u>*Tabesugimashita*</u>.
<u>たべすぎました</u>。
<u>食べ過ぎました</u>。

Day 61 Grammar Cards:

1. **How to / way / method**	I-Form + *kata*	I-Form + かた	I-Form + 方
2. **Suru-Verbs *suru* + *kata***	*no shikata*	のしかた	の仕方
3. **Difficult to**	I-Form + *nikui*	I-Form + にくい	
4. **Easy to**	I-Form + *yasui*	I-Form + やすい	
5. **too much**	I-Form + *sugiru*	I-Form + すぎる	I-Form + 過ぎる

Day 61 Vocabulary:

1. **to fail / to make a mistake**	*shippai suru*	しっぱいする	失敗する
2. **to promise**	*yakusoku suru*	やくそくする	約束する
3. **to reply**	*henji suru*	へんじする	返事する
4. **to explain**	*setsumei suru*	せつめいする	説明する
5. **to fight**	*kenka suru*	けんかする	喧嘩する
6. **to research**	*kenkyuu suru*	けんきゅうする	研究する
7. **to drop**	*otosu*	おとす	落とす
The intransitive version is *ochiru* おちる[落ちる].			
8. **to slip / to slide**	*suberu*	すべる	滑る **(G)**
This can be used as a slang to say *fail a test*. This word is also the verb for *snowboarding*.			
9. **to raise / to bring up**	*sodateru*	そだてる	育てる **(I)**
This refers to raising children.			
10. **to pass / exceed**	*sugiru*	すぎる	過ぎる **(I)**

Day 61 Example Sentences:

1. **With this machine it is easy to make mistakes.**

2. **It's difficult to make promises to her.**

3. **Do you know how to reply to this email?**

4. **I don't know how to explain this.**

5. **That guy fights too much.**

6. **She taught me how to do research.**

7. **I've dropped my phone too much.**

8. **It's easy to slip on the ice.**

9. **Children are difficult to raise.**

10. **We've exceeded 100kmph.**

1. このきかいではしっぱいがおこりやすい。

2. かのじょとやくそくしにくい。

3. このメールへのへんじのしかたがわかりますか。

4. このせつめいのしかたがわからない。

5. あのかれはけんかしすぎる。

6. かのじょはわたしにけんきゅうのしかたをおしえました。

7. けいたいをおとしすぎた。

8. こおりのうえはすべりやすいです。

9. こどもはそだてにくいです。

10. ひゃっキロをすぎました。

1. *Kono kikai de wa shippai ga okoriyasui.*

2. *Kanojo to yakusoku shinikui.*

3. *Kono meeru e no henji no shikata ga wakarimasu ka?*

4. *Kono setsumei no shikata ga wakranai.*

5. *Ano kare wa kenka shisugiru.*

6. *Kanojo wa watashi ni kenkyuu no shikata o oshiemashita.*

7. *Keitai o otoshisugita.*

8. *Koori no ue wa suberiyasui desu.*

9. *Kodomo wa sodatenikui desu.*

10. *Hyakkiro o sugimashita.*

1. この機械では失敗が起こりやすい。

2. 彼女と約束しにくい。

3. このメールへの返事の仕方が分かりますか。

4. この説明の仕方が分からない。

5. あの彼は喧嘩し過ぎる。

6. 彼女は私に研究の仕方を教えました。

7. 携帯を落とし過ぎた。

8. 氷の上は滑りやすいです。

9. 子供は育てにくいです。

10. 百キロを過ぎました。

Day 62: Experiences

To ask about experiences, or to say that you have done something, use the Ta-Form + *koto ga aru* ことがある.

I <u>have been</u> to Japan.	**I <u>have eaten</u> octopus.**
Watashi wa nihon ni <u>itta koto ga arimasu</u>.	*Boku wa tako o <u>tabeta koto ga aru</u>.*
わたしはにほんに<u>いったことがあります</u>。	ぼくはタコを<u>たべたことがある</u>。
私は日本に<u>行ったことがあります</u>。	僕はタコを<u>食べたことがある</u>。

More often than not, people will drop the *ga* が, especially in a casual setting.

I <u>have eaten</u> octopus.
Tako o <u>tabeta koto aru</u>.
タコを<u>たべたことある</u>。
タコを<u>食べたことある</u>。

Day 62 Grammar Card:

1. have done (experiences)	Ta-Form + *koto ga aru*	Ta-Form + ことがある

Day 62 Vocabulary:

1. hair	*kami*	かみ	髪
Careful, this word is a homonym with *kami* かみ[紙] (paper) and *kami* かみ[神] (god).			
2. hair / fur	*ke*	け	毛
This is used for animals.			
3. whiskers / mustache / beard	*hige*	ひげ	髯・髭・鬚
This word is used for all types of facial hair, with the three kanji representing the three English words respectively.			
4. neck	*kubi*	くび	首
5. chest (body)	*mune*	むね	胸
6. back (body)	*senaka*	せなか	背中
7. shoulder	*kata*	かた	肩
8. elbow	*hiji*	ひじ	肘
9. ring	*yubiwa*	ゆびわ	指輪
This literally means *finger circle*.			
10. glove	*tebukuro*	てぶくろ	手袋
This literally means *hand bag*.			

Day 62 Example Sentences:

1. I have never cut my hair myself.

2. I have cut animal fur.

3. I have never grown a beard.

4. I have never touched a giraffe's neck.

5. Have you ever injured your chest?

6. My back has never been injured.

7. I have never seen her shoulder.

8. I have never broken my elbow.

9. I have bought a ring before.

10. I have lost my gloves before.

1. じぶんでかみをきったことがありません。

2. けをきったことある。

3. ひげをのばしたことがないです。

4. キリンのくびをさわったことがありません。

5. むねをけがしたことがありますか。

6. せなかをけがしたことない。

7. かのじょのかたをみたことがない。

8. ひじをおったことがありません。

9. ゆびわをかったことある。

10. てぶくろをうしなったことがあります。

1. *Jibun de kami o kitta koto ga arimasen.*

2. *Ke o kitta koto aru.*

3. *Hige o nobashita koto ga nai desu.*

4. *Kirin no kubi o sawatta koto ga arimasen.*

5. *Mune o kega shita koto ga arimasu ka?*

6. *Senaka o kega shita koto nai.*

7. *Kanojo no kata o mita koto ga nai.*

8. *Hiji o otta koto ga arimasen.*

9. *Yubiwa o katta koto aru.*

10. *Tebukuro o ushinatta koto ga arimasu.*

1. 自分で髪を切ったことがありません。

2. 毛を切ったことある。

3. 鬚を伸ばしたことがないです。

4. キリンの首を触ったことがありません。

5. 胸を怪我したことがありますか。

6. 背中を怪我したことない。

7. 彼女の肩を見たことがない。

8. 肘を折ったことがありません。

9. 指輪を買ったことある。

10. 手袋を失ったことがあります。

Day 63: Intend to, Plan to

To state your intentions, use the U-Form + *tsumori* つもり. This requires adding *da* だ or *desu* です.

I <u>intend to</u> study.	I don't <u>intend to</u> study.
Benkyou suru <u>tsumori</u> desu.	*Benkyou suru <u>tsumori</u> ja nai.*
べんきょうするつもりです。	べんきょうする<u>つもり</u>じゃない。
勉強するつもりです。	勉強する<u>つもり</u>じゃない。

In English, *intend to* has a feeling of strong volition. In Japanese, it is not so strong, and used in many casual situations, including talking about your plans for the future. A more natural translation of the previous sentences would be: *I will study, I'm planning on studying,* or, *I think I might study.*

To say that you have definitive plans to do something, for example, something scheduled on your calendar, use the U-Form + *yotei* よてい[予定]. This can be said affirmatively by adding *da* だ or *desu* です, but in the negative requires saying that the plans do not exist with *aru* ある. In the affirmative, *desu* です is more popular. Study the following examples:

I <u>am planning to</u> study.	I <u>have plans to</u> study.	I <u>am not planning</u> to study.
		I <u>have no plans to</u> study.
Benkyou suru <u>yotei desu</u>.	*Benkyou suru <u>yotei wa aru</u>.*	*Benkyou suru <u>yotei wa nai</u>.*
べんきょうする<u>よてい</u>です。	べんきょうする<u>よてい</u>はある。	べんきょうする<u>よてい</u>はない。
勉強する予定です。	勉強する予定はある。	勉強する予定はない。

Day 63 Grammar Card:

1. **Intend to / will**	U-Form + *tsumori desu*	U-Form + つもりです	
2. **Have plans to / planning to**	U-Form + *yotei desu* *U-Form + yotei wa aru*	U-Form + よていです U-Form + よていはある	U-Form + 予定です U-Form + 予定はある
3. **Have no plans to / not planning to**	U-Form + *yotei wa nai*	U-Form + よていはない	U-Form + 予定はない

Day 63 Vocabulary:

1. **the world**	*sekai*	せかい	世界
2. **politics / government**	*seiji*	せいじ	政治
3. **war**	*sensou*	せんそう	戦争
4. **society**	*shakai*	しゃかい	社会

This is also the school subject *social studies*.

5. **freedom / liberty**	*jiyuu*	じゆう	自由
6. **citizen**	*shimin*	しみん	市民
7. **economics / finance**	*keizai*	けいざい	経済
8. **police**	*keisatsu*	けいさつ	警察

This refers to the organization, not the individual officers.

9. **transportation / traffic**	*koutsuu*	こうつう	交通

This is not used to say the streets are congested, but rather it is referring to the cars and trains themselves. To say the streets are congested, add *juutai* じゅうたい[渋滞]: *koutsuujuutai* こうつうじゅうたい[交通渋滞].

10. **international**	*kokusaiteki*	こくさいてき	国際的 **(Na)**

This is often used as a prefix to other words, and when it is, *teki* てき[的] will be dropped.

1. I have plans to travel around the world.

2. They intend to discuss government.

3. He intends to start a war!

4. I'm planning to study social studies at 7:00.

5. They intend to restrict our freedoms.

6. The citizens intend to revolt!

7. She intends to recover the economy.

8. The police are planning to arrest the criminal.

9. We have no intention to change transportation.

10. I intend to board the international space station.

1. せかいいっしゅうりょこうするよていです。

2. かれらはせいじをはなしあうつもりだ。

3. かれはせんそうをはじめるつもりですよ。

4. しちじにしゃかいをべんきょうするよていです。

5. かれらはわたしたちのじゆうをせいげんするつもりだ。

6. しみんはほうきするつもりですよ。

7. かのじょはけいざいをなおすつもりです。

8. けいさつははんにんをつかまえるつもりだ。

9. わたしたちはこうつうをかえるつもりではありません。

10. こくさいうちゅうステーションにのるつもりです。

1. *Sekai isshuu ryokou suru yotei desu.*

2. *Karera wa seiji o hanashiau tsumori da.*

3. *Kare wa sensou o hajimeru tsumori desu yo!*

4. *Shichiji ni shakai o benkyou suru yotei desu.*

5. *Karera wa watashitachi no jiyuu o seigen suru tsumori da.*

6. *Shimin wa houki suru tsumori desu yo!*

7. *Kanojo wa keizai o naosu tsumori desu.*

8. *Keisatsu wa hannin o tsukamaeru tsumori da.*

9. *Watashitachi wa koutsuu o kaeru tsumori de wa arimasen.*

10. *Kokusai uchuu suteeshon ni noru tsumori desu.*

1. 世界一周旅行する予定です。

2. 彼らは政治を話し合うつもりだ。

3. 彼は戦争を始めるつもりですよ。

4. 時に社会を勉強する予定です。

5. 彼らは私たちの自由を制限するつもりだ。

6. 市民は蜂起するつもりですよ。

7. 彼女は経済を直すつもりです。

8. 警察は犯人を捕まえるつもりだ。

9. 私たちは交通を変えるつもりではありません。

10. 国際宇宙ステーションに乗るつもりです。

Day 64: Adjectives

In Japanese, there are three types of adjectives. They are called I-Adjectives, Na-Adjectives, and No-Adjectives. They each have different rules. For the most part, I-Adjectives will end with *i* い, and Na-Adjectives will not. There are a few exceptions where adjectives ending in *i* い will be Na-Adjectives. No-Adjectives are the rarest, and actually, they are nouns being used as adjectives, not adjectives themselves. Na- and No-Adjectives get their name because the suffix *na* な or *no* の will be added when they come before a noun. Actually, No-Adjectives are using the ownership particle *no* の. For a simple *A is B* type sentence, all adjectives have the same grammar. In Japanese, like English, adjectives come before the noun they modify. Study the following examples:

I-Adjective	**cute**	*kawaii*	かわいい	可愛い
Na-Adjective	**beautiful**	*kirei*	きれい	綺麗

The woman is <u>cute</u>.	**The woman is <u>beautiful</u>.**
Onna no hito wa <u>kawaii</u> desu. おんなのひとは<u>かわいい</u>です。 女の人は<u>かわいい</u>です。	*Onna no hito wa <u>kirei</u> desu.* おんなのひとは<u>きれい</u>です。 女の人は<u>きれい</u>です。
The <u>cute</u> woman is speaking.	**The <u>beautiful</u> woman is speaking.**
<u>Kawaii</u> onna no hito ga hanashite iru. <u>かわいい</u>おんなのひとがはなしている。 <u>かわいい</u>女の人が話している。	*<u>Kireina</u> onna no hito ga hanashite iru.* <u>きれいな</u>おんなのひとがはなしている。 <u>きれいな</u>女の人が話している。

In the last example sentence, *na* な was added to the adjective. This is because *kirei* きれい is a Na-Adjective, and *na* な must be added when it comes before the noun it is modifying.

But wait, what about No-Adjectives? Where are the example sentences with No-Adjectives? The truth is, you've been tricked! All of the previous example sentences had a No-Adjective in them. Can you find it? If you guessed *onna* おんな[女] (woman), you are right! You've actually been using No-Adjectives this whole time without realizing it. In the phrase *onna no hito* おんなのひと[女の人], *onna* おんな[女] (woman) is a No-Adjective that modifies the word *hito* ひと[人] (person). As stated previously, No-Adjectives are nouns that are being used as an adjective. Because of this, many textbooks don't actually consider them adjectives.

One final note. I-Adjectives are what's called quasi-verbs, which means they don't require the copula. In (A) *is* (adjective) type sentences, *da* だ and *desu* です are dropped. However, don't forget that *desu* です can be added to make sentences more polite, so you will still see adjective sentences end in *desu* です.

Na-Adjectives will be noted with a **(Na)**. No-Adjectives are nouns, so nouns won't be noted. However, No-Adjectives that aren't obviously nouns will be noted with **(No)**.

Day 64 Grammar Cards:

1. **Na-Adjectives preceding nouns**	Add *na*	Add な
2. **I-Adjective sentences**	Drop *da* or *desu*	Drop だ or です

Day 64 Vocabulary:

1. **cute**	*kawaii*	かわいい	可愛い **(UK)**
2. **beautiful / clean / pure**	*kirei*	きれい	綺麗 **(Na)(UK)**
3. **long**	*nagai*	ながい	長い
4. **tall / high / expensive**	*takai*	たかい	高い

The *expensive* definition comes from *high price*.

5. **short / small**	*mijikai*	みじかい	短い

This refers to short in length or height.

6. **short / low**	*hikui*	ひくい	低い

This refers to short as in low to the ground.

7. **easy**	*yasui*	やすい	易い
cheap / inexpensive	*yasui*	やすい	安い

The *cheap* definition comes from *easy to buy*.

8. **easy / simple**	*kantan*	かんたん	簡単 **(Na)**
9. **small**	*chiisai*	ちいさい	小さい **(I/Na)**

A slang version of this word is *chicchai* ちっちゃい. As a prefix, the kanji can be attached to nouns to say that the noun is a small version, when this happens, it is pronounced as *shou* しょう[小].

10. **big**	*ookii*	おおきい	大きい **(I/Na)**

If you notice, *big* and *small* can sometimes be both I-Adjectives and Na-Adjectives. As a non-native speaker, you should always use them as I-Adjectives, however, in certain situations, Japanese speakers with use them as Na-Adjectives.

<u>Day 64 Examples Sentences</u>:

1. **I saw a cute baby on TV.**

2. **A beautiful woman lives here.**

3. **This road is long.**

4. **These clothes are expensive.**

5. **This pencil is short.**

6. **This desk is low to the ground.**

7. **I like to eat cheap food.**

8. **This is a simple problem.**

9. **Japanese houses are small.**

10. **The universe is big.**

1. テレビでかわいいあかちゃんをみた。

2. ここはきれいなおんなのひとがすんでいる。

3. このどうろはながい。

4. このふくはたかいです。

5. このえんぴつはみじかい。

6. このつくえはひくいです。

7. やすいたべものがすき。

8. これはかんたんなもんだいです。

9. にほんのいえはちいさい。

10. うちゅうはおおきい。

1. *Terebi de kawaii akachan o mita.*

2. *Koko wa kirei na onna no hito ga sunde iru.*

3. *Kono douro wa nagai.*

4. *Kono fuku wa takai desu.*

5. *Kono enpitsu wa mijikai.*

6. *Kono tsukue wa hikui desu.*

7. *Yasui tabemono ga suki.*

8. *Kore wa kantan na mondai desu.*

9. *Nihon no ie wa chiisai.*

10. *Uchuu wa ookii.*

1. テレビでかわいい赤ちゃんを見た。

2. ここはきれいな女の人が生んでいる。

3. この道路は長い。

4. この服は高いです。

5. この鉛筆は短い。

6. この机は低いです。

7. 安い食べ物が好き。

8. これは簡単な問題です。

9. 日本の家は小さい。

10. 宇宙は大きい。

I-Adjectives are what's called quasi-verbs and will conjugate based on their tense. The conjugations are very similar to verb conjugations. You've actually seen them before. The conjugations are the same as those learned with *want*. This is because *want* is actually an adjective in Japanese, meaning *desired*. Study he following conjugations:

To make an I-Adjective negative, replace the final *i* い with *kunai* くない.

fun → not fun	*tanoshii → tanoshikunai*	たのしい → たのしくない	楽しい → 楽しくない

To make a past tense I-Adjective, replace the final *i* い with *katta* かった.

fun → was fun	*tanoshii → tanoshikatta*	たのしい → たのしかった	楽しい → 楽しかった

To make a past tense negative I-Adjective, replace the final *i* い with *kunakatta* くなかった.

fun → **was not fun**	*tanoshii →* *tanoshikunakatta*	たのしい → たのしくなかった	楽しい → 楽しくなかった

For Na- and No-Adjectives, endings are not used. Instead, *da* だ or *desu* です is conjugated.

beautiful → **not beautiful**	*kirei desu →* *kirei dewa arimasen*	きれいです → きれいではありません
beautiful → **was beautiful**	*kirei desu →* *kirei deshita*	きれいです → きれいでした
beautiful → **was not beautiful**	*kirei desu →* *kirei dewa arimasen deshita*	きれいです → きれいではありませんでした

Day 65 Grammar Cards:

1. not (I-Adjective)	replace *i* with *kunai*	replace い with くない
2. was (I-Adjective)	replace *i* with *katta*	replace い with かった
3. was not (I-Adjective)	replace *i* with *kunakatta*	replace い with くなかった

Day 65 Vocabulary:

1. delicious	*oishii*	おいしい	美味しい
2. unpleasant / bad taste	*mazui*	まずい	不味い
3. many	*ooi*	おおい	多い
4. few	*sukunai*	すくない	少ない

Be careful with this one. The negative form is *sukunakunai* すくなくない[少なくない].

5. a small amount / a little bit	*sukoshi*	すこし	少し

Just like in English, this is actually not an adjective, but a noun. It can sometimes function like an adjective, but requires no special grammar.

6. skillful	*jouzu*	じょうず	上手 (Na)

English speakers usually don't say *skillful*, but rather *good*.

7. unskillful	*heta*	へた	下手 (Na)

Again, for *unskillful*, *bad* is a better translation.

8. early / soon / fast	*hayai*	はやい	早い
fast (speed)	*hayai*	はやい	速い
9. slow / late	*osoi*	おそい	遅い
10. alright / okay / safe	*daijoubu*	だいじょうぶ	大丈夫 (Na)
alright / okay / safe	*heiki*	へいき	平気 (Na)

Daijoubu だいじょうぶ[大丈夫] is the more common word and can be used in more cases. *Heiki* へいき[平気] is usually only used to refer to yourself, not an object or situation. The kanji for *heiki* へいき[平気] mean *peace* and *spirit*.

Day 65 Example Sentences:

1. Breakfast was delicious.

2. Lunch tasted bad.

3. There weren't many drinks.

4. There were few foods.

5. There was a little bit of cake.

6. His singing was good.

7. His dancing was bad.

8. Walking is not fast.

9. The train was (slow / late).

10. Was it okay?

1. あさごはんはおいしかった。

2. ひるごはんはまずかった。

3. のみものはおおくなかった。

4. たべものはすくなかった。

5. ケーキがすこしあった。

6. かれはうたうのがじょうずだった。

7. かれはおどるのがへただった。

8. あるくのははやくない。

9. でんしゃはおそかった。

10. だいじょうぶだったの。

1. *Asagohan wa oishikatta.*

2. *Hirugohan wa mazukatta.*

3. *Nomimono wa ookunakatta.*

4. *Tabemono wa sukunakatta.*

5. *Keeki ga sukoshi atta.*

6. *Kare wa utau no ga jouzu datta.*

7. *Kare wa odoru no ga heta datta.*

8. *Aruku no wa hayakunai.*

9. *Densha wa osokatta.*

10. *Daijoubu datta no?*

1. 朝ご飯は美味しかった。

2. 昼ご飯は不味かった。

3. 飲み物は多くなかった。

4. 食べ物は少なかった。

5. ケーキが少しあった。

6. 彼は歌うのが上手だった。

7. 彼は踊るのが下手だった。

8. 歩くのは速くない。

9. 電車は遅かった。

10. 大丈夫だったの。

Adjectives also have a Te-Form. I-Adjectives require conjugations, which look very similar to verb conjugations. Na- and No-Adjectives just conjugate the *da* だ or *desu* です.

To make the Te-Form of an I-adjective, replace the final *i* い with *kute* くて.

tanoshii → tanoshikute	たのしい → たのしくて	楽しい → 楽しくて

The Te-Form of adjectives is <u>only</u> to say *and*, for example:

The party was <u>fun and</u> interesting.
Paati wa <u>tanoshikute</u> omoshirokatta.
パーティは<u>たのしくて</u>おもしろかった。
パーティは<u>楽しくて</u>面白かった。

Previously, you learned the Te-Form can be used to give commands by adding *kudasai* ください, but with adjectives, commands can not be given with the Te-Form. The following example is <u>incorrect</u>:

Please <u>be kind</u>.
<u>Yasashikute</u> kudasai.
<u>やさしくて</u>ください。
<u>優しくて</u>ください。

Adjective commands will be covered in Day 68.

Day 66 Grammar Card:

1. Te-Form (I-Adjective)	replace *i* い with *kute* くて

Day 66 Vocabulary:

1. good	*yoi / ii*	よい・いい	良い

Good is the only adjective with two different forms. Whenever you conjugate it, use *yoi* よい. Any other time, it's up to the speaker's preference. As an adverb, it can mean *often* in addition to *well*.

2. bad	*warui*	わるい	悪い
3. dangerous	*abunai*	あぶない	危ない
4. new	*atarashii*	あたらしい	新しい
5. old	*furui*	ふるい	古い

This word is not used for people. If you say it, it will be insulting. Instead, use words like *grandma* and *grandpa,* or *roujin* ろうじん[老人] (old person).

6. young	*wakai*	わかい	若い
7. gentle / kind	*yasashii*	やさしい	優しい

This word is also a homonym with *yasashii* やさしい[易しい] (easy / simple), which is an alternate pronunciation of *yasui* やすい[易い] (easy / simple). If you hear *yasashii,* most people will be using it in the context of *kind / gentle.*

8. cool / refreshing	*suzushii*	すずしい	涼しい
9. fun	*tanoshii*	たのしい	楽しい
10. boring	*tsumaranai*	つまらない	詰まらない

Day 66 Example Sentences:

1. Tokyo's atmosphere is good and lively.

2. Yesterday I felt sick and couldn't go to work.

3. This area is dangerous and dirty.

4. I bought a new and bright colored car.

5. I sold my old dirty car.

6. Recently, young people are lazy.

7. Kindly and quickly help your family.

8. This water is really cold and refreshing.

9. Studying Japanese is fun and interesting.

10. Speaking English is boring and not interesting.

1. とうきょうのふんいきがよくてにぎやかです。

2. きのう、わたしはたいちょうがわるくてしごとにいけなかった。

3. このちいきはあぶなくてきたないよ。

4. あたらしくてあざやかないろのくるまをかいました。

5. ふるくてきたないくるまをうりました。

6. さいきん、わかものはなまけもの。

7. かぞくをやさしくてはやくたすけてください。

8. このみずはとてもつめたくてすずしい。

9. にほんごをべんきょうすることはたのしくておもしろいです。

10. えいごをはなすのはつまらなくておもしろくない。

1. *Toukyou no funiki ga yokute nigiyaka desu.*

2. *Kinou, watashi wa taichou ga warukute shigoto ni ikenakatta.*

3. *Kono chiiki wa abunakute kitanai yo.*

4. *Atarashikute azayaka na iro no kuruma o kaimashita.*

5. *Furukute kitanai kuruma o urimashita.*

6. *Saikin, wakamono wa namakemono.*

7. *Kazoku o yasashikute hayaku tasukete kudasai.*

8. *Kono mizu wa totemo tsumetakute suzushii.*

9. *Nihongo o benkyou suru koto wa tanoshikute omoshiroi desu.*

10. *Eigo o hanasu no wa tsumaranakute omoshirokunai.*

1. 東京の雰囲気が良くて賑やかです。

2. 昨日、私は体調が悪くて仕事に行けなかった。

3. この地域は危なくて汚いよ。

4. 新しくて鮮やかな色の車を買いました。

5. 古くて汚い車を売りました。

6. 最近、若者は怠け者。

7. 家族を優しくて早く助けて下さい。

8. この水はとても冷たくて涼しい。

9. 日本語を勉強することは楽しくて面白いです。

10. 英語を話すのは詰まらなくて面白くない。

Day 67: Adverbs, Adjectival Nouns

To make an adverb with I-Adjectives, replace the final *i* い with *ku* く. For Na-Adjectives, add *ni* に.

fast → quickly	quiet → quietly
hayai → hayaku	*shizuka → shizuka ni*
はやい → はやく	しずか → しずかに
早い → 早く	静か → 静かに

Because No-Adjectives are actually nouns, they don't have an adverbial form. Think about the word *woman*, what is the adverb form of it? Womanly? *Womanly* actually means: *like a woman.* Because of this, the grammar is more complex, and will be covered in Volume Two.

When describing a change in something, use the verb *naru* なる[成る] (to become) with adverbs. A sentence like, *It became quietly,* sounds strange in English, but in Japanese, adverbs are used instead of adjectives.

It got big.	It became quiet.
Ookiku natta.	*Shizuka ni narimashita.*
おおきくなった。	しずかになりました。
大きくなった。	静かになりました。

To make an adjectival noun with I-Adjectives, that is, to change the adjective into a noun, replace the final *i* い with *sa* さ.

high → height
takai → takasa
たかい → たかさ
高い → 高さ

In English, there is no opposite word for *height.* Something like *lowness* sounds silly. In Japanese, the opposite word for *takasa* たかさ[高さ] (height) is *hikusa* ひくさ[低さ] (lowness). Actually, both of these words would translate as *height* in Japanese, but with one we are emphasizing the tall height of some object, and the other we are emphasizing the small height.

For some Na-Adjectives, *sa* さ can be added, but not all of them. Some Na-Adjectives already function as nouns, so *sa* さ isn't necessary. No-Adjectives are already nouns, so no changes are necessary.

convenient → convenience
benri → benrisa
べんり → べんりさ
便利 → 便利さ

Day 67 Grammar Cards:

1. Adjective → Adverb (I-Adjective)	replace *i* with *ku*	replace い with く
2. Adjective → Adverb (Na-Adjective)	add *ni*	add に
3. Become / get (adjective)	(adverb) + *naru*	(adverb) + なる
4. Adjective → Noun (I-Adjective)	replace *i* with *sa*	replace い with さ
5. Adjective → Noun (Na-Adjective)	add *sa*	add さ

Day 67 Vocabulary:

1. strong	*tsuyoi*	つよい	強い
2. weak	*yowai*	よわい	弱い
3. hot	*atsui*	あつい	暑い

This word for *hot* as well as the next word for *cold* will only be used when talking about the weather or how your whole body feels.

4. cold	*samui*	さむい	寒い
5. thick	*atsui*	あつい	厚い
6. thin	*hosoi*	ほそい	細い
7. loud	*urusai*	うるさい	煩い

People also use this word to say *shut up*. Literally, they are saying: *Loud!*

8. quiet / calm	*shizuka*	しずか	静か **(Na)**
9. heavy	*omoi*	おもい	重い
10. light	*karui*	かるい	軽い

Day 67 Example Sentences:

1. His strength is amazing!

2. I weakly kicked him.

3. This heat is unbearable.

4. How do they live in that cold?

5. This books thickness is 3cm.

6. The model's thinness makes us worry.

7. That guy is speaking loudly.

8. The students are speaking quietly.

9. This weighs 100kg.

10. I can't believe how light this computer is!

1. かれのつよさはすごいよ。

2. かれをよわくけった。

3. このあつさはたいへん。

4. あのさむさのなかどういきているの。

5. このほんのあつさはさんセンチ。

6. モデルのほそさはしんぱいになる

7. あのかれはうるさくはなしている。

8. がくせいはしずかにはなしている。

9. このおもさはひゃっキロです。

10. このパソコンのかるさはしんじられない。

1. *Kare no tsuyosa wa sugoi yo!*

2. *Kare o yowaku ketta.*

3. *Kono atsusa wa taihen.*

4. *Ano samusa no naka dou ikite iru no?*

5. *Kono hon no atsusa wa san senchi.*

6. *Moderu no hososa wa shinpai ni naru.*

7. *Ano kare wa urusaku hanasanashite iru.*

8. *Gakusei wa shizuka ni hanashite iru.*

9. *Kono omosa wa hyakkiro desu.*

10. *Kono pasokon no karusa wa shinjirarenai!*

1. 彼の強さは凄いよ。

2. 彼を弱く蹴った。

3. この暑さは大変。

4. あの寒さの中どう生きているの。

5. この本の厚さは三センチ。

6. モデルの細さは心配になる。

7. あの彼は煩く話している。

8. 学生は静かに話している。

9. この重さは百キロです。

10. このパソコンの軽さは信じられない。

Day 68: Adjective Commands

Giving commands with adjectives in Japanese is quite difficult because there are many different ways to do it, and depending on the adjective, the rule is different. It's going to take you some trial and error and practice to figure out what rule each adjective uses.

The Te-Form of adjectives is not used to give a command. In most cases, a verb will be used to give an adjective command. For example, to say: *Don't be late,* the verb *okureru* おくれる[遅れる] (to be late) will be used: *okurenaide kudasai* おくれないでください[遅れないで下さい]. It may seem amazing, but Japanese does indeed have a verb for many of its adjectives. Although they don't have the same pronunciation, *osoi* おそい[遅い] (late) and *okureru* おくれる[遅れる] (to be late) share the same kanji. This may help you identify some adjectives as verbs.

Often in English, when we say *be* with an adjective, we actually mean *feel.* Some I-Adjectives that describe feelings can become a verb by changing the final *i* い to *mu* む:

fun → have fun	**sad → be / feel sad**
tanoshii → tanoshimu	*kanashii → kanashimu*
たのしい → たのしむ	かなしい → かなしむ
楽しい → 楽しむ	悲しい → 悲しむ

If there is no verb available to express the command, adjectives can be used. To give an adjective command in Japanese, use the adverb, not the adjective, plus *suru* する. Since these are commands, *suru* する needs to be in the Te-Form: *shite* して. Using *suru* する literally means: *do it ~ly.* The nuance is similar to *keep* or *make* in English. You are asking someone to do that adjective, or stay in the state of that adjective.

I <u>keep / make</u> my room clean.	**Please <u>keep / make</u> the room clean.**	**Please <u>be quiet</u>.**
Heya o kireii ni <u>suru</u>.	*Heya o kireii ni <u>shite</u> kudasai.*	*<u>Shizuka ni shite</u> kudasai.*
へやをきれいに<u>する</u>。	へやをきれいに<u>して</u>ください。	<u>しずかにして</u>ください。
部屋をきれいに<u>する</u>。	部屋をきれいに<u>して</u>下さい。	<u>静かにして</u>下さい。

Because this grammar has a nuance of *keep / make,* it doesn't work with all adjectives. Many adjectives have to be turned into a noun by adding *koto* こと.

Please don't be <u>cruel</u>.
(Lit. Please don't do <u>cruel things</u>.)
<u>Zankoku na koto</u> o shinaide kudasai.
<u>ざんこくなこと</u>をしないでください。
<u>残酷なこと</u>をしないで下さい。

No-Adjectives don't need to add *koto* こと because they are already nouns, and will use *naru* なる instead, commanding the person to *become* or *not become* the noun.

Don't be timid.
Yowaki ni naranaide.
よわきにならないで。
弱気にならないで。

Rarely, some adjectives will use the verb *garu* がる(to feel). I-Adjectives will drop the final *i* い. This verb is actually a bit more complicated, and a detailed explanation of it is given in Volume Two.

Please don't be shy.
Hazukashi garanaide kudasai.
はずかしがらないでください。
恥ずかしがらないで下さい。

Day 68 Grammar Cards:

1. I-Adjective → Verb feeling the adjective	replace *i* with *mu*	replace い with む
2. Keep / make (adjective)	(adverb) + *shite / shinaide*	(adverb) + して・しないで
3. Adjective Commands	(adjective) + *koto* + (*shite / shinaide*)	(adjective) + こと + (して・しないで)
	No-Adjective + (*natte / naranaide*)	No-Adjective + (なって・ならないで)
	Drop final *i*, (adjective) + (*gatte /garanaide*)	Drop final い, (adjective) + (がって・がらないで)

Day 68 Vocabulary:

1. awful / terrible	*hidoi*	ひどい	酷い

This word is most commonly used to say someone has done something bad.

2. hard / solid / stiff	*katai*	かたい	固い・硬い・堅い

The three kanji are for the type of material. The first kanji is general, and means to *harden*, the second is used primarily with wood, the third means with metal or stone.

3. soft	*yawarakai*	やわらかい	軟らかい・柔らかい

The first kanji refers to soft as opposed to hard or stiff. The second refers to a soft material, like a blanket, or as in *tender*, like meat, or a *flexible* person.

4. sad	*kanashii*	かなしい	悲しい
5. embarrassed / shy	*hazukashii*	はずかしい	恥ずかしい
6. strict	*kibishii*	きびしい	厳しい

Like a lot of Japanese adjectives dealing with difficulty, this word can also be used to say you are in a bad situation, or not doing well.

7. complex	*fukuzatsu*	ふくざつ	複雑 (**Na**)
8. correct	*tadashii*	ただしい	正しい

On a cultural note, this kanji is used to count to five, because it has five strokes, similar to the four lines with a one cross used in English.

9. different	*betsu*	べつ	別 (**Na**)

This word can also be the noun: *difference*. When it is, it will be used like a No-Adjective. It is also often attached to words as a prefix and suffix.

10. inconvenient	*fuben*	ふべん	不便 (**Na**)

This word has the prefix *fu* ふ[不] which is used in many adjectives to convey the opposite meaning. In this case, it is the opposite of *benri* べんり[便利] (convenient).

Day 68 Example Sentences:

1. **Don't say such things! Don't be so terrible!**

2. **Please harden the jelly.**

3. **Please tenderize this meat.**

4. **Don't be sad.**

5. **Don't be shy.**

6. **Please don't be so strict.**

7. **This is a complex problem.**

8. **Which is the correct answer?**

9. **That's not him. He is a different person.**

10. **This location is very inconvenient.**

1. そんなこといわないで。そんなにひどいことをしないで。

2. このゼリーをかためてください。

3. このにくをやわらかくしてください。

4. かなしまないでください。

5. はずかしいがらないで。

6. そんなにきびしくしないでください。

7. これはふくざつなもんだいです。

8. このこたえはどっちがただしいですか。

9. あれはかれじゃない。かれはべつじんです。

10. このばしょはとてもふべんです。

1. *Sonna koto iwanaide! Sonnani hidoi koto o shinaide!*

2. *Kono serii o katamete kudasai.*

3. *Kono niku o yawarakaku shite kudasai.*

4. *Kanashimanaide kudasai.*

5. *Hazukashii garanaide.*

6. *Sonnani kibishiku shinaide kudasai.*

7. *Kore wa fukuzatsu na mondai desu.*

8. *Kono kotae wa docchi ga tadashii desu ka?*

9. *Are wa kare ja nai. Kare wa betsujin desu.*

10. *Kono basho wa totemo fuben desu.*

1. そんなこと言わないで。そんなに酷いことをしないで。

2. このゼリーを固めて下さい。

3. この肉を柔らかくして下さい。

4. 悲しまないで下さい。

5. 恥ずかしいがらないで。

6. そんなに厳しくしないで下さい。

7. これは複雑な問題です。

8. この答えはどっちが正しいですか。

9. あれは彼じゃない。彼は別人です。

10. この場所はとても不便です。

Day 69: Comparisons

To say that something is simply better without comparing it to another noun, use the following construction:

A *nohouga* (adjective) *desu.*	A のほうが (adjective) です。

America is <u>bigger</u>.	**Sushi is <u>more delicious</u>.**
Amerika <u>no hou ga ookii</u> desu.	*Sushi <u>no hou ga oishii</u> desu.*
アメリカ<u>のほうがおおきい</u>です。	すし<u>のほうがおいしい</u>です。
アメリカ<u>のほうが大きい</u>です。	寿司<u>のほうが美味しい</u>です。

To say that something is simply worse without comparing it to another noun, use the following construction:

A *yorimo* (adjective) *desu.*	A よりも (adjective) です。

In conversation, *mo* も is almost always dropped, leaving just *yori* より. For example:

Japan is <u>smaller</u>.	**Ramen is <u>less delicious</u>.**
(Lit. Japan is less big.)	*Raamen <u>yori oishii</u> desu.*
Nihon <u>yori ookii</u> desu.	ラーメン<u>より</u>おいしいです。
にほん<u>よりおおきい</u>です。	ラーメン<u>より</u>美味しいです。
日本<u>より大きい</u>です。	

To compare two nouns, combine these phrases, with *nohouga* のほうが attached to the better thing, and *yori* より attached to the lesser thing:

A *nohouga* B *yori* (adjective) *desu.*	A のほうが B より(adjective) です。

The order of A and B can be switched. It doesn't matter which one comes first. Also, *nohouga* のほうが can be replaced with *wa* は, but *yori* より can not. Study the following examples:

America is <u>bigger than</u> Japan.	**Sushi is <u>more delicious than</u> ramen.**
(Lit. As for America, Japan is less big.)	**(Lit. As for sushi, ramen is less delicious.)**
Amerika <u>wa</u> nihon yori <u>ookii</u> desu.	*Sushi wa raamen <u>yori oishii</u> desu.*
アメリカ<u>は</u>にほんより<u>おおきい</u>です。	すしはラーメンより<u>おいしい</u>です。
アメリカ<u>は</u>日本より<u>大きい</u>です。	寿司はラーメン<u>より</u>美味しいです。

To actually say the phrase: *compared to*, use the verb *kuraberu* くらべる[比べる] (to compare) in the Te-Form, in the following construction:

Compared to A, B is (adjective)	A *ni kurabete,* B *wa* (adjective)	A にくらべて、 B は (adjective)	A に比べて、 B は(adjective)

It's a good idea to also attach *no hou ga* のほうが or *yori* より to B, to show it's relationship to A.

> **<u>Compared to</u> ramen, sushi is more delicious.**
> *Raamen <u>ni kurabete</u>, sushi no hou ga oishii desu.*
> ラーメン<u>にくらべて</u>、すしのほうがおいしいです。
> ラーメン<u>に比べて</u>、寿司のほうが美味しいです。

There are also cases in English when the comparative form of adjectives is used even when no comparisons are being made. For example: *Please do it faster.* In Japanese, *motto* もっと (more) can be used to make a comparative adjective.

> **Please do it <u>faster</u>.**
> *<u>Motto hayaku</u> shite kudasai.*
> <u>もっとはやく</u>してください。
> <u>もっと早く</u>してください。

Motto もっと can also be used in place of *no hou ga* のほうが. The dictionary definition is *even more*, so this has a stronger emphasis than using the *yori* より construction.

> **Sushi is <u>even more delicious than</u> ramen.**
> **(Ramen is delicious, but sushi even more so.)**
> *Raamen <u>yori</u>, sushi wa motto oishii desu.*
> ラーメンよりすしは<u>もっと</u>おいしいです。
> ラーメンより寿司は<u>もっと</u>美味しいです。

Day 69 Grammar Cards:

1. (noun) is more (adjective)	(noun) *nohouga* (adjective)	(noun) のほうが (adjective)	
2. (noun) is less (adjective)	(noun) *yorimo* (adjective)	(noun) よりも (adjective)	
3. Compared to A, B is (adjective)	A *ni kurabete* B *wa* (adjective)	A にくらべて、 B は (adjective)	A に比べて、 B は (adjective)
4. More (strong emphasis)	*motto*	もっと	

Day 69 Vocabulary:

1. sweet	*amai*	あまい	甘い
2. difficult	*muzukashii*	むずかしい	難しい
3. round	*marui*	まるい	丸い
4. convenient	*benri*	べんり	便利 **(Na)**
5. wide	*hiroi*	ひろい	広い
6. narrow	*semai*	せまい	狭い
7. near	*chikai*	ちかい	近い
8. far	*tooi*	とおい	遠い
9. spicy	*karai*	からい	辛い
10. thin / weak	*usui*	うすい	薄い

This refers to the dilution of something, like a thin soup, or a weak coffee.

<u>Day 69 Example Sentences</u>:

1. Sugar is sweeter than salt.

2. Japanese is more difficult than English.

3. A circle is rounder than a square.

4. A letter is less convenient than email.

5. My room is wider.

6. My room is less narrow.

7. This convenience store is closer.

8. That station is farther away.

9. Wasabi is spicier than green peppers.

10. This coffee is weaker than water.

1. さとうはしおよりあまいです。

2. にほんごはえいごよりむずかしいです。

3. まるはしかくよりまるいです。

4. てがみよりメールのほうがべんりです。

5. わたしのへやのほうがひろい。

6. わたしのへやよりせまい。

7. このコンビニのほうがちかい。

8. そのえきのほうがとおい。

9. ピーマンよりわさびのほうがからい。

10. このコーヒーはみずよりうすい。

1. *Satou wa shio yori amai desu.*

2. *Nihongo wa Eigo yori muzukashii desu.*

3. *Maru wa shikaku yori marui desu.*

4. *Tegami yori meeru no hou ga benri desu.*

5. *Watashi no heya no hou ga hiroi.*

6. *Watashi no heya yori semai.*

7. *Kono konbini no hou ga chikai.*

8. *Sono eki no hou ga tooi.*

9. *Piiman yori wasabi no hou ga karai.*

10. *Kono koohii wa mizu yori usui.*

1. 砂糖は塩より甘いです。

2. 日本語は英語より難しいです。

3. 丸は四角より丸いです。

4. 手紙よりメールの方が便利です。

5. 私の部屋の方が広い。

6. 私の部屋より狭い。

7. このコンビニの方が近い。

8. その駅の方が遠い。

9. ピーマンより山葵の方が辛い。

10. このコーヒーは水より薄い。

Day 70: Superlative

To say something is *the most* or *the best* in Japanese is very easy. Simply add *ichiban* いちばん[一番] before the adjective. This sort of sounds silly. because you are literally saying something is *the number one!*

Jupiter is <u>the biggest</u> planet.	**Sushi is <u>the most delicious</u> food.**
Mokusei ga <u>ichiban ookii</u> desu.	*Sushi ga <u>ichiban oishii</u> tabemono desu.*
もくせいが<u>いちばんおおきい</u> です。	すしが<u>いちばんおいしい</u>たべものです。
木星が<u>一番大きい</u>です。	寿司が<u>一番美味しい</u>食べ物です。

This is sometimes paired with the phrase *nonakade* のなかで[の中で] when choosing the best from a group or a place.

Japan is the most interesting place <u>on Earth</u>!
<u>Chikyuu nonakade</u> nihon ga ichiban omoshiroi desu.
<u>ちきゅうのなかで</u>にほんがいちばんおもしろいです。
<u>地球のなかで</u>日本が一番面白いです。

To say that something is your *favorite,* combine *ichiban* いちばん[一番] with *suki* すき[好き]. This phrase becomes a Na-Adjective:

Ramen is my <u>favorite</u> food.
Ichiban suki na tabemono wa raamen desu.
いちばんすきなたべものはラーメンです。
一番好きな食べ物はラーメンです。

Ichiban いちばん [一番] is used in casual conversation, and has the nuance of *best* or *number one.* *Mottomo* もっとも[最も] can also be used, which means *most* or *extremely.* *Mottomo* もっとも[最も] is usually used in formal situations or writing. It has the nuance of *extremely,* rather than *best.*

Jupiter is the biggest planet.	**Sushi is the most delicious food.**
(Lit. Jupiter is <u>extremely</u> big.)	**(Lit. Sushi is <u>extremely</u> delicious.)**
Mokusei ga <u>mottomo</u> ookii desu.	*Sushi ga <u>mottomo</u> oishii tabemono desu.*
もくせいが<u>もっとも</u>おおきいです。	すしが<u>もっとも</u>おいしいたべものです。
木星が<u>最も</u>大きいです。	寿司が<u>最も</u>美味しい食べ物です。

The kanji used in *mottomo* もっとも[最も] is often combined with other adjectives to make the superlative form of that adjective. When it does, it will be pronounced with the On-Reading, *sai* さい。

The biggest.	*saidai*	さいだい	最大
The fastest.	*saisoku*	さいそく	最速

Day 70 Grammar Cards:

1. the most	*ichiban / mottomo* (adjective)	いちばん・もっとも (adjective)	一番・最も (adjective)
2. the most (from a group)	(group) *nonakade* (noun) (*wa / ga*) (*ichiban / mottomo*) (adjective)	(group) のなかで (noun) (は・が) (いちばん・もっとも) (adjective)	(group) の中で (noun) (は・が) (一番・最も) (adjective)
3. favorite	*ichiban suki*	いちばんすき	一番好き **(Na)**

Day 70 Vocabulary:

1. busy	*isogashii*	いそがしい	忙しい
2. painful	*itai*	いたい	痛い
3. dirty	*kitanai*	きたない	汚い
4. wonderful / splendid	*kekkou*	けっこう	結構 **(Na)**

This word doesn't actually mean wonderful. It is used in combinations with other adjectives to mean *very.* It is also used to say you have had enough or are satisfied, as in food or drink. Or if you are in a store, and a clerk asks if you need help, you can use this word to say you are *fine,* and don't need help.

5. important	*taisetsu*	たいせつ	大切 **(Na)**
6. huge / very / difficult	*taihen*	たいへん	大変 **(Na)**

The kanji for this word together mean *unusually big.* It almost always is used in a negative context. When used by itself, it will mean you are in a difficult or bad situation.

7. cold (object / touch)	*tsumetai*	つめたい	冷たい

You learned hot and cold before, but this word, as well as the next word, are used for objects, or when something transfers the energy of heat or coldness.

8. hot / warm (object / touch)	*atatakai*	あたたかい	暖かい

Many people will drop the second *ta* た and pronounce this *attakai* あったかい.

9. lukewarm	*nurui*	ぬるい	温い
10. fat	*futoi*	ふとい	太い

Day 70 Example Sentences:

1. **Japanese are the busiest people.**

2. **It was the most painful experience.**

3. **Your room is the dirtiest!**

4. **I saw a wonderfully rare artifact.**

5. **Happiness is the most important thing.**

6. **She has the most difficult life of everyone.**

7. **This dessert is the coldest.**

8. **These french fries are the hottest.**

9. **Lukewarm food tastes the worst.**

10. **Sumo wrestlers are the fattest.**

1. *Nihonjin ga ichiban isogashii desu.*

2. *Are ga ichiban itakatta keiken.*

3. *Anata no heya ga ichiban kitanai yo!*

4. *Kekkou mezurashii shuuzouhin o mita.*

5. *Shiawase ga ichiban taisetsu na mono desu.*

6. *Minna nonakade kanojo no seikatsu ga ichiban taihen da.*

7. *Kono dezaato ga ichiban tsumetai.*

8. *Kono poteto ga ichiban atatakai.*

9. *Nurui tabemono ga ichiban mazui.*

10. *Osumousan ga ichiban futoi.*

1. にほんじんがいちばんいそがしいです。

2. あれがいちばんいたかったけいけん。

3. あなたのへやがいちばんきたないよ。

4. けっこうめずらしいしゅうぞうひんをみた。

5. しあわせがいちばんたいせつなものです。

6. みんなのなかでかのじょのせいかつがいちばんたいへんだ。

7. このデザートがいちばんつめたい。

8. このポテトがいちばんあたたかい。

9. ぬるいたべものがいちばんまずい。

10. おすもうさんがいちばんふとい。

1. 日本人が一番忙しいです。

2. あれが一番痛かった経験。

3. あなたの部屋が一番汚いよ。

4. 結構珍しい収蔵品を見た。

5. 幸せが一番大切なものです。

6. 皆の中で彼女の生活が一番大変だ。

7. このデザートが一番冷たい。

8. このポテトが一番温かい。

9. 温い食べ物が一番不味い。

10. お相撲さんが一番太い。

Today's vocabulary covers the weather. Japan has four distinct seasons. In the summer it is very hot and humid. In the winter it is cold and dry, and it usually snows. It rains quite often, with June being especially rainy, known as the *rainy season*.

Day 71 Vocabulary:

1. weather	*tenki*	てんき	天気
2. to be sunny	*hareru*	はれる	晴れる **(I) (Te-Iru)**

This is indeed a verb and not an adjective. To say, *It is sunny*, say: *Harete iru* はれている[晴れている]. Like most verbs, this can change into a noun to make a different sentence with the same meaning: *Hare desu* はれです[晴れです].

3. to be cloudy	*kumoru*	くもる	曇る

To say, *It is cloudy*, use the noun: *kumori desu* くもりです[曇りです].

4. rain	*ame*	あめ	雨

In Day 31 you learned the word *furu* ふる[降る] (to fall). Use this verb with rain to say *It's raining*.

5. wind	*kaze*	かぜ	風

To say, *It's windy*, use the verb *fuku* ふく[吹く] (to blow), or *sugoi kaze desu* すごいかぜです[すごい風です].

6. snow	*yuki*	ゆき	雪
7. indoors	*shitsunai*	しつない	室内 **(No)**
8. outside	*soto*	そと	外 **(No)**
9. place / location	*basho*	ばしょ	場所

This word is used for physical locations, not abstractly.

10. place / spot	*tokoro*	ところ	所

This word is often used abstractly, and also in a few grammar constructions, which will be covered in Volume Two.

Day 71 Example Sentences:

1. **The weather is nice today, isn't it?**

2. **It's very sunny today!**

3. **Yesterday was cloudy.**

4. **Will it rain tomorrow?**

5. **It's really windy!**

6. **I like snow.**

7. **On rainy days, I stay inside.**

8. **On sunny days, I go outside.**

9. **This place is warm when it snows.**

10. **What kind of place is Yokohama?**

1. きょうのてんきはいいですね。

2. きょうはすごいはれているよ。

3. きのうはくもりだった。

4. あしたはあめがふっていますか。

5. すごいかぜです。

6. ゆきがすきです。

7. あめのひはわたしはしつないにいる。

8. はれのひはわたしはそとにいきます。

9. ゆきがふれば、このばしょはあったかいです。

10. よこはまはどんなところですか。

1. *Kyou no tenki wa ii desu ne.*

2. *Kyou wa sugoi harete iru yo!*

3. *Kinou wa kumori datta.*

4. *Ashita wa ame ga futte imasu ka?*

5. *Sugoi kaze desu!*

6. *Yuki ga suki desu.*

7. *Ame no hi wa watashi wa shitsunai ni iru.*

8. *Hare no hi wa watashi wa soto ni ikimasu.*

9. *Yuki ga fureba, kono basho wa attakai desu.*

10. *Yokohama wa donna tokoro desu ka?*

1. 今日の天気は良いですね。

2. 今日は凄い晴れているよ。

3. 昨日は曇りだった。

4. 明日は雨が降っていますか。

5. 凄い風です。

6. 雪が好きです。

7. 雨の日は私は室内にいる。

8. 晴れの日は私は外に行きます。

9. 雪が降れば、この場所は温かいです。

10. 横浜はどんな所ですか。

Day 72: Vocabulary Practice

Today's lesson deals with colors. Most colors are I-Adjectives. A few are No-Adjectives. For the I-Adjectives, when just referring to the color itself, drop the *i* い. For example, the color *red* is *aka* あか[赤], but the adjective *red* is *akai* あかい[赤い]. Notice, *orange* isn't in today's list because it is a katakana word borrowed from English: *orenji* オレンジ, which is a No-Adjective. It is listed at the very beginning of this book.

Day 72 Vocabulary:

1. red	*aka*	あか	赤
2. yellow	*kiiro*	きいろ	黄色
3. green	*midori*	みどり	緑 **(No)**

Green is a relatively recent color in Japanese. Before it's introduction, Japanese people saw blue and green as the same color. This word can also refer to *greenery,* as in plants.

4. blue	*ao*	あお	青
5. purple	*murasaki*	むらさき	紫 **(No)**
6. brown	*chairo*	ちゃいろ	茶色 **(No)**

This refers to a light brown color and literally means *tea color*. For a darker brown, use the katakana word *buraun* ブラウン.

7. black	*kuro*	くろ	黒
8. white	*shiro*	しろ	白
9. bright	*akarui*	あかるい	明るい
10. dark	*kurai*	くらい	暗い

This word can also mean gloomy or depressing.

Day 72 Example Sentences:

1. The Japanese flag has a red circle.

2. This shirt is yellow and blue.

3. She is wearing a green shirt.

4. His eye is blue.

5. I am wearing a purple hat.

6. That team has a brown mascot.

7. I like black and white movies.

8. The American flag is red, white, and blue.

9. These are bright and expensive.

10. These are dark and boring.

1. にほんのはたはあかいまるがあります。

2. このシャツはきいろとあおです。

3. かのじょはみどりのしゃつをきています。

4. かれのめはあおい。

5. わたしはむらさきのぼうしをかぶっています。

6. あのチームはちゃいろのマスコットがいます。

7. しろくろえいががすきです。

8. アメリカのはたはあかとしろとあおです。

9. これらあかるくてたかいです。

10. これらはくらくてつまらないです。

1. *Nihon no hata wa akai maru ga arimasu.*

2. *Kono shatsu wa kiiro to ao desu.*

3. *Kanojo wa midori no shatsu o kite imasu.*

4. *Kare no me wa aoi.*

5. *Watashi wa murasaki no boushi o kabutte imasu.*

6. *Ano chiimu wa chairo no masukotto ga imasu.*

7. *Shirokuro eiga ga suki desu.*

8. *Amerika no hata wa aka to shiro to ao desu.*

9. *Korera wa akarukute takai desu.*

10. *Korera wa kurakute tsumaranai desu.*

1. 日本の旗は赤い丸があります。

2. このシャツは黄色と青です。

3. 彼女は緑のシャツを着ています。

4. 彼の目は青い。

5. 私は紫の帽子を被っています。

6. あのチームは茶色のマスコットがいます。

7. 白黒映画が好きです。

8. アメリカの旗は赤と白と青です。

9. これらは明るくて高いです。

10. これらは暗くてつまらないです。

Day 73 Vocabulary:

1. beside / next to	soba	そば	側 (No)
2. next to / next door to	tonari	となり	隣 (No)
3. side	yoko	よこ	横 (No)

This refers to a horizontal position or movement, like laying on your side, or shaking your head side to side.

4. straight ahead / straight forward	massugu	まっすぐ	真っ直ぐ (Na)
5. opposite side / over there	mukou	むこう	向こう (No)
6. front side	omote	おもて	表 (No)
7. back side	ura	うら	裏 (No)
8. both sides	ryouhou	りょうほう	両方 (No)
9. to move	ugoku	うごく	動く
10. to dance	odoru	おどる	踊る

1. **It's beside the table.**

2. **She is in the next room.**

3. **Please lay on your side.**

4. **Please go straight ahead.**

5. **The convenience store is on the other side.**

6. **The front side of the building is under construction.**

7. **The entrance is in the back side.**

8. **Both sides of my body hurt.**

9. **I can't move my legs!**

10. **Do you like dancing?**

1. それはテーブルのそばです。

2. かのじょはとなりのへやにいます。

3. よこになってください。

4. まっすぐにいってください。

5. コンビニはむこうです。

6. ビルのおもてはこうじちゅうです。

7. げんかんはうらにあります。

8. からだのりょうほうがいたいです。

9. あしをうごかせないよ。

10. おどるのがすきですか。

1. *Sore wa teburu no soba desu.*

2. *Kanojo wa tonari no heya ni imasu.*

3. *Yoko ni natte kudasai.*

4. *Massugu ni itte kudasai.*

5. *Konbini wa mukou desu.*

6. *Biru no omote wa koujichuu desu.*

7. *Genkan wa ura ni arimasu.*

8. *Karada no ryouhou ga itai desu.*

9. *Ashi o ugokasenai yo!*

10. *Odoru no ga suki desu ka?*

1. それはテーブルの側です。

2. 彼女は隣の部屋にいます。

3. 横になって下さい。

4. 真っ直ぐに行って下さい。

5. コンビニは向こうです。

6. ビルの表は工事中です。

7. 玄関は裏にあります。

8. 体の両方が痛いです。

9. 足を動かせないよ。

10. 踊るのが好きですか。

Day 74 Vocabulary:

1. disagreeable / unpleasant	*iya*	いや	嫌 **(Na)**

This word is also used to say *no*, or *no way*: *iya da* いやだ[嫌だ]. It often just sounds like *yada* やだ.

2. interesting / strange	*omoshiroi*	おもしろい	面白い

This word can cause some confusion, because it is often used in a negative sense to mean something is strange or weird, so context is important.

3. robust / durable / strong	*joubu*	じょうぶ	丈夫 **(Na)**
4. lively / bustling	*nigiyaka*	にぎやか	賑やか **(Na)**
5. famous	*yuumei*	ゆうめい	有名] **(Na)**
6. popular	*ninki*	にんき	人気 **(Special)**

Technically, the definition for this word is *popularity*. It can be used like a No- or Na-Adjective. To say something is popular, say *popularity exists*, *ninki ga aru* にんきがある[人気がある].

7. slowly / at ease	*yukkri*	ゆっくり	**(Special)**

This word is different from *osoi* おそい[遅い] (slow / late) in that it means to do something calmly, the opposite of flustered. It is very special in that it uses the particle *to* と instead of *na* な or *no* の. The *to* と is often dropped in conversation.

8. splendid / elegant	*rippa*	りっぱ	立派 **(Na)**
9. oneself	*jibun*	じぶん	自分 **(No)**

To say that you *did something by yourself*, use *jibun de* じぶんで[自分で].

10. sleepy	*nemui*	ねむい	眠い

This adjective comes from the the verb *nemuru* ねむる[眠る].

1. There's no way I'll eat natto.

2. I watched an interesting movie.

3. This is a durable material.

4. Tokyo is a bustling city.

5. He is a famous singer.

6. This is a popular restaurant.

7. Please speak at ease.

8. She is a splendid person.

9. I made it myself.

10. I couldn't sleep, so I'm sleepy.

1. なっとうをたべるのはぜったいいやだ。

2. おもしろいえいがをみました。

3. これはじょうぶなざいりょうです。

4. とうきょうはにぎやかなとしです。

5. かれはゆうめいなかしゅです

6. このレストランはにんきがあります。

7. ゆっくりとはなしてください。

8. かのじょはりっぱなひとです。

9. じぶんでつくりました。

10. ねむれなかったから、ねむいです。

1. *Nattou o taberu no wa zettai iya da.*

2. *Omoshiroi eiga o mimashita.*

3. *Kore wa joubu na zairyou desu.*

4. *Toukyou wa nigiyaka na toshi desu.*

5. *Kare wa yuumei na kashu desu.*

6. *Kono resutoran wa ninki ga arimasu.*

7. *Yukkuri to hanashite kudasai.*

8. *Kanojo wa rippa na hito desu.*

9. *Jibun de tsukurimashita.*

10. *Nemurenakatta kara, nemui desu.*

1. 納豆を食べるのは絶対嫌だ。

2. 面白い映画を観ました。

3. これは丈夫な材料です。

4. 東京は賑やかな都市です。

5. 彼は有名な歌手です。

6. このレストランは人気があります。

7. ゆっくりと話して下さい。

8. 彼女は立派な人です。

9. 自分で作りました。

10. 眠れなかったから、眠いです。

Day 75: Vocabulary Practice

Day 75 Vocabulary:

1. the same	onaji	おなじ	同じ (No)
2. various	iroiro	いろいろ	色々 (Na)(UK)
3. caution	chuui	ちゅうい	注意
4. For example.	tatoeba	たとえば	例えば
5. Oh I see. / I understand now.	naruhodo	なるほど	
This is used to say that you now understand information that was previously unclear.			
6. enough	juubun	じゅうぶん	十分 (Na)
This literally means *ten parts*.			
7. impossible	muri	むり	無理 (Na)
8. disappointment	zannen	ざんねん	残念 (Na)
Said by itself, this is used to express your sorrow, similar to: *That's too bad,* or, *What a pity.*			
9. polite	teinei	ていねい	丁寧 (Na)
10. after a long time	hisashiburi	ひさしぶり	久しぶり (Na)
Said by itself, this means *long time no see.*			

Day 75 Example Sentences:

1. **We are wearing the same shirt.**

2. **I like various things.**

3. **Please be careful.**

4. **I like meat. For example, chicken.**

5. **He is married? Oh, now I understand.**

6. **I have enough money already.**

7. **He's flying! That's impossible!**

8. **They divorced? That's too bad.**

9. **Speak politely to your mother.**

10. **Long time no see. How are you?**

1. わたしたちはおなじシャツをきています。

2. いろいろなものがすきです。

3. ごちゅういください。

4. にくがすき。たとえば、チキン。

5. かれはけっこんしていますか。なるほど。

6. もうじゅうぶんおかねがあります。

7. かれはとんでいる。そんなことはむりでしょう。

8. かれらはりこんしましたか? ざんねんです。

9. おかあさんにはていねいにはなしなさい。

10. ひさしぶり。げんきですか。

1. *Watashitachi wa onaji shatsu o kite imasu.*

2. *Iroiro na mono ga suki desu.*

3. *Gochuui kudasai.*

4. *Niku ga suki. Tatoeba, chikin.*

5. *Kare wa kekkon shite imasu ka? Naruhodo.*

6. *Mou juubun okane ga arimasu.*

7. *Kare wa tonde iru! Sonna koto wa muri deshou!*

8. *Karera wa rikon shimashita ka? Zannen desu.*

9. *Okaasan ni wa teinei ni hanashinasai.*

10. *Hisashiburi. Genki desu ka?*

1. 私たちは同じシャツを着ています。

2. いろいろなものが好きです。

3. ご注意下さい。

4. 肉が好き。例えば、チキン。

5. 彼は結婚していますか。なるほど。

6. もう十分お金があります。

7. 彼は飛んでいる。そんなことは無理でしょう。

8. 彼らは離婚しましたか? 残念です。

9. お母さんには丁寧に話しなさい。

10. 久しぶり。元気ですか。

Day 76: Vocabulary Practice

Day 76 Vocabulary:

1. scary	*kowai*	こわい	怖い
2. lonely	*sabishii*	さびしい	寂しい
3. kind / kindness	*shinsetsu*	しんせつ	親切 (**Na**)

This word is both the adjective and the noun.

4. terrific / amazing	*sugoi*	すごい	凄い

This is probably the most popular word to use in Japanese to say things like *great, awesome, wonderful*. The definition is *terrible*, but it is usually used in a positive sense, just like *terrific* is a positive word in English that is derived from the negative word *terror*. It is also combined with other adjectives to mean *very*.

5. special	*tokubetsu*	とくべつ	特別 (**Na**)

This word is a bit special because it can sometimes use *no* の instead of *na* な, and also sometimes no particle is necessary.

6. usual / normal	*futsuu*	ふつう	普通 (**No**)
7. bitter	*nigai*	にがい	苦い

This refers to flavor, not a person's temperament.

8. strange / crazy	*hen*	へん	変 (**Na**)
9. rare / precious	*mezurashii*	めずらしい	珍しい
10. beautiful	*utsukushii*	うつくしい	美しい

This is usually used for things like nature and art, whereas *kirei* きれい[綺麗] (beautiful) is used for people.

Day 76 Example Sentences:

1. His face is scary.	1. かれのかおはこわいです。
2. I get lonely at night.	2. よるにはさびしくなる。
3. I met a kind man.	3. しんせつなおとこのひとにあいました。
4. This curry is amazing!	4. このカレーはすごいおいしいです。
5. I didn't do anything special.	5. とくべつなことはしませんでした。
6. I live a normal life.	6. ふつうのせいかつをおくっています。
7. I like bitter chocolate.	7. にがいチョコが好すきです。
8. That guy always says crazy things.	8. あのかれはいつもへんなことをいいます。
9. This rare jewel is expensive.	9. このめずらしいほうせきはたかいです。
10. I really like beautiful forests.	10. うつくしいもりがだいすきです。

1. *Kare no kao wa kowai desu.*	1. 彼の顔は怖いです。
2. *Yoru ni wa sabishiku naru.*	2. 夜には寂しくなる。
3. *Shinsetsu na otoko no hito ni aimashita.*	3. 親切な男の人に会いました。
4. *Kono karee wa sugoi oishii desu.*	4. このカレーは凄い美味しいです。
5. *Tokubetsu na koto wa shimasen deshita.*	5. 特別なことはしませんでした。
6. *Futsuu no seikatsu o okutte imasu.*	6. 普通の生活を送っています。
7. *Nigai choko ga suki desu.*	7. 苦いチョコが好きです。
8. *Ano kare wa itsumo hen na koto o iimasu.*	8. あの彼はいつも変なことを言います。
9. *Kono mezurashii houseki wa takai desu.*	9. この珍しい宝石は高いです。
10. *Utsukushii mori ga daisuki desu.*	10. 美しい森が大好きです。

Day 77: Vocabulary Practice

Many of the words today are actually adverbs, not adjectives.

Day 77 Vocabulary:

1. together	*issho*	いっしょ	一緒
This is almost always paired with the particle *ni* に.				
2. all	*zenbu*	ぜんぶ	全部 **(No)**
3. whole amount / everything	*subete*	すべて	全て **(No)**
This is interchangeable with *zenbu* ぜんぶ[全部] in many contexts, just as *all* and *every* are interchangeable in English.			
4. many	*takusan*	たくさん	沢山 **(Na)(UK)**
5. very	*totemo*	とても	
6. other / the rest	*hoka*	ほか	他 **(No) (UK)**
This is often paired with the particle *ni* に.			
7. again	*mata*	また	
8. absolutely	*zettai*	ぜったい	絶対
9. at all / entirely / completely	*zenzen*	ぜんぜん	全然
This can be used with both positive and negative sentences, however, is most often used negatively. When used alone, it means *not at all*.			
10. truth	*hontou*	ほんとう	本当
This is often paired with *ni* に to say *truly*, or as a response to information, as in, *Really?*			

<u>Day 77 Example Sentences</u>:

1. Let's go together.

2. Is this all?

3. Let's buy everything.

4. I have many siblings.

5. This is very good.

6. Are there any other questions?

7. Let's meet again.

8. We will absolutely win this time!

9. I can't speak Japanese at all.

10. I truly did my best.

1. いっしょにいこう。

2. これはぜんぶですか。

3. すべてをかいましょう。

4. きょうだいはたくさんいます。

5. これはとてもいいです。

6. ほかにしつもんがありますか。

7. またあいましょう。

8. こんかいはぜったいわたしたちのかちだ！

9. おれはにほんごをぜんぜんはなせません。

10. わたしはほんとうにがんばりました。

1. *Issho ni ikou.*

2. *Kore wa zenbu desu ka?*

3. *Subete o kaimashou.*

4. *Kyoudai wa takusan imasu.*

5. *Kore wa totemo ii desu.*

6. *Hoka ni shitsumon ga arimasu ka?*

7. *Mata aimashou.*

8. *Konkai wa zettai watashitachi no kachi da!*

9. *Ore wa nihongo o zenzen hanasemasen.*

10. *Watashi wa hontou ni ganbarimashita.*

1. 一緒に行こう。

2. これは全部ですか。

3. 全てを買いましょう。

4. 兄弟はたくさんいます。

5. これはとても良いです。

6. 他に質問がありますか。

7. また会いましょう。

8. 今回は絶対私たちの勝ちだ！

9. 俺は日本語を全然話せません。

10. 私は本当に頑張りました。

Day 78: Numbers

Numbers in Japanese are quite complex. The numbers introduced today are used for counting. Some are actually derived from Chinese and English, and will be referred to as the Foreign numbers. In the next lesson, native Japanese numbers will be covered.

0	*rei / zero*	れい・ゼロ	零
1	*ichi*	いち	一
2	*ni*	に	二
3	*san*	さん	三
4	*shi / yon*	し・よん	四
5	*go*	ご	五
6	*roku*	ろく	六
7	*shichi / nana*	しち・なな	七
8	*hachi*	はち	八
9	*kyuu*	きゅう	九
10	*juu*	じゅう	十

The reason why four and seven have two different numbers is because the verb *to die* in Japanese is *shinu* しぬ[死ぬ], and people don't want to associate numbers with death. On that note, the number four is unlucky in Japan, similar to thirteen in Western cultures. Traditional Japanese is text is written top to bottom, right to left. However, when it is written horizontally, like in this book, the kanji for numbers is not written, only the numeral. That being said, in order to practice seeing the kanji written, that rule will be broken in this book.

To make higher numbers is very easy. To say *eleven* in Japanese, simply say *ten-one*. *Twelve* is *ten-two* and so on:

11	*juu ichi*	じゅういち	十一
12	*juu ni*	じゅうに	十二

To make the deca-numbers, like *twenty* and *thirty*, simply say *two-ten*, or *three-ten*. This means that words like twenty-two are said as *two-ten-two*.

20	*ni juu*	にじゅう	二十
22	*ni juu ni*	にじゅうに	二十二

Day 78 Vocabulary:
Today there are technically eleven words, but there are no sentences to practice. It's good to memorize these kanji, because they are fairly simple.

1. one	*ichi*	いち	一
2. two	*ni*	に	二
3. three	*san*	さん	三
4. four	*shi / yon*	し・よん	四
5. five	*go*	ご	五
6. six	*roku*	ろく	六
7. seven	*shichi / nana*	しち・なな	七
8. eight	*hachi*	はち	八
9. nine	*kyuu*	きゅう	九
10. ten	*juu*	じゅう	十
11. zero	*rei / zero*	れい・ゼロ	零

The following list is the native Japanese pronunciation of numbers:

1	*hito*	ひと	一
2	*futa*	ふた	二
3	*mi*	み	三
4	yo	よ	四
5	*itsu*	いつ	五
6	*mu*	む	六
7	*nana*	なな	七
8	*ya*	や	八
9	*kokono*	ここの	九
10	*too*	とお	十

The alternative numbers for four and seven are derived from this list. These numbers only go up to ten. These numbers aren't used for general counting, the Foreign numbers are used for that. Even when the Japanese numbers are used in certain constructions, numbers higher than ten will always use the Foreign numbers.

Day 79 Vocabulary:

1. one	*hito*	ひと	一
2. two	*futa*	ふた	二
3. three	*mi*	み	三
4. four	yo	よ	四
5. five	*itsu*	いつ	五
6. six	*mu*	む	六
7. seven	*nana*	なな	七
8. eight	*ya*	や	八
9. nine	*kokono*	ここの	九
10. ten	*too*	とお	十

Day 80: Numbers, Part 3

Higher numbers like *hundreds* and *thousands* can be made the same way as the deca-numbers. Simply say how many of each number you have. Study the following numbers:

100	*hyaku*	ひゃく	百
1000	*sen*	せん	千
10,000	*man*	まん	万
100,000,000	*oku*	おく	億

Did you notice something? Where is one million? In English and other western countries, numbers are separated in intervals of three, that is, every three zeros gives us a new number. In Japanese, they use intervals of four zeros. There is no word for *million*, instead, a Japanese speaker will say *a hundred ten-thousands: hyaku man* ひゃくまん[百万].

The word for *numbers* in Japanese is *bangou* ばんごう[番号]. You can attach *ban* ばん[番] as a suffix to Foreign numbers to literally say things like: *number one, number two*. The suffix *me* め[目] can be attached to *ban* ばん[番] to indicate rank: *first, second, third*. Study the following examples:

number one	*ichiban*	いちばん	一番
first	*ichibanme*	いちばんめ	一番目
number two	*niban*	にばん	二番
second	*nibanme*	にばんめ	二番目

For numbers with a decimal point, simply say it as you would in English. The word for *point* is *ten* てん. Except for *ni* に[二] (two), if the number ends with a vowel, then *ten* てん changes to *tten* ってん. One and eight also have special pronunciations.

4.5	*yon ten go*	よんてんご	四点五
2.8	*ni ten hachi*	にてんはち	二点八
1.3	*itten san*	いってんさん	一点三
8.1	*hatten ichi*	はってんいち	八点一

For fractions, say the denominator first followed by the numerator - the opposite of English. Instead of *over* or *th*, use *bun no* ぶんの[分の], which literally means *part of.*

| **2/5, two over five, two-fifths (Lit. Five parts of two)** | *go bun no ni* | ごぶんのに | 五分の二 |

Day 80 Grammar Cards:

1. number X	X *ban*	X ばん	X 番
2. X rank	X *ban me*	X ばんめ	X 番目
3. X.Y	X *ten* Y	X てん Y	X 点 Y
4. X / Y	Y *bun no* X	Y ぶんの X	Y 分の X

Day 80 Vocabulary:

1. hundred	*hyaku*	ひゃく	百
2. thousand	*sen*	せん	千
3. ten thousand	*man*	まん	万
4. hundred million	*oku*	おく	億
5. number (numeric)	*bangou*	ばんごう	番号
6. arithmetic	*sansuu*	さんすう	算数

The kanji in this word are quite common. The first kanji means *to calculate* and is used in many compound words where calculations are done. The second kanji means *number* and is used in many compound words with numbers.

7. to add	*tasu*	たす	足す

The word *addition* can be made by combining this word with the kanji *to calculate*, which creates the word *tashizan* たしざん[足し算].

8. to subtract	*hiku*	ひく	引く

This is the same word as *to pull*. *Subtraction* is *hikizan* ひきざん[引き算].

9. to multiply	*kakeru*	かける	掛ける

Do you recognize this word? That's right! It's yet another meaning for *kakeru! Multiplication* is *kakezan* かけざん[掛け算].

10. to divide	*waru*	わる	割る

Division is *warizan* わりざん[割り算].

Day 80 Example Sentences:

1. I can count to one hundred.

2. That was a thousand years ago.

3. The price of this game is ten thousand yen.

4. I have one hundred million yen in savings.

5. Which number is it?

6. I'm not so good at arithmetic.

7. Two plus two is four.

8. Five minus one is four.

9. Three times seven is twenty-one.

10. One hundred divided by ten is ten.

1. ひゃくまでかぞえられる。

2. あれはせんねんまえでした。

3. このゲームのねだんはいちまんえんです。

4. おれのちょきんはいちおくえんです。

5. ばんごうはどれですか。

6. さんすうはにがてです。

7. にたすにはよん。

8. ごひくいちはよん。

9. さんかけるななはにじゅういちです。

10. ひゃくわるじゅうはじゅう。

1. *Hyaku made kazoerareru.*

2. *Are wa sen nen mae deshita.*

3. *Kono geemu no nedan wa ichi man en desu.*

4. *Ore no chokin wa ichi oku en desu.*

5. *Bangou wa dore desu ka?*

6. *Sansuu wa nigate desu.*

7. *Ni tasu ni wa yon.*

8. *Go hiku ichi wa yon.*

9. *San kakeru nana wa nijuuichi desu.*

10. *Hyaku waru juu wa juu.*

1. 百まで数えられる。

2. あれは千年前でした。

3. このゲームの値段は一万円です。

4. 俺の貯金は一億円です。

5. 番号はどれですか。

6. 算数は苦手です。

7. 二足す二は四。

8. 五引く一は四。

9. 三掛ける七は二十一です。

10. 百割る十は十。

Day 81: Counting

Counting objects in Japanese is complicated. An appropriate ending must be added to the number, based on the type of object. There are about twenty different ways to do this! The most useful ones will be covered in this book. You may think this is silly, but actually, this happens in English too, with things like *flights* of stairs, or *bundles* of sticks.

The general counter is made by adding the suffix *tsu* つ to the native Japanese numbers. If you don't know what kind of counter to use for some object, use this one, and a Japanese person will understand you. From ten and up, numbers don't get the suffix, and will use the Foreign numbers. For example, *thirty-five things* is *sanjuugo* さんじゅうご[三十五]. Study the following list:

1 thing	*hitotsu*	ひとつ	一つ
2 things	*futatsu*	ふたつ	二つ
3 things	*mittsu*	みっつ	三つ
4 things	*yottsu*	よっつ	四つ
5 things	*itsutsu*	いつつ	五つ
6 things	*muttsu*	むっつ	六つ
7 things	*nanatsu*	ななつ	七つ
8 things	*yattsu*	やっつ	八つ
9 things	*kokonotsu*	ここのつ	九つ
10 things*	*too*	とお	十

The counter for people uses the suffix *nin* にん[人] added to the Foreign numbers, with exceptions for *one person, two people*, and *four people*. *Seven people* can be said with both the Foreign and Japanese numbers. For numbers of people higher than ten, just add the suffix *nin* にん[人] to the number.

1 person*	*hitori*	ひとり	一人
2 people*	*futari*	ふたり	二人
3 people	*sannin*	さんにん	三人
4 people*	*yonin*	よにん	四人
5 people	*gonin*	ごにん	五人
6 people	*rokunin*	ろくにん	六人
7 people*	*nananin / shichinin*	ななにん・しちにん	七人
8 people	*hachinin*	はちにん	八人
9 people	*kyuunin*	きゅうにん	九人
10 people	*juunin*	じゅうにん	十人

For cylindrical objects, like chopsticks or cans, use the suffix *hon* ほん[本] with the Foreign numbers. This one is a little tricky because there are some pronunciation changes.

1 cylinder*	*ippon*	いっぽん	一本
2 cylinders	*nihon*	にほん	二本
3 cylinders*	*sanbon*	さんぼん	三本
4 cylinders	*yonhon*	よんほん	四本
5 cylinders	*gohon*	ごほん	五本
6 cylinders*	*roppon / rokuhon*	ろっぽん・ろくほん	六本
7 cylinders	*nanahon*	ななほん	七本
8 cylinders*	*happon*	はっぽん	八本
9 cylinders	*kyuuhon*	きゅうほん	九本
10 cylinders*	*juppon*	じゅっぽん	十本

For small, usually round objects, use the suffix *ko* こ[個] with the Foreign numbers.

1 small thing*	*ikko*	いっこ	一個
2 small things	*niko*	にこ	二個
3 small things	*sanko*	さんこ	三個
4 small things	*yonko*	よんこ	四個
5 small things	*goko*	ごこ	五個
6 small things*	*rokko*	ろっこ	六個
7 small things	*nanako*	ななこ	七個
8 small things*	*hachiko / hakko*	はちこ・はっこ	八個
9 small things	*kyuuko*	きゅうこ	九個
10 small things*	*jukko*	じゅっこ	十個

For small flat objects, like paper, use the suffix *mai* まい[一枚] with the Foreign numbers.

1 flat thing	*ichimai*	いちまい	一枚
2 flat things	*nimai*	にまい	二枚
3 flat things	*sanmai*	さんまい	三枚
4 flat things	*yonmai*	よんまい	四枚
5 flat things	*gomai*	ごまい	五枚
6 flat things	*rokumai*	ろくまい	六枚
7 flat things	*nanamai*	ななまい	七枚
8 flat things	*hachimai*	はちまい	八枚

9 flat things	*kyuumai*	きゅうまい	九枚
10 flat things	*juumai*	じゅうまい	十枚

For years of life, use the suffix *sai* さい[才・歳] with the Foreign numbers. Note that there are two possible kanji for this. The first kanji is an abbreviation of the second. The age twenty is the year of adulthood in Japan, and it is pronounced *hatachi* はたち.

1 year old*	*issai*	いっさい	一才
2 years old	*nisai*	にさい	二才
3 years old	*sansai*	さんさい	三才
4 years old	*yonsai*	よんさい	四才
5 years old	*gosai*	ごさい	五才
6 years old	*rokusai*	ろくさい	六才
7 years old	*nanasai*	ななさい	七才
8 years old*	*hassai*	はっさい	八才
9 years old	*kyuusai*	きゅうさい	九才
10 years old*	*jussai*	じゅっさい	十才

To say the number of times, use the suffix *kai* かい[回] with the Foreign numbers.

1 time*	*ikkai*	いっかい	一回
2 times	*nikai*	にかい	二回
3 times	*sankai*	さんかい	三回
4 times	*yonkai*	よんかい	四回
5 times	*gokai*	ごかい	五回
6 times*	*rokkai*	ろっかい	六回
7 times	*nanakai*	ななかい	七回
8 times*	*hachikai / hakkai*	はちかい・はっかい	八回
9 times	*kyuukai*	きゅうかい	九回
10 times*	*jukkai*	じゅっかい	十回

To say the floors of a building is actually the exact same pronunciation as to say the number of times you have done something, with the exception being *sangai* さんがい[三階] for the third floor, and an additional alternate pronunciation for the eighth floor, *hakkai* はっかい[八階].

Day 81 Grammar Cards:

1. general counter	Japanese numbers + *tsu*	Japanese numbers + つ	
2. people counter	Foreign numbers + *nin*	Foreign numbers + にん	Foreign numbers + 人
3. cylinder counter	Foreign numbers + *hon*	Foreign numbers + ほん	Foreign numbers + 本
4. small object counter	Foreign numbers + *ko*	Foreign numbers + こ	Foreign numbers + 個
5. flat object counter	Foreign numbers + *mai*	Foreign numbers + まい	Foreign numbers + 枚
6. years old counter	Foreign numbers + *sai*	Foreign numbers + さい	Foreign numbers + 才・歳
7. times counter	Foreign numbers + *kai*	Foreign numbers + かい	Foreign numbers + 回
floor counter	Foreign numbers + *kai*	Foreign numbers + かい	Foreign numbers + 階

Day 81 Vocabulary:

1. one person	*hitori*	ひとり	一人
This can also be used to say that you are *alone*, as well as the idiomatic expression *one by one*, *hitorihitori* ひとりひとり[一人一人].			
2. two people	*futari*	ふたり	二人
3. twenty years old	*hatachi*	はたち	二十歳
4. to count	*kazoeru*	かぞえる	数える **(I)**
5. number / amount / count	*kazu*	かず	数
This is the noun of the previous verb.			
6. number / figure / digit	*suuji*	すうじ	数字
This refers to digits 0-9 themselves.			
7. to earn (salary)	*kasegu*	かせぐ	稼ぐ
8. account / finance / accountant	*kaikei*	かいけい	会計
This can refer to a company's accounts as well as a person who does accounting. This is actually the same word you learned for *bill*.			
9. stock / shares (finance)	*kabu*	かぶ	株
10. to invest	*toushi suru*	とうしする	投資する

Day 81 Example Sentences:

1. **I'm alone.**

2. **I saw two people on the street.**

3. **Next year I will be twenty years old.**

4. **I can count to ten with my hands.**

5. **The number of humans has reached seven billion.**

6. **These reports have a lot of figures.**

7. **I want to earn a lot of money.**

8. **My younger brother is an accountant.**

9. **I have never bought stocks.**

10. **Investing is dangerous.**

1. ひとりです。

2. みちでふたりをみました。

3. らいねんはたちになる。

4. てでじゅうまでかぞえることができる。

5. にんげんのかずはななひゃくおくにたっしました。

6. このほうこくはすうじがたくさんです。

7. たくさんかせぎたいです。

8. おとうとはかいけいしです。

9. かぶをかったことがありません。

10. とうしするのはあぶないです。

1. *Hitori desu.*

2. *Michi de futari o mimashita.*

3. *Rainen hatachi ni naru.*

4. *Te de juu made kazoeru koto ga dekiru.*

5. *Ningen no kazu wa nana hyaku oku ni tasshimashta.*

6. *Kono houkoku wa suuji ga takusan desu.*

7. *Takusan kasegitai desu.*

8. *Otouto wa kaikeishi desu.*

9. *Kabu o katta koto ga arimasen.*

10. *Toushi suru no wa abunai desu.*

1. 一人です。

2. 道で二人を見ました。

3. 来年二十歳に成る。

4. 手で十まで数えることが出来る。

5. 人間の数は七百億に達しました。

6. この報告は数字がたくさんです。

7. たくさん稼ぎたいです。

8. 弟は会計士です。

9. 株を買ったことがありません。

10. 投資するのは危ないです。

To count the first ten days of a month, add the suffix *ka* か[日] to the Japanese numbers. The first of the month is an exception, and most of the days have small changes to the pronunciation:

First*	*tsuitachi*	ついたち	一日
Second*	*futsuka*	ふつか	二日
Third*	*mikka*	みっか	三日
Fourth*	*yokka*	よっか	四日
Fifth	*itsuka*	いつか	五日
Sixth*	*muika*	むいか	六日
Seventh*	*nanoka*	なのか	七日
Eighth*	*youka*	ようか	八日
Ninth	*kokonoka*	ここのか	九日
Tenth	*tooka*	とおか	十日

For the rest of the days of the month, add the suffix *nichi* にち[日] to the number:

Eleventh	*juuichinichi*	じゅういちにち	十一日
Twenty-fifth	*nijuugonichi*	にじゅうごにち	二十五日

The fourteenth and the twenty-fourth will use *ka* か instead of *nichi* にち, and the twentieth has a completely different pronunciation:

Fourteenth	*juuyokka*	じゅうよっか	十四日
Twenty-fourth	*nijuuyokka*	にじゅうよっか	二十四日
Twentieth	*hatsuka*	はつか	二十日

To say the months of the year, use the number of the month plus the suffix *gatsu* がつ[月]. Although most people say *yon* よん and *nana* なな for four and seven, with months, people use the alternate pronunciation, *shi* し and *shichi* しち. September also has a special pronunciation.

January	*ichigatsu*	いちがつ	一月
April	*shigatsu*	しがつ	四月
July	*shichigatsu*	しちがつ	七月
September*	*kugatsu*	くがつ	九月

To say the year, add the suffix *nen* ねん[年] to the number. Unlike English, in Japanese, they will say the thousand and hundreds place of a year, and not separate it. 1963 will be pronounced as *year one thousand nine hundred sixty-three*:

1963	*sen-kyuuhyaku-rokujuu-san-nen*	せんきゅうひゃくろくじゅうさんねん	千九百六十三年

Also, people will usually just write the numeral and not the kanji, so this previous example would actually just be written out as 1963 年. On a cultural note, Japan also has their own year recording system that goes along with the reign of current Emperor. As of the writing of this book, Japan is currently in the Heisei Era, which began in 1988, so the year 2015 in Japan is also known as Heisei 27.

Day 82 Grammar Cards:

1. Days of the month 1-10	Japanese numbers + *ka*	Japanese numbers + か	Japanese numbers + 日
2. Days of the month 11-31	Foreign numbers + *nichi*	Foreign numbers + にち	Foreign numbers + 日
First of the month	*tsuitachi*	ついたち	一日
fourteenth	*juuyokka*	じゅうよっか	十四日
twentieth	*hatsuka*	はつか	二十日
twenty-fourth	*nijuuyokka*	にじゅうよっか	二十四日
3. Months	Foreign numbers + *gatsu*	Foreign numbers + がつ	Foreign numbers + 月
4. Years	Foreign numbers + *nen*	Foreign numbers + ねん	Foreign numbers + 年

Day 82 Vocabulary:

1. today	*kyou*	きょう	今日
2. tomorrow	*ashita*	あした	明日
3. yesterday	*kinou*	きのう	昨日
4. the day before yesterday	*ototoi*	おととい	一昨日
5. the day after tomorrow	*asatte*	あさって	明後日
6. day	*hi*	ひ	日
7. week	*shuu*	しゅう	週
8. month	*getsu*	げつ	月
9. year	*toshi*	とし	年
10. time	*toki*	とき	時
time	*jikan*	じかん	時間

The first word is the concept of time, used in phrases like *at that time*. The second is an interval of time, used in phrases like *we have time*.

1. **The weather is nice today.**

2. **I will go to a park tomorrow.**

3. **I couldn't sleep well yesterday.**

4. **The day before yesterday I met my friend.**

5. **I will go on a trip the day after tomorrow.**

6. **I'm busy that day.**

7. **This week was tough.**

8. **This month I will start my diet.**

9. **Every year I travel abroad.**

10. **We have no time.**

1. きょうはいいおてんきです。

2. あしたはこうえんにいきます。

3. きのうはよくねむれなかった。

4. おとといはともだちとあいました。

5. あさってりょこうします。

6. そのひはいそがしいです。

7. こんしゅうはたいへんだった。

8. こんげつからダイエットをはじめます。

9. まいとしわたしはかいがいにりょこうします。

10. じかんがない。

1. *Kyou wa ii otenki desu.*

2. *Ashita wa kouen ni ikimasu.*

3. *Kinou wa yoku nemurenakatta.*

4. *Ototoi wa tomodachi to aimashita.*

5. *Asatte ryokou shimasu.*

6. *Sono hi wa isogashii desu.*

7. *Konshuu wa taihen datta.*

8. *Kongetsu kara daietto o hajimemasu.*

9. *Maitoshi watashi wa kaigai ni ryokou shimasu.*

10. *Jikan ga nai.*

1. 今日は良いお天気です。

2. 明日は公園に行きます。

3. 昨日は良く眠れなかった。

4. 一昨日は友達と会いました。

5. 明後日旅行します。

6. その日は忙しいです。

7. 今週は大変だった。

8. 今月からダイエットを始めます。

9. 毎年私は海外に旅行します。

10. 時間がない。

Day 83: Dates, Part 2

Today's lesson covers the days of the week. If you are having trouble with the meanings, try to remember the literal meanings, which will be included.

Day 83 Vocabulary:

1. morning	*asa*	あさ	朝
2. daytime	*hiru*	ひる	昼
3. evening	*yuugata*	ゆうがた	夕方
4. night	*yoru*	よる	夜
5. Sunday	*nichiyoubi*	にちようび	日曜日
This means day of the Sun.			
6. Monday	*getsuyoubi*	げつようび	月曜日
This means day of the Moon.			
7. Tuesday	*kayoubi*	かようび	火曜日
This means day of fire.			
8. Wednesday	*suiyoubi*	すいようび	水曜日
This means day of water.			
9. Thursday	*mokuyoubi*	もくようび	木曜日
This means day of trees.			
10. Friday	*kinyoubi*	きんようび	金曜日
This means day of gold.			
11. Saturday	*doyoubi*	どようび	土曜日
This means day of earth.			

Day 83 Example Sentences:

1. I eat breakfast in the morning.

2. I exercise in the afternoon.

3. In the evenings I watch TV.

4. At night I go out to eat.

5. I go to church on Sunday.

6. I hate Mondays.

7. I have to work on Tuesday.

8. I will meet my friends on Wednesday.

9. I go bowling on Thursdays.

10. There is a party on Friday.

11. I have plans on Saturday.

1. あさちょうしょくをたべます。

2. わたしはひるにうんどうします。

3. ゆうがたにはテレビをみます。

4. よるたべにいきます。

5. にちようびにきょうかいにいく。

6. げつようびがきらい。

7. かようびはしごとしなければならない。

8. すいようびはともだちとあいます。

9. もくようびはボウリングにいきます。

10. きんようびはパーティがある。

11. どようびはよていがあります。

1. *Asa choushoku o tabemasu.*

2. *Watashi wa hiru ni undou shimasu.*

3. *Yuugata ni wa terbi o mimasu.*

4. *Yoru tabe ni ikimasu.*

5. *Nichiyoubi ni kyoukai ni iku.*

6. *Getsyoubi ga kirai.*

7. *Kayoubi wa shigoto shinakerba naranai.*

8. *Suiyoubi wa tomodachi to aimasu.*

9. *Mokuyoubi wa bouringu ni ikimasu.*

10. *Kinyoubi wa paati ga aru.*

11. *Doyoubi wa yotei ga arimasu.*

1. 朝朝食を食べます。

2. 私は昼に運動します。

3. 夕方にはテレビを見ます。

4. 夜食べに行きます。

5. 日曜日に教会に行く。

6. 月曜日が嫌い。

7. 火曜日は仕事しなければならない。

8. 水曜日は友達と会います。

9. 木曜日はボウリングに行きます。

10. 金曜日はパーティがある。

11. 土曜日は予定があります。

Day 84: Dates, Part 3

Like English, Japanese uses prefixes with time words:

every	*mai*	まい	毎
last	*sen* / *saku*	せん・さく	先・昨
next	*rai* / *myou*	らい・みょう	来・明

Saku さく[昨] is the more formal version of *sen* せん[先], usually used in writing rather than conversation. The only exception is *sakunen* さくねん[昨年] (last year), which seems to be used just as often as *kyonen* きょねん[去年]. The same applies to *rai* らい[来] and *myou* みょう [明]. In words where they can both be used, *myou* みょう [明] is the more formal version. There are a couple of exceptions that use completely different words. Study the following lists:

Every morning	*maiasa*	まいあさ	毎朝
Every day	*mainichi*	まいにち	毎日
Every night	*maiban*	まいばん	毎晩
Every week	*maishuu*	まいしゅう	毎週
Every month	*maitsuki / maigetsu*	まいげつ・まいつき	毎月
Every year	*maitoshi / mainen*	まいとし・まいねん	毎年
Yesterday morning	*sakuchou*	さくちょう	昨朝
Instead of *sakuchou* さくちょう [昨朝], many people will use the *no* の particle with *yesterday*: *kinou no asa* きのうのあさ[昨日の朝] (yesterday's morning)			
Last night*	*yuube*	ゆうべ	夕べ・昨夜
The second kanji for *yuube* has an alternate pronunciation, *sakuya* さくや.			
Last night	*sakuban*	さくばん	昨晩
Last week	*senshuu*	せんしゅう	先週
Last week	*sakushuu*	さくしゅう	昨週
Last month	*sengetsu*	せんげつ	先月
Last year*	*kyonen*	きょねん	去年
Last year	*sakunen*	さくねん	昨年
Tomorrow	*myounichi*	みょうにち	明日
Notice, this is the same kanji for *ashita* あした[明日].			
Tomorrow morning	*myouchou*	みょうちょう	明朝
Most people will just say *ashita no asa* あしたのあさ[明日の朝].			

Tomorrow night	*myouban*	みょうばん	明晩
Most people will just say *ashita no yoru* あしたのよる[明日の夜]			
Next week	*raishuu*	らいしゅう	来週
Next month	*raigetsu*	らいげつ	来月
Next year	*rainen*	らいねん	来年
Next year	*myounen*	みょうねん	明年

The prefix *issaku* いっさく[一昨] means *one previous*. Though, the special pronunciation *oto* is used more often.

The day before yesterday	*issakujitsu / ototoi*	いっさくじつ・おととい	一昨日
The year before last	*issakunen / ototoshi*	いっさくねん・おととし	一昨年

The prefix *sarai* さらい[再来] means *after next*. *Day* has its own special word.

The day after tomorrow*	*asatte / myougonichi*	あさって・みょうごにち	明後日
The week after next	*saraishuu*	さらいしゅう	再来週
The month after next	*saraigetsu*	さらいげつ	再来月
The year after next	*sarainen*	さらいねん	再来年

The prefix *kon* こん[今] means *this*:

This morning*	*kesa*	けさ	今朝
This day	*konnichi*	こんにち	今日
This evening	*konban*	こんばん	今晩
This week	*konshuu*	こんしゅう	今週
This month	*kongetsu*	こんげつ	今月
This year*	*kotoshi*	ことし	今年

Day 84 Grammar Cards:

1. every (time)	prefix *mai*	まい	毎
2. last (time)	prefix *sen / saku*	せん・さく	先・作
3. next (time)	prefix *rai / myou*	らい・みょう	来・明
4. one previous (day / year)	*prefix issaku*	いっさく	一作
Usually pronounced *oto* おと			
5. (week / month / year) after next	prefix *sarai*	さらい	再来
6. the day after tomorrow	*asatte*	あさって	明後日
7. this (time)	prefix *kon*	こん	今

Day 84 Vocabulary:

1. last night	*yuube*	ゆうべ	夕べ・昨夜
Again, the second kanji for *yuube* has an alternate pronunciation, *sakuya* さくや.			
last night	*sakuban*	さくばん	昨晩
2. last year	*kyonen*	きょねん	去年
last year	*sakunen*	さくねん	昨年
3. year before last	*issakunen / ototoshi*	いっさくねん・おととし	一昨年
4. this morning	*kesa*	けさ	今朝
5. this year	*kotoshi*	ことし	今年
6. Spring	*haru*	はる	春
7. Summer	*natsu*	なつ	夏
8. Fall	*aki*	あき	秋
9. Winter	*fuyu*	ふゆ	冬
With the seasons, adding *yasumi* やすみ[休み] means a vacation during that season. For example, *natsuyasumi* なつやすみ[夏休み] (summer vacation). *Yasumi* やすみ[休み] is the noun of the verb *yasumu* やすむ[休む] (to rest), and it can mean *day off* or *holiday*.			
10. season	*kisetsu*	きせつ	季節

1. **I drank too much last night.**

2. **Last year I went to France.**

3. **The year before last I lived in Japan.**

4. **This morning I felt sick.**

5. **This year I'm going to work hard.**

6. **Flowers bloom in the Spring.**

7. **Summers in Japan are humid.**

8. **It gets cold in the Fall.**

9. **What will you do for winter vacation?**

10. **What is your favorite season?**

1. ゆうべはのみすぎました。

2. きょねんフランスにいった。

3. おととしはにほんにすんでいました。

4. けさはぐあいがわるかった。

5. ことしははたらきます。

6. はなははるにさきます。

7. にほんのなつはむしあついです。

8. あきにはさむくなる。

9. ふゆやすみはなにをしますか。

10. いちばんすきなきせつはどれですか。

1. *Yuube wa nomisugimashita.*

2. *Kyonen furansu ni itta.*

3. *Ototoshi wa nihon ni sunde imashita.*

4. *Kesa wa guai ga warukatta.*

5. *Kotoshi wa hatarakimasu.*

6. *Hana wa haru ni sakimasu.*

7. *Nihon no natsu wa mushiatsui desu.*

8. *Aki ni wa samuku naru.*

9. *Fuyuyasumi wa nani o shimasu ka?*

10. *Ichiban suki na kisetsu wa dore desu ka?*

1. 夕べは飲み過ぎました。

2. 去年フランスに行った。

3. 一昨年は日本に住んでいました。

4. 今朝は具合が悪かった。

5. 今年は働きます。

6. 花は春に咲きます。

7. 日本の夏は蒸し暑いです。

8. 秋には寒くなる。

9. 冬休みは何をしますか。

10. 一番好きな季節はどれですか。

Day 85: Time

In Japan they use a 24-hour clock, so that means at midnight, the time is 0:00 or 24:00. Sometimes, when referring to early morning hours, even higher numbers than 24 are used. For example 25:00 refers to 1:00am, and 28:00 refers to 4:00am.

To mark the hour, use *ji* じ[時]. Pay close attention to four and seven o'clock:

1:00am	*ichiji*	いちじ	一時
4:00am	*yoji*	よじ	四時
7:00am	*shichiji*	しちじ	七時
12:00pm	*juuniji*	じゅうにじ	十二時
Midnight	*reiji*	れいじ	零時
Midnight	*nijuuyoji*	にじゅうよじ	二十四時

Though most people will say the 24-hour clock based number, the words for *am* and *pm* are *gozen* ごぜん[午前] and *gogo* ごご[午後], respectively. They are placed <u>before</u> the time:

5:00am	*gozen goji*	ごぜんごじ	午前五時
5:00pm	*gogo goji*	ごごごじ	午後五時

For minutes you will use *fun* ふん[分] / *pun* ぷん[分]. This word has a different pronunciation based on the number it is next to:

:01	*ippun*	いっぷん	一分
:02	*nifun*	にふん	二分
:03	*sanpun*	さんぷん	三分
:04	*yonpun / yonfun*	よんぷん・よんふん	四分
:05	*gofun*	ごふん	五分
:06	*roppun / rokufun*	ろっぷん・ろくふん	六分
:07	*nanafun*	ななふん	七分
:08	*happun hachifun*	はっぷん・はちふん	八分
:09	*kyuufun*	きゅうふん	九分
:10	*juppun*	じゅっぷん	十分

For thirty, *han* はん[半] can be used, which literally means *half*.

10:30	*juujihan*	じゅうじはん	十時半

For seconds, use *byou* びょう[秒]. There are no exceptions or alternate pronunciations.

In English, the preposition *at* is used with time. In Japanese, *ni* に is used.

It starts <u>at</u> seven.
Shichiji <u>ni</u> hajimarimasu.
しちじにはじまります。
七時に始まります。

Day 85 Grammar Cards:

1. hour (time)	suffix *ji*	じ	時
2. minute (time)	suffix *fun / pun*	ふん・ぷん	分
3. second (time)	suffix *byou*	びょう	秒

Day 85 Vocabulary:

1. am	*gozen*	ごぜん	午前
pm	*gogo*	ごご	午後
These words can also be used to mean *morning* and *afternoon*.			
2. half	*han*	はん	半
3. now	*ima*	いま	今
4. sometimes	*tokidoki*	ときどき	時々
5. often	*tabitabi*	たびたび	度々
6. rarely	*mettani*	めったに	滅多に
This is used with a negative verb.			
7. usually	*taitei*	たいてい	大抵 (UK)
8. gradually / soon	*sorosoro*	そろそろ	
This means something will happen soon, *any minute now*.			
9. soon / instantly / immediately	*suguni*	すぐに	直ぐに (UK)
This means *very soon*.			
10. soon	*mousugu*	もうすぐ	もう直ぐ (UK)
This word is more along the lines of the English meaning of *soon*.			

1. It is now 7:30am.

2. Let's meet at 1:30pm.

3. What time is it now?

4. I sometimes eat cake.

5. I often study Japanese.

6. I rarely drink alcohol.

7. I usually don't drive.

8. Spring is coming soon.

9. She will arrive very soon.

10. He will come soon.

1. いまはごぜんしちじはんです。

2. じゅうさんじはんにあいましょう。

3. いまなんじですか。

4. ときどきケーキをくう。

5. たびたびにほんごをべんきょうします。

6. おさけはめったにのみません。

7. たいていうんてんしません。

8. そろそろはるがきます。

9. かのじょはすぐにつきます。

10. かれはもうすぐきます。

1. *Ima wa gozen shichiji han desu.*

2. *Juu san ji han ni aimashou.*

3. *Ima nanji desu ka?*

4. *Tokidoki keeki o kuu.*

5. *Tabitabi nihongo o benkyou shimasu.*

6. *Osake wa mettani nomimasen.*

7. *Taitei unten shimasen.*

8. *Sorosoro haru ga kimasu.*

9. *Kanojo wa sugu ni tsukimasu.*

10. *Kare wa mousugu kimasu.*

1. 今は午前七時半です。

2. 十三時半に会いましょう。

3. 今何時ですか。

4. 時々ケーキを食う。

5. 度々日本語を勉強します。

6. お酒は滅多に飲みません。

7. 大抵運転しません。

8. そろそろ春が来ます。

9. 彼女はすぐに着きます。

10. 彼はもう直ぐ来ます。

Day 86: Time, Part 2

The prepositions *from* and *until* are *kara* から and *made* まで respectively.

The department store is open <u>from</u> 7:00am <u>until</u> 10:00pm.
Depaato wa shichi ji <u>kara</u> nijuuni ji <u>made</u> akemasu.
デパートはしちじからにじゅうにじまであけます。
デパートは七時から二十二時まで開けます。

Japanese speakers will also use *kara* から in places where English speakers use *at / from,* to indicate when something begins:

It starts <u>at / from</u> seven.
Shichiji <u>kara</u> hajimarimasu.
しちじからはじまります。
七時から始まります。

The expression *ima kara* いまから[今から] means *from now on,* or, *starting from now.*

Let's do our best <u>from now on</u>.
Ima kara ganbarimashou.
いまからがんばりましょう。
今から頑張りましょう。

Kara から can sometimes mean *after* when used with events or something that takes place. In this sense it means: *at the end of this.*

Let's go <u>after</u> this.
Kore <u>kara</u> ikimashou.
これからいきましょう。
これから行きましょう。

Kara から can also be used in all the other contexts where *from* is used in English. For example: *This present is from Jim,* or, *I came back from Japan.*

To talk about a time interval, add the suffix *kan* かん[間]. This word literally means *interval*. It can be used to show how long something took or lasted.

One hour (<u>long</u>).	One minute (<u>long</u>).
Ichi ji <u>kan</u>.	*Ippun <u>kan</u>.*
いちじ<u>かん</u>。	いっぷん<u>かん</u>。
一時<u>間</u>。	一分<u>間</u>。
One second (<u>long</u>).	**Two years (<u>long</u>).**
Ichibyou <u>kan</u>.	*Ni nen <u>kan</u>.*
いちびょう<u>かん</u>。	にねん<u>かん</u>。
一秒<u>間</u>。	二年<u>間</u>。
One week (<u>long</u>).	**Two weeks (<u>long</u>).**
Isshuu <u>kan</u>.	*Nishuu <u>kan</u>.*
いっしゅう<u>かん</u>。	にしゅう<u>かん</u>。
一週<u>間</u>。	二週<u>間</u>。

Intervals of days and months are a bit different. For an interval of a day, simply say the date on the calendar:

Three days (long).
The third of the month.
Mikka.
みっか。
三日。

For months, use the suffix *kagetsu* かげつ[ヶ月]. One month long has a special pronunciation:

One month (<u>long</u>).	Two months (<u>long</u>).
Ikkagetsu.	*Nikagetsu.*
いっ<u>かげつ</u>。	に<u>かげつ</u>。
一<u>ヶ月</u>。	二<u>ヶ月</u>。

Day 86 Grammar Cards:

1. from / until	kara / made	から・まで	
2. from now on / after (this)	ima kara / (kore) kara	いまから・(これ) から	
3. general time interval (long)	kan	かん	間
4. month time interval (long)	kagetsu	かげつ	ヶ月

Day 86 Vocabulary:

1. the future (far)	mirai	みらい	未来

This usually refers to the far future, with spaceships and robots.

2. the future (near)	shourai	しょうらい	将来

This usually refers to the foreseeable future.

3. the last / end / final	saigo	さいご	最後
4. the first / start / beginning	saisho	さいしょ	最初

This is also used in the idiomatic phrase, *first things first*: *ichiban saisho* いちばんさいしょ[一番最初].

5. the past / ancient times / a long time ago	mukashi	むかし	昔

This refers to things that happened long ago. But because time is relative, if it feels like a long time for the speaker, even a few days or weeks can feel like ancient times.

6. the past	kako	かこ	過去

This refers to the more recent past.

7. local train	kakuekiteisha	かくえきていしゃ	各駅停車

This word means *a train that stops at all stations*. When the train operator is speaking, they will use this word, however, on the signs for the next coming train, they sometimes use a different kanji: *futsuu* ふつう[普通] (usual / normal). The reason is because there are two major train operators in Japan - JR and the Metro. The next three words are for the different types of trains.

8. semi-express train	junkyuu	じゅんきゅう	準急
rapid train	kaisoku	かいそく	快速

Though these are two different words, these trains are faster than local trains, but slower than the express trains. JR will use *semi-express* while the Metro will use *rapid*.

9. express train	kyuukou	きゅうこう	急行
10. limited express train	tokkyuu	とっきゅう	特急

This is the fastest of the trains and sometimes requires a premium. However, it is not often, and usually when it does, the train will look different than the other trains, so don't worry about getting on a train without paying enough.

1. **In the future, we won't use oil.**

2. **I'm going to move to Tokyo in the future.**

3. **This is the last chocolate.**

4. **In the beginning, I didn't understand anything.**

5. **A long time ago democracy didn't exist.**

6. **Don't think about the past.**

7. **This train will become a local train starting from Shibuya station.**

8. **Hurry! We won't make the rapid train!**

9. **The express train is late.**

10. **The limited express train takes thirty minutes.**

1. みらいではせきゆをつかいません。

2. しょうらいとうきょうにひっこしします。

3. これはさいごのチョコです。

4. さいしょはぜんぜんわかりませんでした。

5. むかしはみんしゅしゅぎがありませんでした。

6. かこをかんがえないでください。

7. このでんしゃはしぶやえきからかくえきていしゃになります。

8. いそいで。かいそくでんしゃにまにあいませんよ。

9. きゅうこうでんしゃはおくれた。

10. とっきゅうでんしゃではさんじゅっぷんかかります。

1. *Mirai de wa sekiyu o tsukaimasen.*

2. *Shourai toukyou ni hikkoshimasu.*

3. *Kore wa saigo no choko desu.*

4. *Saisho wa zenzen wakarimasen deshita.*

5. *Mukashi wa minshushugi ga arimasen deshita.*

6. *Kako o kangaenaide kudasai.*

7. *Kono densha wa shibuya eki kara kakuekiteisha ni narimasu.*

8. *Isoide! Kaisoku densha ni maniaimasen yo!*

9. *Kyuukou densha wa okureta.*

10. *Tokkyuu densha de wa sanjuppun kakarimasu.*

1. 未来では石油を使いません。

2. 将来東京に引っ越します。

3. これは最後のチョコです。

4. 最初は全然分かりませんでした。

5. 昔は民主主義がありませんでした。

6. 過去を考えないで下さい。

7. この電車は渋谷駅から各駅停車になります。

8. 急いで。快速電車に間に合いませんよ。

9. 急行電車は遅れた。

10. 特急電車では三十分かかります。

Day 87: Already, Still, Yet, About, Approximately

To say that something *has already been done, is already underway,* or to ask if something *is yet to be done,* use the word *mou* もう. The correct translation of this word can easily be understood from context. Study the following examples:

I have <u>already</u> eaten dinner. *Mou bangohan o tabemashita.* もうばんごはんをたべました。 もう晩ご飯を食べました。	**I am <u>already</u> eating dinner.** *Mou bangohan o tabete imasu.* もうばんごはんをたべています。 もう晩ご飯を食べています。
Have you eaten dinner <u>yet</u>? **(Lit. Have you already eaten dinner?)** *Mou bangohan o tabemashita ka?* もうばんごはんをたべましたか？ もう晩ご飯を食べましたか？	

Mou ichido もういちど[もう一度] and *mou ikkai* もういっかい[もう一回] are idiomatic expressions that both mean: *one more time.*

Let's review <u>one more time</u>. *Mou ikkai fukushuu shimashou.* もういっかいふくしゅうしましょう。 もう一回復習しましょう。

To say *still* or *not yet*, use *mada* まだ:

I am <u>still</u> eating dinner. *Mada bangohan o tabete imasu.* まだばんごはんをたべています。 まだ晩ご飯を食べています。	**I <u>haven't</u> eaten dinner <u>yet</u>.** *Mada bangohan o tabete inakatta.* まだばんごはんをたべていなかった。 まだ晩ご飯を食べていなかった。

Kurai くらい means *about* in relation to time and numbers. It can also be pronounced as the voiced version *gurai* ぐらい. A more formal version is *yaku* やく[約], which translates as *approximately.* Unlike *kurai* くらい, *yaku* やく[約] is placed <u>before</u> the word it modifies.

It starts at <u>about</u> eight. *Hachiji <u>gurai</u> hajimarimasu.* はちじぐらいはじまります。 ８時ぐらい始まります。	**<u>Approximately</u> ten people were there.** *<u>Yaku</u> juunin ga imashita.* やくじゅうにんがいました。 約１０人がいました。

Day 87 Grammar Cards:

1. still / not yet	mada	まだ	
2. one more time	mou ichido / mou ikkai	もういちど・もういっかい	もう一度・もう一回
3. about	kurai / gurai	くらい・ぐらい	
4. approximately	yaku	やく	約

Day 87 Vocabulary:

1. already / yet (question)	mou	もう	
2. gradually / soon	dandan	だんだん	段々 (UK)
3. occasionally	tamani	たまに	
4. previous / before / ahead / future	saki	さき	先

This can be confusing because it has two completely opposite meanings. However, from the tense of the sentence you should be able to understand which meaning it is.

5. now / current / present	genzai	げんざい	現在
6. finally / at last	yatto	やっと	
7. to be late	okureru	おくれる	遅れる (I)
8. recently	saikin	さいきん	最近

This is the most basic word for *recently*.

9. the other day / recently	kono aida	このあいだ	この間

This word literally means *during this interval*.

10. nowadays	kono goro	このごろ	この頃

This word literally means *around this time*.

1. **I already did that.**

2. **I gradually got used to my new apartment.**

3. **I occasionally eat an expensive steak.**

4. **Please go ahead of me.**

5. **The current conditions are alright.**

6. **Finally I can meet her!**

7. **That guy is always late.**

8. **Recently I visited my mother.**

9. **I met her by chance the other day.**

10. **Nowadays I've become a bit lazy.**

1. それはもうした。

2. あたらしいアパートはだんだんなれました。

3. たかいステーキをたまにたべます。

4. さきにいってください。

5. げんざいのじじょうはだいじょうぶです。

6. やっとかのじょとあえるよ。

7. あのかれはいつもおくれます。

8. さいきんおかあさんをたずねた。

9. このあいだはぐうぜんかのじょとあいました。

10. このごろはちょっとなまけものになったんだ。

1. *Sore wa mou shita.*

2. *Atarashii apaato ni dandan naremashita.*

3. *Takai suteeki o tamani tabemasu.*

4. *Saki ni itte kudasai.*

5. *Genzai no jijou wa daijoubu desu.*

6. *Yatto kanojo to aeru yo!*

7. *Ano kare wa itsumo okuremasu.*

8. *Saikin okaasan o tazuneta.*

9. *Kono aida wa guuzen kanojo to aimashita.*

10. *Kono goro wa chotto namakemono ni natta nda.*

1. それはもうした。

2. 新しいアパートはだんだん慣れました。

3. 高いステーキをたまに食べます。

4. 先に行って下さい。

5. 現在の事情は大丈夫です。

6. やっと彼女と会えるよ。

7. あの彼はいつも遅れます。

8. 最近お母さんを訪ねた。

9. この間は偶然彼女と会いました。

10. この頃はちょっと怠け者になったんだ。

Day 88: Before, After, In, During, While, When

Some of the time expressions studied today will be followed by *ni* に. If they follow a noun, they will be preceded by *no* の. In conversation, both of these can sometimes be dropped.

To say that something happened *before* something else, use *mae* まえ[前].

Before I sleep, I brush my teeth.	**Before the meeting, I prepared.**
Neru mae ni, ha o migakimasu.	*Kaigi no mae ni, junbi o shimashita.*
ねる<u>まえに</u>、はをみがきます。	かいぎのまえにじゅんびをしました。
寝る<u>前に</u>、歯を研きます。	会議の前に準備をしました。

Similarly, to say that something happened *after* something else, use *ato* あと[後]. In English, the verb used with *after* can be in the present or past tense, but in Japanese, the verb used with *ato* あと[後] will always be in the past tense. Remember, the tense of the entire sentence is controlled by the final verb.

After I take a walk, I read a book.	**After the fight, the mood suddenly changed.**
Sanpo o shita ato ni, hon o yomimasu.	*Kenka no ato, kibun ga kyuu ni kawarimashita.*
さんぽをした<u>あとに</u>、ほんをよみます。	<u>けんかのあと</u>、きぶんがきゅうにかわりました。
散歩をした<u>後に</u>、本を読みます。	喧嘩の後、気分が急に変わりました。

If something happens very shortly after, *ato* あと[後] sounds less natural. The Te-Form + *kara* から is better for actions that immediately proceed each other. This doesn't use the particles *no* の and *ni* に:

Right after I brush my teeth, I sleep.
Ha o migaite kara, nemasu.
はを<u>みがいてから</u>、ねます。
歯を<u>磨いてから</u>、寝ます。

Ato あと[後] can be used as a prefix with nouns or time, to say how much of something is remaining. This doesn't use kanji.

There are five minutes <u>left until</u> it starts.	**I have a year <u>left until</u> I can graduate.**
Ato gofun de hajimarimasu.	*Ato ichinenkan de sotsugyou dekiru.*
<u>あと</u>ごふんではじまります。	<u>あと</u>いちねんかんでそつぎょうできる。
<u>あと</u>五分で始まります。	<u>あと</u>一年間で卒業できる。

The kanji 後 can also be used as a suffix with time to say *in* or *after,* but uses the pronunciation *go* ご[後].

It starts <u>in</u> five minutes.	**<u>After</u> two weeks, he finally arrived.**
Gofungo ni hajimarimasu.	*Nishuukango, kare wa yatto touchaku shimashita.*
ごふん<u>ご</u>にはじまります。	にしゅうかん<u>ご</u>、かれはやっととうちゃくしました。
五分<u>後</u>に始まります。	二週間<u>後</u>、彼はやっと到着しました。

To say *during* or *while*, use *aida* あいだ[間]. *Aida* あいだ[間] literally means *interval* and is used to to say that two things happened during a certain time interval. When talking about physical location, *aida* あいだ[間] means *between*.

During the game, I chatted with my friend.	The cheese is **between** the meat and bread.
Shiai no aida ni tomodachi to shabetta.	*Chiizu wa niku to pan no aida ni arimasu.*
しあいのあいだにともだちとしゃべった。	チーズはにくとぱんのあいだにあります。
試合の間に友達と喋った。	チーズは肉とパンの間にあります。

When using *aida* あいだ[間] with verbs, the verb must be in the present continuous tense. Again, the final verb in the sentence controls the tense of the sentence:

While I **was watching** the game, I chatted with my friend.
Shiai o miteriru aida ni, tomodachi to shabetta.
しあいみているあいだに、ともだちとしゃべった。
試合を見ている間に、友達と喋った。

Another way to say *while* is to use the I-Form plus *nagara* ながら, this doesn't use the particles *no* の and *ni* に. Using *nagara* ながら emphasizes that two things happened at the same time.

While I **walk**, I listen to music.
Arukinagara, ongaku o kiku.
あるきながら、おんがくをきく。
きながら、音楽を聞く。

To talk about past events using the word *when*, use *toki* とき[時]. This literally means *at the time of*. *Koro* ころ[頃] can also be used, which means *approximately when*. The two are interchangeable but *koro* ころ[頃] is more vague.

When I was a student, I couldn't cook for myself.
Gakusei no toki wa, jisui dekinakatta.
がくせいのときは、じすいできなかった。
学生の時は、自炊出来なかった。

Around the time I was a student, I couldn't cook for myself.
Gakusei no koro wa, jisui dekinakatta.
がくせいのころは、じすいできなかった。
学生の頃は、自炊出来なかった。

When said after *ji* じ[時], *koro* ころ will become the voiced version, *goro* ごろ, and means *approximately* or *about*.

It starts **at about seven**.
Shichiji goro ni hajimarimasu.
しちじごろにはじまります。
七時頃に始まります。

Day 88 Grammar Cards:

1. before	*mae*	まえ	前
2. after	*ato* (past tense verb)	あと	後
3. immediately after	Te-Form + *kara*	Te-Form + から	
4. remaining	prefix *ato*	あと	
5. in / after	suffix *go*	ご	後
6. during	*aida*	あいだ	間
during (verb)	Present continuous + *aida*	Present continuous + あいだ	間
7. while doing	I-Form + *nagara*	I-Form + ながら	
8. when (past event)	*toki*	とき	時
when (approximately)	*koro*	ころ	頃

Day 88 Vocabulary:

1. this time / next time / another time	*kondo*	こんど	今度
This can sometimes be confusing because it can refer to an action taking place now, or be used to say to do something another time, so pay attention to the context.			
2. next	*tsugi*	つぎ	次 (No)
3. recently (before)	*kono mae*	このまえ	この前
This is another word that means *recently*. This word explicitly states the the thing has happened recently *before*. In English this can be expressed by saying *just recently*.			
4. a little while / in a moment	*shibaraku*	しばらく	暫く (UK)
5. era	*jidai*	じだい	時代
As stated previously, at the time of this book's publication, Japan is in the Heisei Era: *heisei jidai* へいせいじだい[平成時代]. However, this is usually only added to eras more than 100 years old.			
6. modern times / the present day	*gendai*	げんだい	現代
7. urgent / sudden / steep	*kyuu*	きゅう	急 (Na)
This can mean an *urgent* matter, as well as a *steep* hill.			
8. less than / below / under	*ika*	いか	以下
This is not used for comparisons. But rather, to show limits and expectations.			
9. more than	*ijou*	いじょう	以上
This is also not used for comparisons. An idiomatic usage of this word, is to say it at the end of a speech, or when ordering food, to say: *That's all*.			
10. within	*inai*	いない	以内
This is used for time intervals to say some event occurred within an allotted time frame.			

Day 88 Example Sentences:

1. I'm tired so let's do it next time.

2. The next person, please.

3. I just recently tidied up my room.

4. We will reach Kyoto station in a moment.

5. Japan changed a lot during the Meiji Era.

6. We live in the information age.

7. After the fight, the mood suddenly changed.

8. When I was a child, toys cost under five dollars.

9. While I was waiting, I saw more than one hundred people.

10. When I lived in Japan, I could run a kilometer in three minutes.

1. つかれたから、こんどやりましょう。

2. つぎのかた、どうぞ。

3. このまえ、へやをかたづけた。

4. しばらくすると、きょうとえきにつきます。

5. めいじじだいのあいだににほんはだいぶかわりました。

6. げんだいはじょうほうかじだいだ。

7. けんかのあと、きぶんがきゅうにかわりました。

8. こどものとき、おもちゃのねだんはごドルいかだった。

9. まっているあいだ、ひゃくにんいじょうのひとをみました。

10. にほんにすんでいたとき、いちキロをさんぷんいないではしれました。

1. *Tsukareta kara, kondo yarimashou.*

2. *Tsugi no kata, douzo.*

3. *Kono mae ,heya o katazuketa.*

4. *Shibaraku suru to, kyouto eki ni tsukimasu.*

5. *Meiji jidai no aida ni nihon wa daibu kawarimashita.*

6. *Gendai wa jouhouka jidai da.*

7. *Kenka no ato, kibun ga kyuu ni kawarimashita.*

8. *Kodomo no toki, omocha no nedan wa go doru ika datta.*

9. *Matte iru aida, hyaku nin ijou no hito o mimashita.*

10. *Nihon ni sunde ita toki, ichi kiro o sanpun inai de hashiremashita.*

1. 疲れたから、今度やりましょう。

2. 次の方、どうぞ。

3. この前、部屋を片付けた。

4. しばらくすると、京都駅に着きます。

5. 明治時代の間に日本は大分変わりました。

6. 現代は情報化時代だ。

7. 喧嘩の後、気分が急に変わりました。

8. 子供の時、おもちゃの値段は五ドル以下だった。

9. 待っている間、百人以上の人を見ました。

10. 日本に住んでいた時、一キロを三分以内で走れました。

Day 89: Honorific and Humble Speech

As mentioned in the first few lessons of this book, Japanese has two extra polite forms of words called Honorific and Humble Speech. The differences between the two depends on the subject of the sentence. Use Honorific Speech when talking about someone else, and Humble Speech when talking about yourself. This makes sense because you don't want to honor yourself, that's narcissistic!

While learning honorific and humble speech is not the most important part of Japanese, there are a few words that are very common that you will hear a lot. You may never be in a situation where you have to use these words, however, if you are a customer, a company will most likely use these words when they talk to you. Because these words are extra polite, they will always be used in the Masu-Form, after all, what's the point of using an extra polite word without the polite ending?

Day 89 Vocabulary:

1. honorific speech	*sonkeigo*	そんけいご	尊敬語
2. humble speech	*kenjougo*	けんじょうご	謙譲語
3. to come / to go / to be	*irassharu**	いらっしゃる	**(honorific)**
This is the most common honorific word you will hear, perhaps because it has three different meanings. It is the honorific form of *kuru* くる[来る], *iku* いく[行く], and *iru* いる.			
4. to come / to go / to be	*oide ni naru*	おいでになる	お出でになる **(honorific)(UK)**
This word is also the honorific form of *kuru* くる[来る], *iku* いく[行く], and *iru* いる, and is interchangeable with the previous word, but it is used less often. One more common usage is to tell someone to *follow you,* or *come to you,* by saying *oide* おいで[お出で].			
5. to come / to go	*mairu*	まいる	参る **(G) (humble)**
This word can be confusing because it also has some non-humble homonyms which use the same kanji. They include *to be madly in love, to be defeated, to be annoyed.* You will hear this word often at train stations.			
6. to do	*itasu*	いたす	致す **(humble)**
Just a reminder, this is the humble form of *suru* する.			
7. to do	*nasaru**	なさる	為さる**(honorific)(UK)**
This is where the command ending *nasai* なさい is derived.			
8. to see / to look	*goran ni naru*	ごらんになる	ご覧に成る **(honorific)**
9. to say	*ossharu**	おっしゃる	仰る **(honorific)(UK)**
10. to eat / to drink / to receive	*itadaku*	いただく	頂く **(humble)**
This is actually one of the first words you learned, used before eating something.			

*There's one more thing that needs to be covered. A few of the words have special conjugations in the Masu-Form. For *irassharu* いらっしゃる(to come, to go, to be), *nasaru* なさる[為さる] (to do), and *ossharu* おっしゃる[仰る] (to say), replace *ru* る with *i* い before adding *masu* ます. You don't really need to memorize this, as you will almost never use these words in speech other than their common uses, which you've actually already been doing, with the command *nasai* なさい, which is short for *nasaimasu* なさいます, and *gozaimasu* ございます, which is the Masu-Form of the honorific verb *gozaru* ござる, and also *irashaimase* いらっしゃませ, which is the E-Form of *irasharu* いらしゃる combined with the Masu-Form.

Day 89 Example Sentences:

1. Young people don't use honorific speech.

2. Humble speech was used a lot in ancient times.

3. She came to the temple.

4. Hey, you, come here.

5. I'm sorry, I will come in five minutes.

6. I will be married next week.

7. There's no reason to worry.

8. Please look to the right.

9. She said nothing.

10. I ate a lot. Thank you so much.

1. わかものはけいごをつかわない。

2. むかしはけんじょうごがよくつかわれました。

3. かのじょはおてらにいらっしゃいました。

4. ね、あなた、おいで。

5. もうしわけございません、あとごふんでまいります。

6. わたくしはらいしゅうけっこんいたします。

7. ごしんぱいなさるにはおよびません。

8. みぎがわをごらんになってください。

9. かのじょはなにもおっしゃいませんでした。

10. たくさんいただきました。どうもありがとうございました。

1. *Wakamono wa keigo o tsukawanai.*

2. *Mukashi wa kenjougo ga yoku tsukawaremashita.*

3. *Kanojo wa otera ni irasshaimashita.*

4. *Ne, anata, oide.*

5. *Moushiwake gozaimasen, ato go fun de mairimasu.*

6. *Watakushi wa raishuu kekkon itashimasu.*

7. *Goshinpai nasaru ni wa oyobimasen.*

8. *Migigawa o goran ni natte kudasai.*

9. *Kanojo wa nanimo osshaimasen deshita.*

10. *Takusan itadakimashita. Doumo arigatou gozaimashita.*

1. 若者は敬語を使わない。

2. 昔は謙譲語がよく使われました。

3. 彼女はお寺にいらっしゃいました。

4. ね、あなた、お出で。

5. 申し訳ございません、あと五分で参ります。

6. 私は来週結婚致します。

7. ご心配なさるには及びません。

8. 右側をご覧になって下さい。

9. 彼女は何も仰いませんでした。

10. たくさん頂きました。どうもありがとうございました。

Day 90: False Cognates

Today's lesson will cover some *katakana* カタカナ words that have different meanings that what you might think.

Day 90 Vocabulary:

1. Never mind. / Don't worry about it.	*donmai*	ドンマイ
This word comes from *don't mind*, but is used to tell someone to *not worry about something*, that *it's not important*.		
2. excited / high energy	*hai tenshon*	ハイテンション
People will often drop the *hai* ハイ and just say *tenshon* テンション, which, in English, is only used negatively, as in, tension between two people. In Japanese this refers to a high energy or excited state, like a child opening a new gaming system on Christmas morning and becoming crazy with excitement.		
3. condominium complex	*manshon*	マンション
This comes from the word *mansion* in English, but doesn't refer to a large house, but rather a building with multiple apartments or condominiums. These types of buildings are very popular in Japan.		
4. TV star	*tarento*	タレント
This refers to people on TV, many of whom are famous for nothing other than being on TV.		
5. woman pleaser	*feminisuto*	フェミニスト
This word does not refer to a woman's rights advocate, but quite the opposite. It refers to a man who pampers and takes care of women, often financially.		
6. mixed race	*haafu*	ハーフ
Though the word *half* is used, it doesn't necessarily mean you are only half mixed race, and usually, it is only used to refer to a mixed race Japanese person. Many Americans are mixed, but this isn't generally used when talking about Americans. Be careful, because the word *nyuuhaafu* ニューハーフ refers to a transgender man.		
7. sticker	*shiiru*	シール
This doesn't refer to *seals* but rather *stickers*.		
8. electric outlet	*konsento*	コンセント
Not *consent,* but rather an electric outlet.		
9. motorcycle	*baiku*	バイク
Japanese people will become very confused if you refer to your *bicycle* as a *bike*.		
10. playing cards	*toranpu*	トランプ
While *trump* is indeed a game you can play with cards, in Japanese it refers to the cards themselves.		